Kent Beck's
guide to
Better
Smalltalk

SIGS Reference Library

Additional Volumes in Preparation

Kent Beck's
Guide to
Better
Smalltalk
A *SORTED* COLLECTION

Kent Beck
First Class Software, Inc.

CAMBRIDGE
UNIVERSITY PRESS

SIGS
BOOKS

PUBLISHED BY THE PRESS SYNDICATE OF THE UNIVERSITY OF CAMBRIDGE
The Pitt Building, Trumpington Street, Cambridge CB2 1RP, United Kingdom

CAMBRIDGE UNIVERSITY PRESS
The Edinburgh Building, Cambridge CB2 2RU, UK
http://www.cup.cam.ac.uk
40 West 20th Street, New York, NY 10011-4211, USA
http://www.cup.org
10 Stamford Road, Oakleigh, Melbourne 3166, Australia

Published in association with SIGS Books

First published in 1999

Design and composition by Kevin Callahan/BNGO Books
Cover design by Yin Moy and Tom Jezek
Printed in the United States of America

A catalog record for this book is available from the British Library.

Library of Congress Cataloging-in-Publication Data

Beck, Kent.
    Kent Beck's guide to Better Smalltalk / Kent Beck
        p.   cm. -- (SIGS Reference Library Series ; 14)
        ISBN 0-521-64437-2 (pbk.)
        1. Smalltalk (Computer program language) I. Title. II. Series
QA76.73.S59B425 1998
005.12'3 --dc21

98-39476
ISBN 0-521-64437-2 paperback

"A Diagram for Object-Oriented Programs," ©1986
"A Laboratory for Teaching Object-Oriented Thinking," ©1989
"Playground: An Object-Oriented Simulation System with Agent Rules
for Children of All Ages," ©1989
Reprinted courtesy of the Association for Computing Machinery

"Think Like an Object," reprinted courtesy of *Unix Review,* ©1991

"Patterns Generate Architecture," *ECOOP '94—Object-Oriented Programming,* W. Olthoff (Ed.),
reprinted courtesy of Springer-Verlag Publishing, ©1994

"Patterns and Software Development," reprinted courtesy of *Dr. Dobb's Journal,* ©1994

To Cindee

CONTENTS

FOREWORD

ALTHOUGH I FIRST got interested in Smalltalk when I read the 1981 *Byte* issue, I didn't get an opportunity to start using it until 1995. I was hooked right away. OOPSLA '96 was exciting because it was the first time I got to meet practicing Smalltalkers. I was thrilled to find people who were crazier than I was. One of them was Kent. Kent was working at the Tektronix labs at the time, and I spent a day there after OOPSLA was over, meeting Kent and Ward and lots of other Smalltalkers. They were bold, adventurous, experienced; they were pushing Smalltalk to its limits. I wanted to be like them.

Over the years, I've gotten to know Kent better than I ever expected. He has made me eat sushi, jump out of a redwood, and write about patterns. I've always felt that I was following where he had broken the trail. It's been a good path to follow.

Kent has always epitomized the spirit of Smalltalk to me. He is an intellectual and a nonconformist, yet he is an intensely practical person. He is concerned with making the world a better place for others, and not just for himself. He is open and sharing. Smalltalk is like that, too.

These articles not only show the thinking of a leading Smalltalker, they show his progression from a techie to someone focusing on the human side of software development. Kent has gone from trying to figure out how to make a computer behave to trying to help people to be more successful. Reading his articles will help you along that path.

If you have saved all the back issues of the *Smalltalk Report,* go back and read his articles. Otherwise, read this book!

—Ralph Johnson
Champaign, Illinois

PREFACE

"**I**'M NOT DEAD YET.**" That's what I thought when Don Jackson at SIGS offered to put my articles together into a book. It's probably that every book I've ever seen with "Complete" or "Collected" in the title is no longer with us. Last I checked, I'm still here.

Having established that I am alive enough to be typing this, let's get to the point of the Preface—convincing you to buy this book. You are standing here trying to decide whether to spend your hard-earned dinero for that exquisite literature you saw with the swords and dragons and stuff on the cover or a collection of my articles. Here's my pitch—my entire career has been spent learning how to communicate with other people about programs. This book chronicles how I learned what I know and how I learned to tell people stories about it.

I just finished my first book, *The Smalltalk Best Practice Patterns*. It is easy to see how a book written end to end can have a single theme. This book has no such theme. It has a story—no, two stories.

The first story could be called "Kent Discovers the Importance of People." I got into computing to avoid having to deal with people. As a sophomore in high school, I took physics instead of biology so I wouldn't have to try to understand "all that squishy stuff." The rest of my academic career was spent in search of deeper understanding of the mechanics of things, whether the topic was computing or music. The sequence of articles you're about to read shows how I shed my focus on mechanics, how I awoke to the importance of community.

The second story could be called "Kent Learns to Write." Learning to write is odd. Sometimes stuff just comes out and it's great, sometimes it comes out easily and it's crap, and sometimes it doesn't come out at all. I started out pretty well, rapidly lost ground as I started thinking too much about what I was doing, and only recently returned to my early form (this is a common pattern in my learning, but the cycle doesn't often take ten years).

As you might expect from a collection of articles, I don't reach any grand conclusions about the problem of human communication. Instead, herein you will find recorded the experiences of one blind man groping one elephant for eight years and trying to talk about his experiences as he goes along.

Introduction

I HAVE STARTED AND STOPPED working on this book several times. Each time I began writing the introduction to a paper, I looked at it about half way through and said, "This seems awfully arrogant and self-centered. It's all about me, not about Smalltalk. Who wants to read about me?" I gave myself a good old-fashioned Puritan lecture about the virtues of self-efface-ment, and quit writing.

Recently I got Natalie Goldberg's second book about writing, *Wild Mind.* Her first book, *Writing Down the Bones,* was a collection of exercises for freeing the flow of ideas from mind to paper. I was reading *Wild Mind* sit-ting on a smooth teak bench in the Rose Garden of the Royal Botanical Gar-dens in Sydney. The yellowy autumn morning sun was baking the smell out of the roses. I read a comment another author made about the first book: "Why Natalie, this book should be very successful. When you are done with it, you know the author better. That's all a reader really wants, to know the author better. Even if it's a novel, they want to know the author."

Creaking teak as I sat back. A flutter of wings as the gathered ibis around me took off. I blinked my eyes, hard. If a novel is about getting to know the author, and a book of writing exercises is about getting to know the author, then why shouldn't a book of Smalltalk essays be about getting to know the author? Just because the author is me, that doesn't make it a stupid idea.

By the time the lightning had finished zipping around in my brain, the smoke curling from my ears had dissipated, and the light bulbs flashing above my head had slowed their flashing, I had decided to use this book to intro-duce myself to you.

The Articles

I have arranged the articles chronologically by date of publication. I tried several different ways of organizing them, but finally realized that any other organization would be a lot more work and not really buy you that much. If you want information carefully organized by topic, read *The Smalltalk Best Practice Patterns.* Putting these articles in time sequence gives you a better chance to watch how my thinking and writing change over time.

One issue I really grappled with was whether to edit the articles. I tended to sprinkle "last month we talked about"s and "next month we'll talk about"s liberally in my Smalltalk Report columns. Once again, I have opted to pretty much leave well enough alone. If there is something in an article I disagree with now, or if I lie about a coming article, I'll notify you in the introduction to that article.

How to Read Them

I have thought of two ways to read these articles:

1. **Intros only.** As a way of getting to know more about me, you could read just the introductions to the articles. Each introduction tells the story of what I can remember of writing the article, what I learned from it, what I would do or say differently now, and sometimes a little sideline about someone who has influenced my living or thinking.

2. **Beginning to end.** By following the articles from first to last, you can see some of the development of my thinking over time. Really, though, you can only see the development of my writing. My thinking has always been far in advance of what I've been able to, or had the courage to, write about.

1

A Diagram for Object-Oriented Programs

WITH WARD CUNNINGHAM
OOPSLA '86 Proceedings

M*y programming partner Ward Cunningham taught me to avoid complexity. In spite of my blue-chip, Silicon Valley brat credentials, I was never a very good programmer. Ward has more programming talent than I do, but he still programs simpler stuff, not because he must, but because he chooses. That is a big part of my success to date—picking development priorities and ignoring interesting side issues.*

This was my first technical article. I was lucky to write it with Ward, because he had a pretty good handle on how to focus an article. That was the lesson of this paper for me—focus. I can remember discussing for days what the one single point was we wanted a reader to take away. That was a powerful lesson, and a bit painful, too. Ward and I had been working on lots of exciting stuff. I wanted to talk about all of it. Ward leaned and leaned on finding the one point that stood above all others. Finally we hit on this one.

The article introduces the Cunningham Diagram, a diagram with much the same information in it as Jacobson's Interaction Diagram, but (to my eyes, anyway) much more artistically rendered. As far as impact goes, this paper was a dud. The two good ideas here—the diagram itself and a tool for constructing it from running code—both disappeared without a trace. Oh well, first you have to start talking, then folks have to start listening.

One other bit of story here. I can keenly remember sweating blood with Ward one Saturday to get the paper into the approved OOPSLA format. We had an early Macintosh with MacWrite and MacDraw. We spent hours and hours getting all the details right. At the end I was convinced that there was something to the Mac, but it sure wasn't there yet.

W E INTRODUCE A NOTATION for diagramming the message sending dialogue that takes place between objects participating in an object-oriented computation. Our representation takes a global point of view which emphasizes the collaboration between objects implementing the behavior of individuals. We illustrate the diagram's usage with examples drawn from the Smalltalk-80™ virtual image. We also describe a mechanism for automatic construction of diagrams from Smalltalk code.

INTRODUCTION

The Smalltalk-80 virtual image [Goldberg 83] has many examples of expertly organized programs, many of which play an important role in the Smalltalk-80 system. These are worthy objects of study for at least two reasons. First, they often provide exquisite examples of the style and idiom unique to object-oriented programming. As valuable as a concise definition of object-oriented programming might be, it could not replace the corpus of code in the virtual image for illuminating the range of application of the object-oriented style. Students of object-oriented programming should be grateful that the implementors of Smalltalk pushed the object metaphor to the limit, building their system out of nothing but objects. Their result offers a guide to the "objectification" of even the most elusive algorithms. One learns by doing and one does Smalltalk by browsing the world of other programmers. Second, many Smalltalk objects are directly reusable—an even more compelling reason to study their behavior. To the degree that one's application mimics Smalltalk's own implementation, one will find useful objects in the image, preprogrammed, waiting to be used. Smalltalk's reputation as a user-interface-prototyping environment stems from its wealth of reusable user-interface components.

We sought a way of presenting the computations employed in Smalltalk's modular user interface. We developed a representation, a diagram, that emphasized the object nature of the interface components. The essence of an object-oriented computation is the dialog carried out by the objects involved. With this in mind, we consciously omitted from the diagram indications of state or sequence. So reduced, a single diagram shows the cascade of messages that result, for example, from a user interaction. The diagrams are not unique to user-interface codes, though, they are unique to object-oriented computations. We have since applied the diagramming technique to many of the more esoteric examples from the Smalltalk-80 image. The result has solidified our own understanding of object-oriented programming, and enabled us to teach others more clearly about Smalltalk-80.

In this paper we will introduce the notations of our diagramming technique and apply them to several examples from the Smalltalk-80 image. Later examples are drawn from behaviors in the image that are often misunderstood. We hope in this way to make a convincing demonstration of the diagrams' usefulness. Also, the reader can expect to see glimpses of the unique suitability of objects in implementing user-interfaces. We close with a discussion of an automatic technique for the construction and formatting of publication quality diagrams.

THE DIAGRAM

We begin with objects. Objects accept responsibility for their own behavior. As a convenience, the code that implements this behavior is collected into a common place for all objects of the same class. Further, objects of one class might vary in behavior only slightly from those of another class. A new class is said to refine another if it implements only the variant behavior while relying on the other class for the remainder.

We represent an object as a box (See Figure 1-1a). A message sent to an object excites behavior specific to that object. We draw a message-send as a di-

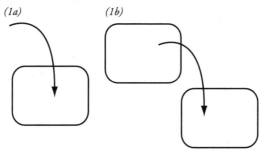

Figure 1-1a) An object receiving a message.
b) An object sending a message to another object.

rected arc landing within the receiving object. If more than one object partic-ipates in a computation then there will be more than one box in the diagram (see Figure 1-1b). When one object invokes a computation in another object through a message send, we show that send as an arc originating in the send-ing object and landing in the receiving object. With the message goes a trans-fer of control. That is, the computation of the sender is suspended until the computation of the receiver is completed. Control returns backward along a message arc along with the answer to the message, if any. So far this mimics the usual semantics of procedure call. Note that we draw a particular message arc only once, even if the message is sent repeatedly, in a loop or otherwise.

An object will exhibit behavior appropriate for the specific message it re-ceives. The various computations are implemented by distinct methods, each labeled with a method selector. We place the selector of methods invoked by messages at the receiving end of a message arc (see Figure 1-2a). It is impor-tant to note that the method invoked by a message will depend on the selec-tor and the receiving object. The same selector might select different methods when received by different objects. In Figure 1-2b, for example, we cannot tell whether the two methods labeled "gamma" are the same. We need to know more about the objects involved.

We identify an object in a diagram by its class. Recall that all members of a class share the same methods. The methods of the objects in Figure 1-3 are all exactly determined because we know the selector and the receiver's class for all of the messages. Recall also that objects of one class might inherit methods from another class. When methods are inherited from other classes (when a class does not implement a method, but one of its superclasses does) we di-vide the receiver into layers representing the classes involved and locate the method selector in the appropriate layer. Figure 1-3b shows two objects of two different classes (Senator and Plebe) each refining a third class (Citizen). The method for "gamma" invoked by each is in fact the same method, the one both inherit from Citizen. Of course, the same method won't necessarily ex-ecute in the same way in both cases; it is being executed on behalf of distinctly different objects. Figure 1-3c shows a revised Plebe. This time Plebes provide their own method for "gamma" which overrides the default implementation inherited by all Citizens.

We draw message arcs so that they always enter an object from above. When an arc travels across a layer of methods before finding its selector in a deeper layer, this suggests an opportunity to override that has not been exploited. The

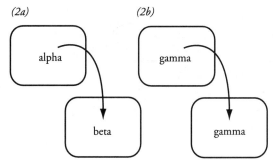

Figure 1-2 *a) One method for "alpha" invokes another for "beta". b) One method for "gamma" invokes another for "gamma".*

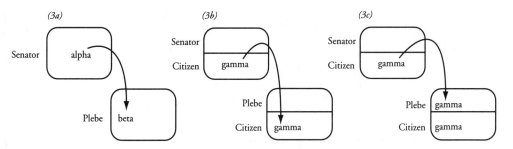

Figure 1-3 *a) A Senator's method for "alpha" invokes a Plebe's method for "beta". b) A Senator's method for "gamma" invokes a Plebe's method for "gamma", in this case the same method inherited by all Citizens. c) A variant of b) where a Plebe overrides the inherited implementation of "gamma".*

top layer will be that of the object's own class. Deeper layers will be superclasses. The bottom layer (if shown) will be the root of the hierarchy-class Object.

Note the contradictory use of the "elevation" metaphor by the terms "override" and "superclass". Which way is up? Some observers have complained that it is non-intuitive to place subclasses above superclasses in our characterizations of objects. We judge overriding the more important concept and like to think of method-lookup searching deeper for an implementation if none is provided by the surface class. Besides, we tried drawing the diagrams upside-down. They looked lifeless with their arcs limply dangling between method selectors.

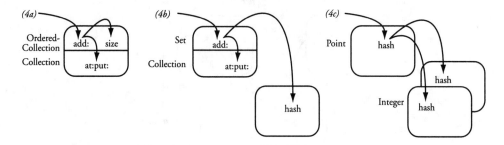

Figure 1-4 a) Adding to an OrderedCollection. b) Adding to a Set.
c) Hashing a Point.

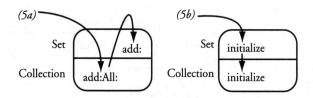

Figure 1-5 a) Adding all of one Collection to another.
b) An initialization method invokes a similar method
in a superclass.

Consider an example drawn from the Smalltalk-80 image. The class Collection includes refinements for many commonly used aggregate data structures-arrays, sets, linked lists and the like. An OrderedCollection, for example, implements a flexibly sized array. An OrderedCollection responds to the message "add: anElement" by adding anElement at the next available location within itself. A slightly simplified diagram of this operation appears in Figure 1-4a. We can see that the add method makes use of two more elementary methods, size and at:put. The diagram doesn't exactly explain why, but one could guess that size is used to determine where to put the new element and at:put is used to put it there. Contrast this to the implementation of add: for Sets in Figure 1-4b. This time the index is found by hashing the new element. Note that computing a hash function is the responsibility of the new element, not of the Set. All objects can hash themselves. Points, for example, compute their hash from their x and y coordinates as illustrated in Figure 1-4c.

We have now seen two examples of recursive behavior. In Figure 1-3b the "gamma" method for one Citizen invoked itself for another. This style of recursion is common in Smalltalk especially when the objects are organized into a tree or list. In Figure 1-4a we see a distinctly different kind of self reference. One method (add:) invokes others (size and at:put:) on behalf of the same object. This is done by addressing messages to "self". This is an idian in Smalltalk since it is the mechanism by which complex methods are decomposed into simpler ones. Figure 1-5 illustrates some particularly interesting variations on this theme. The method "addAll:" works by adding each element of another Collection, one at a time. The algorithm works for all refinements that implement an appropriate method for "add:". We draw messages to self as arcs arching up and back down through the refining layers of an object, emphasizing the refinement's opportunity to override.

Smalltalk-80 provides a mechanism for a refinement to directly address methods of its superclasses. By addressing a message to "super" an overriding method can employ the method it is overriding as part of its implementation. We show a typical application in Figure 1-5b. Note the absence of arch in this message arc. This visual distinction helps to make clear the difference in the way the method is found by the interpreter during a call to super, in contrast to the mechanism used in calls to self or other objects.

ADVANCED EXAMPLES

For more challenging examples we turn to the Smalltalk-80 user-interface. Smalltalk applications present themselves as windows on a bit-mapped display. A window may be divided into a number of panes, each displaying a different aspect of the application. By convention, keystrokes and mouse buttons are interpreted in the context of the pane touched by the cursor. Objects of class View and Controller accept responsibility for displaying output and interpreting input, respectively. A pair of objects, a View and a Controller, is allocated to each pane and another pair to the window as a whole. All of these are organized into a tree where the root represents the whole window, and the leaves represent individual panes. Finally, an object called the model accessible to all of the Views and Controllers, represents the state and behavior of the application.

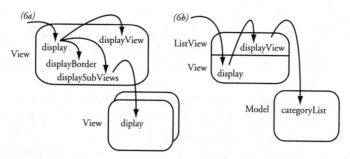

Figure 1-6 a) A View displays itself and its subviews.
b) A specialized View displays a list acquired from its model.

A window displays itself by recursively traversing its Views. Each View displays its border, its own contents, and any Views it might contain (see Figure 1-6a). In practice, an application would employ refinements of View specialized for the needs of each particular pane. For example, a pane displaying a list might use a ListView that overrides displayView with the method for displaying lists. The actual contents of the list would be acquired from the model as shown in Figure 1-6b. Note that the task of displaying a window has been decomposed using three separate programming techniques. First, several objects collaborate in the task. Second, the task is broken into parts for each object. Third, specialized objects can override any one of the parts. All of these techniques are visible in Figure 1-6.

As a user interacts with an application's window, changes made to the model from one pane may require updates in others. The general mechanism for this is outlined in Figure 1-7. A Controller recognizes user inputs as part of its controlActivity. When an input activity is complete, the Controller notifies the model that it has been changed. In response, the model notifies all of its registered dependents (Views always register themselves as a dependent of their model) of the need to update. The process of updating is left to the Views.

All Controllers cooperate to insure that the most appropriate Controller interprets the user's input at any given time. A Controller that wants control (because its View contains the current cursor point) gets control with the message "startUp." Figure 1-8 shows how this message eventually invokes the Controller's controlActivity. The controlLoop does the controlActivity repeatedly as long as the Controller remains active. In Figure 1-8 we see the default implementation of controlActivity searching among its sub-Controllers

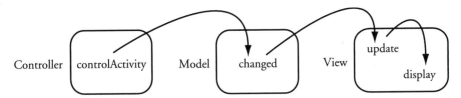

Figure 1-7 Views are advised of a change by a model.

for the appropriate controller for the moment. Refinements of Controller differ primarily in the implementation of controlActivity. Like the example of Figure 1-6, this is simply a recursive traversal of the tree of panes. Both examples pass control to a critical method which can be overriden to implement specialized behaviors. Both will still inherit the behavior required to participate in the collaborative implementation of a user interface.

Comparing these diagrams with the Smalltalk-80 visual image will reveal that we have bent the truth on many occasions. Yet, we argue, we have remained faithful to the style of the actual code. Our focus has been on the relationship between objects participating in a computation—a relationship that can be difficult to see when exploring objects one at a time. This is, in fact, the essence of object-oriented programming.

CREATING DIAGRAMS

Our notation emphasizes the cooperation of objects participating in a computation. We freely omit portions of the computation judged unimportant.Such judgement comes easily enough when drawing a diagram by hand or with a general purpose drafting program as in Figures 1-1 through 1-8. Our strategy for automating the drafting process had to admit intentional and esthetic considerations. Furthermore,we reasoned that only in the debugger [Goldberg 84], or more correctly, the simulation capability of the debugger, do the raw materials of the diagrams come together in one place. That is, to collect the information required for constructing diagrams we must do at least as much work as the debugger does when it steps a computation. The observation was fortuitous in that the debugger also had a user-interface that allowed one to step around computations judged uninteresting.

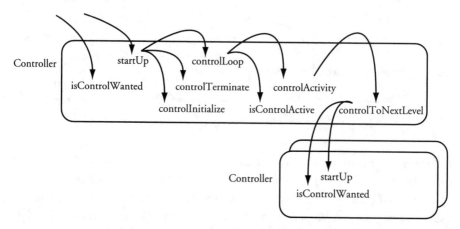

Figure 1-8 Control leads to controlActivity. The default controlActivity recursively passes control to a sub-Controller.

The Smalltalk-80 debugger lists the activation records on the run-time stack, shows the source code of the selected activation, and provides two inspectors, one on the current object, the other on arguments and temporary variables. The debugger's menu has two commands to advance the computation, step and send. Step continues computing until the impending message returns a value. Send retains control so the user can watch the execution of the invoked method.

We chose an extension of the debugger as our drafting user interface. The modified debugger has an additional pane on the right is a special purpose diagram editor. The objects in the diagram can be moved around by dragging them with the mouse. Information is added to the diagram by menu commands step and send, which duplicate the ordinary debugger commands except that they record the message in the diagram. Objects and selectors are added to the diagram on demand. Objects acquire an initial placement by the user, selectors are positioned automatically.

To create a diagram one uses the step and send menu commands from the diagram pane to record the messages judged important. The original debugger commands can be used to locate the desired context without modifying the diagram. Other mouse operations are used to adjust the objects in the diagram until it is visually balanced and clearly conveys the computation.

A prepared diagram can be saved as a bitmap or as a high-resolution image encoded as PostScritptm [Adobe 85] function calls. The PostScript page description language provides a flexible way of specifying the contents of a type-set page. We wrote PostScript functions for each graphical element: arc, box, selector and class. A diagram is compactly encoded as a sequence of calls on these functions.

We were struck by the dynamics of the diagrams as they developed on-screen, in the debugger. The objects in the diagram provided a helpful spatial reference to the objects involved in the computation. In this regard our work is similar to Brad Meyers visualizations in Incense [Meyers 85]. We found that by highlighting the currently executing object we were able to trace much more complicated computations than with the unmodified debugger. The facility proved helpful in locating a long standing bug in Smalltalk's coordinate transformation code. (The bug involved the inappropriate division of responsibilities between panes of a window.) Without the diagram, we had had trouble keeping track of which pane in the computations had done what when. Unlike the debugger's runtime stack display, which reflects only the current state of the computation, the extended debugger's diagram accumulated information throughout the debugging session.

As we pointed out early on, our notation does not explicitly represent the sequence of a computation. However, since the debugger obviously follows a sequence, and our diagrams accumulate in the debugger, our notation represents sequence when viewed over time. Inspired by related work in program animation by Ralph London and Rob Duisberg [London 85], we tried recording the dynamic behavior of a diagram as constructed. We hoped that this, played back at high speed, would add further insight into a computation. Playback involved first displaying the objects in the diagram, then, for each recorded message, drawing or redrawing the message arc and the receiving selector. Replaying diagrams has yet to substantially improve our understanding of a computation, probably because we have yet to view an animation that we haven't just finished recording. Replaying is sufficiently promising that we intend to try it in an instructional context using projection display equipment.

CONCLUSION

We have presented a way of diagramming object-oriented computations. Objects in a diagram are represented by boxes, labeled by the object's class and possibly its superclasses. The classes are listed with the most concrete class at the top, giving a natural interpretation to the term "overriding". Messages are represented by directed arcs from the sending object to the receiving object. Selector names at either end of an arc identify the sending and receiving methods. Furthermore, selector placement within an object indicates the class in which it is defined.

We have used these diagrams to teach beginning and advanced object-oriented programming to more than one hundred students. We feel that their use enhances our students' ability to understand some of the more esoteric examples in the Smalltalk-80 image. Those programs which rely on a dialog of several objects are much easier to understand with diagrams than just by examining source code. The user interface code, recognized to be some of the most difficult to understand, is particularly amenable to a diagrammatic treatment.

We have also extended the Smalltalk-80 system to automatically collect information for diagrams, and we have provided an editing and formatting facility for the result. We implemented this as an extension to an existing utility, the debugger, to provide a familiar user interface. We have in the process enhanced the utility of the debugger.

In conclusion, we feel that the use of diagrams such as these can help teach the concepts and practice of object-oriented programming to naive users. In addition, we feel they can give more experienced programmers insight into how a complicated object-oriented system, such as the Smalltalk-80 virtual image, divides the responsibility of a computation. This insight is critical in a system like Smalltalk which series on reuse to enhance programmer productivity.

REFERENCES

[Adobe 85] Adobe Systems Incorporated. PostScript Language Reference Manual. Addison-Wesley, 1985.

[Goldberg 83] Goldberg, A. J., Robson, D. Smalltalk-80: *The Language and its Implementation.* Addison-Wesley, 1983.

[Goldberg 84] Goldberg, A. J. Smalltalk-80: *The Interactive Programming Environment.* Addison-Wesley, 1984.

[London 85] London, R. L, Duisberg, R. A. *Animating Programs Using Smalltalk.* IEEE Computer 18(8):61-71, Aug 1985.

[Myers 85] Myers, B. A. *Incense: A System for Displaying Data Structures.* Computer Graphics: SIGGRAPH '85 Conference Proceedings, pp. 115-125. ACM, July 1985.

2

CONSTRUCTING ABSTRACTIONS FOR OBJECT-ORIENTED APPLICATIONS

JOOP, JULY–AUGUST, 1989

There are two notable points to make about this paper. First, it is one of the first times Ward and I published any pattern-related material (we presented some stuff at OOPSLA 87 in Orlando, I in Norm Kerth's "Where Do Objects Come From" workshop, Ward on a panel). Second, it argues that the worst problem of reuse is one of communication, not technology or economics.

The paper started out life as a Tektronix technical report. Ward and I had the habit of writing up just about everything we did as a TR. After we had written this, I think we submitted it as a position paper for some conference or workshop. Somehow, JOOP got hold of a copy and contacted us about publishing it.

The paper can be summed up as: "We created two sets of abstractions. The first was communicated as literate source code. The second was communicated as patterns for its reuse. The first set of objects was misused; the second was used correctly. We conclude that the problem of reuse is one of effectively communicating the intent of the code."

MAKING ABSTRACTIONS

We have found Smalltalk's notion of objects communicating with messages an effective vehicle for the express of algorithms and data structures in a form isolated from the details of an application program. The process of isolation, called abstraction, is emerging as a principal activity of programmers. The promise that motivates the activity is the widespread reuse of well developed algorithms and data structures and, consequently, the increased productivity of programmers in general.

We view computer programming as a problem-solving activity. Productivity in specification, design, and implementation of computer programs might well be measured in correct decisions per hour. Here correctness implies that a decision need not be revisited before the successful completion of a project. An abstraction bundles resolved decisions. Once selected, an abstraction partially completes each of the programming phases—specification, design, and implementation. The decision to use an abstraction replaces the decisions resolved by the abstraction. Abstractions increase productivity when the former decisions are more easily resolved than the latter.

Smalltalk successfully serves as a vehicle for expressing abstractions. Features of Smalltalk that have proven useful include: (1) message sending, (2) hierarchical factoring, and (3) storage reclamation. Let us consider each in turn.

Message sending requires that all participants in a computation accept responsibility for interpreting and responding to messages drawn from a predetermined set called protocol. The participants are free to issue further messages in the course of discharging their responsibilities. In this environment an abstraction can accept as much or as little responsibility as is appropriate.

Hierarchical factoring allows responsibilities common to a number of participants to be collected, resolved once, and then inherited by all.

Finally, automatic storage reclamation (garbage collection) insures that accountability for allocated storage does not "leak out" of an abstraction and become the responsibility of a client.

We have come to rely heavily on each of these features. Their simultaneous presence in Smalltalk has renewed our and others' interest in packaging reusable abstractions.

Satisfied as we are with Smalltalk's ability to record and delineate a collection of well-made decisions, we find that the abstractions so produced may still fail to earn their keep in the economic balance of decision substitution. The application programmer's problem-solving tasks are made immediately more complex by the simple existence of the abstraction. Is it of use? How and when? Such concerns offset the decision value of abstractions. Potential solutions are ignored because it takes too much time to establish their value. It becomes easier to do it over.

Blame is often directed at the consumer when such failures of reuse occur.

Not Invented Here (NIH) syndrome, for example, presumes that the consumer simply wanted the prestige of doing everything alone. That is rarely the case. We suspect a Take It or Leave It (TILI) syndrome is more likely at fault. TILI occurs when a programmer produces a general solution but does not suggest to potential users the context in which it solves a problem. Abstraction producers must provide sound guidance in the appropriate application of their work or users will resolve their own problems, not out of perversity, but because it is truly easier to understand and solve a problem than try to second-guess someone else's solution. The guidance must be concrete, not open to interpretation, for interpretation also places a decision burden on potential consumers. Guidance increases the value of abstractions, making them more likely to be reused.

In this article, we will review our participation in an application programming effort taking place within Tektronix. In the next section, we summarize two abstractions we created in the course of our work. We take a case-history point of view to illustrate our interactions with the other programmers involved. In the third section, we analyze the guidance we provided with the abstractions. Some strategies we used appear novel and worthy of further investigation.

TWO CASE STUDIES

The best insight into the production of programs comes in the course of producing programs. With this in mind, we were pleased to have the opportunity to participate in a large product development effort within Tektronix. We spent several months working as part of a pioneering development team responsible for constructing a specialized programming environment. Tektronix, a producer of semiconductor testers used in the manufacture of integrated circuits, recognized a problem in that test program development costs were approaching design costs for many circuits. The solution recognizes the unique activities of test programmers and provides them with specialized tools and resources to facilitate their programming efforts. The design was loosely modeled on Smalltalk and would be implemented in Smalltalk on a Tektronix 4400 series workstation.

The Program Development System (PDS) is implemented as a programming environment written in Smalltalk and an incremental compiler written in C. Both run on the workstation and communicate with the tester control software (also in C) over a local area network. By the time we joined the project the protocols were in place to deliver unformatted bytes between each of these subsystems. Our first case study reviews an abstraction for communicating structured information over an unformatted channel.

We judged existing solutions to the object formatting problem [Vegd86] too complex and unique to Smalltalk. Similarly, the Sun XDR protocol [Sun86] was overly specific to C programs. We sought instead to represent only objects of well understood type in a format that recognized the limitations of each language involved. We chose fixed-size or count-controlled representations to simplify processing in C. We included a type tag with each datum as a step toward objects in Smalltalk. We use a heterogeneous array as the only aggregate type. The external formats we employed are summarized in Figure 2-1. We implemented this formatting in Smalltalk in a class called DataStream. DataStreams were placed as a direct descendant of Stream in the Stream hierarchy.

```
Object
    Stream
        DataStream ('byteStream')
        PositionableStream ('collection' 'position' 'readLimit')
            ReadStream
            WriteStream ('writeLimit')
                ReadWriteStream ()
                    ExternalStream ()
                        FileStream ('name' 'directory'...)
```

This location reflects the fact that DataStreams store structured objects and cannot be randomly positioned. DataStreams provide concrete implementa-

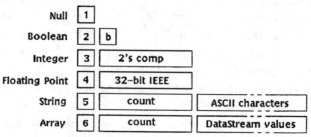

Figure 2-1 DataStream Representations.

tions of **next** and **nextput**: where the conversion of objects to bytes and vice versa takes place. DataStreams delegate their actual I/O responsibilities to an ExternalStream that they manage as their sole internal state.

We coded our implementation as a literate program in the style of Knuth [Knut83] using a specialized browser [Beck86a]. We wanted the implementation approach to be obvious since we could not rule out the need for subsequent modification. We had, after all, only mentioned to our colleagues that we were looking into Smalltalk communication support. We had, however, established that (1) binary formats were necessary to meet performance requirements and (2) a memory image of C structures would be inappropriate since the two compilers in use disagreed on memory format. We included a library of C functions for reading and writing DataStream formats as an appendix to our implementation [Beck86b]. We introduced the abstraction in design meetings by identifying the problems it solved as they came up in discussion. One omission was noted: transparent transmission of unformatted bytes. We added binary as a seventh count-controlled format.

The DataStream case represents a bottom-up abstraction in that the solution was formulated before the need was totally perceived. The reverse was true of our next abstraction.

The PDS was conceived of as a template substitution of per-chip meters into a relatively stable shell program. A prototype implementation had been constructed in Smalltalk using its standard user-interface components. The prototype had been well received at a testing conference. Specific feedback from users and our own application specialists raised issues that were not adequately addressed.

We joined a team of application specialists who undertook to review and more completely specify the behavior of the PDS from user's point of view. Although the prototype had been well received, there was a strong tendency to dramatically alter the appearance of the interface, in many cases, we felt, departing from well established precedents. The application specialists showed a tendency to write typical character-oriented output: draw a box around it and call it a window. They obviously needed more guidance in the design of window-based interfaces. Also, it was clear that the necessary user-interface behavior would require the addition of new types of panes, i.e., new Smalltalk Views, but that a proliferation of new panes would bury the software engineering team in coding details.

We first placed a limit on the variety of panes. In particular, all windows would be constructed from text, list, table, and waveform panes. We cre-

Spec for voh of M3422						
	pin	min	max	vcc	input	vector
alpha	d3	4.5	4.8	5.0	23	1231
beta	d4	4.3	4.9	5.0	34	2341
gamm	d5	4.5	4.9	5.0	23	1231
	d6	4.3	4.8	5.0	34	1234
	d7	4.5	4.8	5.0	23	1234
	d8	4.5	4.9	5.0	23	2342

Figure 2-2 Example Table Pane.

ated the table pane abstraction then and there. It and the already developed waveform pane would be added to the text and list panes supported by Smalltalk. The exact nature of a table evolved as the product specification was completed. We wanted the interaction to suggest a spreadsheet with the semiconductor tester serving as the calculator. A sample table is shown in Figure 2-2.

The table abstraction was implemented in the form of three Smalltalk classes: a pluggable TableView, its corresponding TableController, and an aggregate data structure called a Table. The Tableview communicates with its model by passing whole Tables or by incrementally entering and validating individual table entries. Typing is directed to the currently selected cell. The view manages a scrollable window into the table and is careful to insure that the appropriate column and row labels are always visible.

We began the implementation of the table abstraction before the system specification that used it was complete. We asked one of the project software engineers to join us in the implementation effort. Together we spent about a week building the three classes required and an example of their use.

ACCEPTING THE ABSTRACTOR'S RESPONSIBILITY

The roles individuals assume in the course of collaborative efforts will be as dynamic and as varied as the people involved. We will for the purpose of further discussion find it convenient to describe the role of an abstractor, the role we played in the two cases reviewed above. The abstractor, in short, comprehends a problem space, isolates a portion of the space for which a general solution is possible, and provides a reusable solution.

To avoid TILI, the abstractor has to communicate the context within which an abstraction solves a problem to potential users. Looking at the examples above, we see two styles of providing guidance to the users of an abstraction.

In the DataStream case, we provided guidance in the form of two well documented implementations and a sample application. While this contributed to the value of the abstraction, we found that the users of DataStream did not take full advantages of their capabilities. For instance, in communicating the scope of compound statements in a C function, the C compiler produced a linear list of start–stop character positions. A better use of DataStreams would have been to use their recursive nature to reflect the recursive structure of the scopes. In this case, we failed to communicate fully the value of our abstraction.

With tables we used a different style of guidance, namely, rules for their use in the context of a window-based interface. These rules empowered a group of application experts who had never before designed an interface of this type to specify an interface that was both effective at solving the given problem and implementable in the time available. We can summarize the rules as follows:

1. Window Per Task
2. Few Panes Per Window
3. Standard Panes
4. Short Menus
5. Nouns and Verbs

We mentioned the use of standard panes in the previous section. This requirement is reflected in Rule 3 (Standard Panes) above. Rules 1 (Windows Per Task) and 2 (Few Panes Per Window) provide a context for satisfying Rule 3. Rule 1 requires that each window provide all necessary panes to complete a user task. Rule 2 demands that the task be simple enough to be well supported with a minimum number of panes. Having first satisfied these, Rule 3 proved easy to satisfy with the repertoire of panes we have already discussed. Further, the three rules together provide for easy satisfaction of even more specific rules such as Rule 4 (Short Menus), calling for single-level menus with no more than seven entries; and Rule 5 (Nouns and Verbs), objects (nouns) selected from list panes and action (verbs) invoked from menus.

We did not invent this concept of rules completely ad hoc. We had been studying for some time the work of Christopher Alexander [Alex 77, Alex 791], an architect who has been studying for the last twenty years ways for laymen to design buildings for their own use. We felt that his work applied to the construction of computer systems as well, but we had had no chance to test our hypothesis. Therefore, we created our rules in a similar way to Alexander's "patterns" as needed (primarily when the application experts did something wrong in designing the interface). We were pleased with how well the crude set of rules we created on the spot worked, as they allowed the application engineers to design an interface that was superior to anything we (as self-professed "interface experts") could have done. Borrowing from the field of architecture, where practitioners have faced for many years the problem of building for a client a product that will intimately affect their life, is a fruitful place for further investigation.

In conclusion, we feel that Smalltalk provides the opportunity for the reuse of code through abstractions, but that there is much work to be done in developing strategies for communicating them. In particular, even careful documentation of an abstraction will be insufficient to make clear the intended scope of the solution; rather, an abstraction must be presented within a framework of concrete advice. In this way, an abstractor shares responsibility for choosing which abstractions will be of use in an application.

ACKNOWLEDGMENT

This article is Technical Report No. CR-87-25 of Tektronix, Inc.

REFERENCES

[Alex77] Christopher Alexander et al., *A Pattern Language,* Oxford University Press, New York, 1977.

[Alex79] Christopher Alexander et al., *The Timeless Way of Building,* Oxford University Press. New York, 1979.

[Beck86a] Kent Beck, Ward Cunningham, and Larry Morindi, *DataStreams for Structured Communications: Definition and Implementation*, CR-86-63, Computer Research Laboratory, Tektronix, Inc.

[Beck86b] Kent Beck and Ward Cunningham, *The Literate Program Browser*, CR-86-52, Computer Research Laboratory, Tektronix, Inc.

[Knut84] Donald Knuth, Literate Programming, *Computer Journal*, 27(2):97–111. May 1984.

[Sun86] *Networking with the Sun Workstation*, Sun Microsystems, Part number 800-1324-03, February 1986.

[Vegd86] Steven Vegdahl, Moving Structures Between Smalltalk Images, OOPSLA '86, *The First ACM Conference on Object-Oriented Systems, Languages, and Applications*, 466–471, October 1986.

3

PLAYGROUND: AN OBJECT-ORIENTED SIMULATION SYSTEM WITH AGENT RULES FOR CHILDREN OF ALL AGES

WITH JAY FENTON
OOPSLA '89 Proceedings

I got my name on this paper kind of by accident. I was a late arrival on the Vivarium project. Jay Fenton had been doing some very interesting work on programming languages for kids. He wanted to write something up for OOPSLA. I offered to help him.

I ended up reorganizing the paper enough that he offered to put my name on as an author. I felt a little funny, especially since the paper had been accepted with only Jay's name and I was the program chair and besides, I already had another paper in the conference, but I accepted anyway.

The next year, I was on the ECOOP program committee. We had our meeting in Paris. I remember eating lunch in the Xerox cafeteria. Next to me sat a bright, eager Ph.D. student. He began grilling me about the paper and the research behind it. Turns out his class had been given the assignment of figuring out how they would extend existing research, and the Playground paper was one of the three they could pick to extend. This was a shock, because I don't consider myself a scholar. Really I'm more of a talkative engineer. However, it was fun to be noticed.

Technically, I'm amazed at the prescience of Playground. Alan Kay was absolutely convinced that direct control structures, like Smalltalk's message send, would run out of gas and that "pulling" -style would come into vogue (even though the Internet apps call it "pushing"). Now, probably fifteen years after he first began working on this idea, we still don't have purely pulling-style programming languages, although it seems to me only a matter of time.

PROGRAMMING LANGUAGES FOR CHILDREN have been limited by primitive control and data structures, indirect user interfaces, and artificial syntax. Playground is a child-oriented programming language that uses objects to structure data and has a modular control structure, a direct-manipulation user, and an English-like syntax. Integrating Playground into the curriculum of a classroom of 9- to 10-year-olds has given us valuable insights from the programs intended users, and confirms many of our design decisions.

The Apple Computer Vivarium Project was started in 1986 by Ann Marion and Alan Kay and represents a broad research initiative to investigate the phenomena of learning. To provide a living laboratory for study and experimentation, Apple established a relationship with the Open School, a public school in the Los Angeles Unified School District. As part of this research program, we have created the Playground programming system.

Playground is an object oriented programming environment that allows children to construct simulations by endowing graphical objects with laws to obey. Playground is inspired by our intuition that biology provides a good metaphor for understanding complex dynamic systems. Children will write programs by constructing artificial animals and turning them loose in an environment. Each object is a separate creature, with sensors, effectors, and processing elements, that can act of its own accord.

Our exposition begins with a demonstration of Playground as it would be experienced by a new user. The language is then presented in terms of examples. Next, we consider the influences that led us to adopt agent rules as out unit of computation. The following section deals with implementation details: how we make agent rules work and how they make animation and communication easy. We then recount our experiences teaching this language to children and conclude with our ideas for future directions.

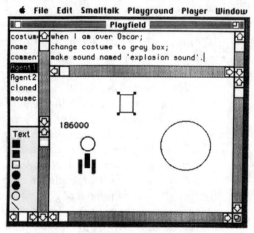

Figure 3-1 Playfield Overview

OVERVIEW

The basic elements of the Playground environment are illustrated by the program's screen display as shown in Figure 3-1.

When first started, Playground behaves like an object oriented drawing program, permitting the user to construct pictures using geometric primitives. Circles, squares, bitmaps, text, and composite objects can be placed anywhere on the screen. Any object or collection of objects can be selected and manipulated through menus. Objects can be opened up and their constituents browsed.

In Playground, objects occupy a planar surface called the *Playfield*. The Playfield can be viewed as a world inhabited by organisms. Each organism in the environment is a *Playground Object*. The Playfield mediates the interactions between the objects within it. Any object can be opened up and investigated, becoming itself a Playfield with constituents. To introduce an object, select a prototype from the gallery of predefined objects. Then click on the Playfield to introduce a copy. This object can then be selected, moved, or resized. When an object is selected, the editing area above the Playfield becomes active, permitting the user to edit the agent rules.

Agent rules describe cause-and-effect relationships that apply to the simulation. When an appropriate set of circumstances comes up, the agent rule is triggered and the designated sequence of operations is followed. Agent rules run in parallel.

As the rules execute, they can move an object or change its appearance. The animation code reacts to these changes by repainting the screen as needed to achieve a real time presentation.

Agent rules are entered using the *caption pane,* which is displayed above the Playfield. The appropriate agent name is selected in the *agent name list pane* on the left. The caption pane applies to whatever object is selected on the Playfield.

In Figure 3-1, the user has selected Agent 1 for the square object. This is indicated by the system highlighting the agent name in the pane on the left, and drawing small rectangles called "birdies" at the corners of the selected object. By moving the birdies the user can resize or reshape the object.

Each organism controls how it is presented to the outside world. This is done by donning a *costume,* a generic shape such as a circle or square, or a bitmap graphic. A costume defines both the physical appearance of an object and how it interacts with the user. For example, graphical objects can be resized, while text objects can have their font changed. An object can also move, change size or color, font, etc. under control of agent rules.

An object can sense the presence of other objects on the Playfield in various ways. Playground provides functions that return sets of objects that are nearby, are of a certain type, that overlap, and so on.

All Playground objects may avail themselves of a background of predefined behaviors which implement a useful naive physics [Gardin, 1989] of location and motion over time. Each object has a heading and velocity which control motion across the Playfield according to the rules of turtle geometry as defined on the Logo programming language [Papert, 1980].

LANGUAGE

In our experience with children, we have found that a surface syntax that closely resembles that of a natural language makes teaching a programming language easier. Playground is defined by a phrasal grammar that uses a syntax closely resembling that of a natural language. Each Playground clause corresponds to a "message send" in a conventional object oriented language. The user program is parsed according to these phsasal grammar rules, which then generate Smalltalk 80 code for compilation. References to undeclared names are allowed, and are resolved at run time using a dynamic binding function. Here are some sample Playground sentences:

Change costume to black box.
Move arrow to 30 @ 50;Make sound 'loud growl'.

In the first example sentence the current object, or self, is commanded to change its costume into a black box. In the second sentence, the object named "arrow" is commanded to move to the given coordinate, and then the 'loud growl' sound is triggered.

The semicolon serves as the non-yielding statement separator. The period designates a yield point. During each simulation cycle, every active agent run up to the next period. Thus proves multiplexing occurs at predictable places.

We have implemented several diverse models in Playground to test its range. Figure 3-2 illustrates a simple "shooting gallery" video game. Note that if an agent rule does not specify a condition, it runs continuously. Figure 3-3 shows a predator/prey simulation, with a fixed number of predators.

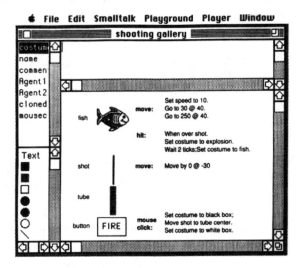

Figure 3-2

Predator/Prey example:

Predator

Wander	Set angle to 360 random; Set speed to 40. Wait 2 seconds.
Hunger	Set hunger to hunger + 1 When hunger > 10 excite 'go to food'.
Goto Food	Set angle to my bearing to food.
Find Food	Set food to nearest prey object
Eat	When I am over food then remove food; Set hunger to 0.

Prey

Wander	Set angle to 360 random. Go forward 4 steps
Flee	Inhibit Wander. Set angle to (my bearing to predator)-180. Go forward 6 steps.
Avoid	Set predator to nearest predator object
Reproduce	When 30 random = 1 then Clone yourself.

Figure 3-3 Predator/Prey

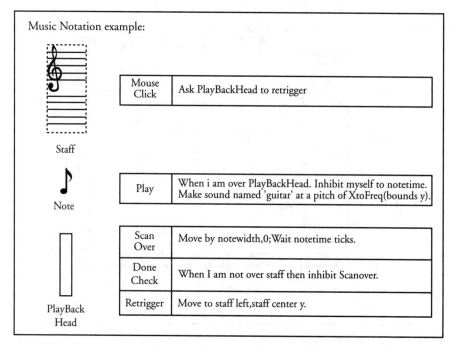

Figure 3-4 Music Sequencer

Figure 3-4 illustrates a conventional music notation editor with real-time playback. In this example, musical note symbols placed on the staff are triggered by the playback head object in sequence, playing melody in real time. The sequence can be edited while it is playing.

While the previous examples give some idea of the expressive power of the Playground system, to delve deeper we must consider the background influences that led us to this formulation.

INFLUENCES

We have studied many fields in searching for the ideas in Playground. A review of these sources of inspiration will help explain the decisions presented in the rest of the paper.

ANIMAL BEHAVIOR MODELS

Since Playground uses the metaphor of biology, it is instructive to study some of the theories of animal behavior that the field of biology offers. Biology is, of course, a vast and fascinating field, riddled with controversy. For a general introduction, see [Grier, 1984]. We take particular interest in the cognitive mechanisms humans have applied in analyzing animal behavior. This means even ideas that are wrong are interesting, if they give insight into how humans grapple with understanding behavior.

> Classical ethology is concerned with observing and describing the behavior of animals. In the classic theory, the organism detects *sign stimuli*, a particular configuration of sensory input, occurring in the environment. These stimuli then influence the organism's innate releasing mechanisms, or *drive centers*. Each drive center has an energy level. These drive centers are organized in a hierarchy, so that drive conflicts can be resolved. The path through the hierarchical tree is determined by the drive centers with the highest energy level.

When a drive is stimulated and permitted control of the organism; a fixed action pattern is undertaken that "releases" the drive energy. There is a close correspondence between the classical ethological theory and the rule-based expert system approach to artificial intelligence.

For example, in the three-spined stickleback fish, if a male detects another fish with a red belly assuming the vertical threat posture, the fighting drive center is stimulated. If no high-priority drive, such as hunger, overrides the fighting drive, the fixed-action pattern for fighting is undertaken. [Tinbergen, 1951]

SOCIETY OF MIND

The massively parallel organization implied by neurobiology has inspired the "Society of Mind" theory [Minksy, 1985]. Each mind consists of a swarm of communicating agents, each running in parallel, attending to aspects of the problem at hand. These agents are organized hierarchically, and are composed

Figure 3-5 Classical,Theory taken from [Grier, 1984]

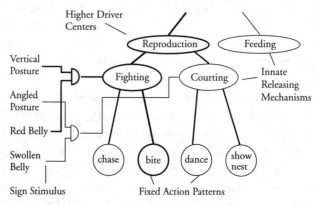

Figure 3-6 Stickleback Behavior

of networks of subagents, the primitive components of which are neurons. Specialized agents attend to memory storage and retrieval, command and control, symbolic processing, and so on.

While the Society of Mind theory has yet to be established by neurobiological evidence, it holds out hope for the unification of symbolic and connectionist theories of Artificial Intelligence. As we propose plausible explanations for how such internal societies must function, we again reveal how the mind attempts to comprehend highly parallel systems.

AGENT RULES

Playground seeks to combine ethological and Society of Mind theories by adopting the agent rule [Travers, 1988] as the fundamental unit of computation. An agent rule is an independently executing entity sensitive to particular sign stimuli. This rule can be excited or inhibited by other agents to achieve purposeful control of the organism. When a rule fires, it then triggers a sequence of operations.

Agent rules differ from conventional expert system rules in several ways.

Agent rules can be gated by excitation and inhibition mechanisms. They are seen as being strongly situated and are encouraged to use specific references rather than variables. An agent rule may contain a state that persists over time; thus separate instantiations of an agent rule must exist for discrete organisms.

OTHER INFLUENCES

Another influence on Playground's development has been the theory of Idealized Conceptual Models [Fauconnier, 1985] [Lakoff, 1987], or ICMs. In ICMs, abstract theories are represented metaphorically using objects and relations grounded in direct experience. We hope, therefore, to be able to model a wide range of phenomena by prefabricating a world with the same properties, operators, and relations as human direct experience, and providing facilities for the construction of metaphors.

There are, of course, a vast array of other influences. The list includes: The philosophy of scientific reasoning and modeling; gaming techniques; ontological engineering; intelligence gathering and analysis; graphical representations of models; audio, film, and video production; air traffic control systems; comic books; magic, and linguistic theory.

TECHNICAL DESIGN

Playground has been implemented in C and Smalltalk/V.

Playground objects are universal particles of identity to which any combination of relations or agents can be attached. Instead of having rigid classes, the capability of objects are patched together on the fly. This requires a very flexible object system. Every Playground object can contain an arbitrary collection of properties. These can include the source code and compiled code for all locally defined agent rules, the list of active processes for a particular object, animation control tables, and any other attached objects or relations.

Any number of agents can be attached to an object. The code for the agent is either stored locally or reached through other objects that have been designated as examples.

The user can branch from one Playfield to another by programming agent rules. It is also possible to write agent rules that connect one Playfield to another, serving as editors or to characterize functional transformations. Every Playground object can also be a Playfield if desired. By using appropriate linking instructions in agent rules, Playground can function as a multimedia hypertext system.

The Playfield serves as a bounded universe for causality. Objects on the Playfield affect each other through orderly mechanisms. New forms of causality can be added by creating new types of events and adding agent rules that react to these event messages.

The rules attached to an object can reach across environment boundaries in a limited way. Thus objects can be created which cause general properties to be introduced into the environment they occupy. For example, it is possible to introduce objects into a Playfield which add physical laws that all objects within the Playfield are to obey, in the manner of the Alternate Reality Kit [Smith, 1986].

SERIALIZATION, PUSHING, AND PULLING

A network of parallel agent rules can be simulated sequentially. This is of course required on conventional serial computers, and is useful for parallel systems as well. For example, most fixed action patterns enumerate a sequence of actions that take place over time. While this can be modeled in parallel hardware, it is much more compact and convenient to construct a sequencing automation that triggers each operation in turn. Algorithms can be created to compile parallel dataflow diagrams into sequential instruction streams; se Fabrik [Ingalls, 1988].

There are two fundamental ways to drive a simulation based on agent rules: pushing and pulling. In *pulling*, or event polling, an agent rule tests for conditions explicitly, hoping to detect appropriate configurations in other objects that would enable it to run. In pushing, or dependency tracing, when another object generates an event, it notifies the objects that are interested in the change.

Each method has its advantages and disadvantages. Pulling can waste time checking for conditions that have not changed, while pushing requires overhead to track the dependency relationships among objects.

Playground supports a mixed mode strategy. Each agent rule can test for the events and situations under which it is to run. When a rule is posted, the condition part is inspected and—if appropriate—the rule is registered with the system so that it runs only when the appropriate events have taken place. These events can be user interface events, events generated explicitly by other objects, or changes of values for a given object. A program may also trigger an agent explicitly, an operation similar to sending a message in a conventional object oriented language.

Facets

A Playground object is composed of one or more facets. A *facet* is a conventional object with a fixed slot structure that represents a class of properties attached to an identity. The facet idea is an adaptation of the multi-valued relation scheme of KODIAK [Wilensky, 1987]. Some examples of facets used in Playground are: Physical Appearance, Motion, Symbolic Meaning, and Process Header. All identities, including those used by Smalltalk, can have other facets attached to them. Facets help avoid the guilt of having too many NIL instance variables!

All Playground facets share a common super-class of PlayObject. each facet has a timestamp field, a list of subfacets, and a backpointer to the primary identity this object is a facet for. Each facet kind can add its own fixed and optional slots to this base structure. For example, any object can be given visual appearance, motion, symbolic meaning, etc., when it is convenient to do so, only incurring overhead for such properties when required.

The Playground system comes with a set of predefined facets implementing a wide range of mundane properties of universal utility. These predefined facets can be specialized or overridden as desired. Whenever any value for a slot in a facet is changed, the timestamp field is updated and any other agents that are watching the value of this facet are notified.

Rule Compilation

The Playground language is implemented using a phrasal parser. This design was suggested by the phrasal lexicon theory described by [Becker, 1975].

The language is specified by a large set of shallow production rules which enumerate the phrases the language will accept. There are two kinds of rules: phrasal rules and nonphrasal rules. A *phrasal rule* must contain one or more terminal symbols. A *nonphrasal rule* mentions only abstract grammatical categories.

Playground rules are entered as text strings in the edit pane. Playground converts these textual strings into an array of tokens such as word, number, special character, etc. The terminal symbols in the phrasal rules are matched against the tokens, giving a list of nonterminal symbols to seek.

This list is run down, and successful phrase matches are retained on the parse chart for further analysis. Analysis then proceeds from the top down, seeking a coherent overall structure. The result is a parse tree. Each phrasal rule contains information on how to convert its meaning into a Smalltalk/V expression. The compiler then transverses the tree, activating the "generate expressions," converting our phrasal syntax into conventional Smalltalk. At appropriate places in the code, special yield messages are inserted. The result is submitted to the Smalltalk/V compiler, giving a Smalltalk method which, when executed, generates an instance of a Playground lightweight process.

For example, the Playground agent script:

```
When I am over nest;
Change costume to black box.
Make sound from file 'meow sound'.
```

when compiled against the phrasal grammar:

```
COMMAND ::= when VALUE
    generate: 'self when: &2'.
FUNCTION ::= i am over VALUE
    generate: '(self over: &4)'.
COMMAND ::= change costume to VALUE
    generate: '(self costume: &4)'.
COMMAND ::= make sound from file VALUE
    generate: '(self sound: &5)'.
NAME ::= black box
    generate: 'BlackBox'.
```

will generate the following sequence of Smalltalk/V code:

```
temporaryMethod
I codeSeq procObject I
codeSeq:= [(procObject semaphore0 wait.
    self when: (self over: (self bindingAt: #nest)).
    self costume: BlackBox. Processor yield.
    self sound: 'meow sound'.
    procObject noteDone].
procObject:= (PlayAgentProcess new: nil running:
codeSeq).
procObject setAutoRepeat.
^procObject.
```

Whenever a given agent becomes active, this process generator method is executed, which adds a Playground lightweight task to the run list for the host object. These tasks exploit the multitasking capability of Smalltalk/V.

ANIMATION AND COMMUNICATION

Every viewable graphical object has abounding rectangle, a depth coordinate, and a costume. The bounding rectangle and depth coordinate give the location in the Playfield that the object occupies. The costume points to a costume object, which can be a string, form, primitive shape, or composite. An object can change its costume at will, to animate or to present different editing capabilities to the user. Whenever the costume is changed, the bounds are adjusted to accurately describe the extent of the costume.

One type of useful Playground object is called an *observable collection*. An agent can allocate an observable collection and add other Playground objects to it, and automatically receive notification of any changes occurring to its members. This is how animation and telecommunications are accomplished.

The animation code uses an observable collection to track all objects on the Playfield. When any object changes, it is added to a list of changed objects. During each animation cycle, this list is retrieved and examined. For each object that has changed, the old and new object boundaries are accumulated into a dirty region list of non-overlapping rectangles. For each dirty cluster, the screen is redrawn in back-to-front order in an offscreen buffer, which is then copied onto the user's display screen (see Figure 3-7).

A similar method is used to accomplish telecommunications. Each object to be shared with remote stations is added to an observable collection, which again accumulates a list of those objects that have changed recently. The telecommunications code goes down this list, comparing the present slot values for the object with previous values, broadcasting the changes discovered. The receiving code likewise keeps a list of changes received, which it then applies locally.

Both the animation and telecommunications methods require that two copies be kept of each object, one giving the current state, the other representing the previous state.

Figure 8 shows how the telecommunications mechanism informs observers at remote stations about the motion of the fish and bubble objects.

HISTORY

Work on Playground began during the summer of 1986. During the past three years, three distinct versions of the program have been created and tested.

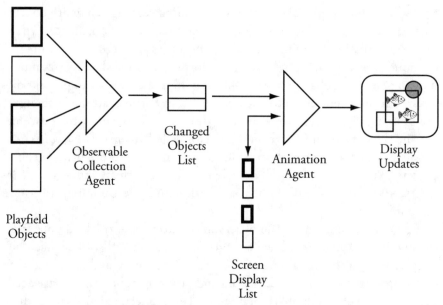

Figure 3-7 Animation Process

Playground 1 is coded in Lightspeed C for the Macintosh. The Playground 1 programming language used a functional notation similar to LISP but with few parentheses. Program statements were tokenized, then interpreted using recursive descent. Playground 1 achieved high animation and telecommunications performance.

Playground 2 is implemented in Digitalk Smalltalk/V [Digitalk, 1988] running on the Macintosh II series of computers. The high interpretation overhead of Smalltalk forced us to emphasize language experiments at the expense of animation and communication. The first language tried was a modified SELF syntax [Ungar, 1987]. A SELF style delegation scheme was also tried and dropped in favor of a direct copying scheme.

Playground 3 is also implemented in Smalltalk/V and uses the operating environment created for Playground 2. The language was changed to the more natural syntax previously described in this paper.

The following table shows the same statement written in the three versions of Playground:

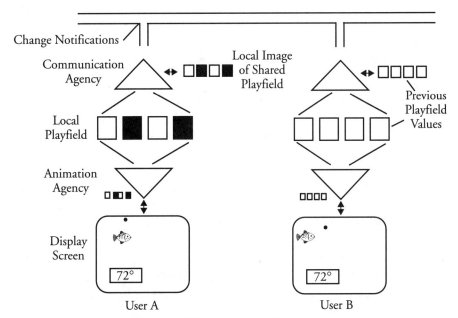

Figure 3-8 Telecommunications Process

Version 1: mousedown: moveto (shot,mousex,150).
Version 2: notice: MouseDown.shot moveTo: (MouseX@150).
Version 3: On mouse clock move shot to MouseX @ 150.

We have found children to be most demanding and stimulating test subjects. In early testing with a more artificial concrete syntax, some children were still able to construct simulations of surprising complexity.

SCHOOL TESTING

Playground has undergone testing using groups of children at the Open School. Generally we do exploratory testing using small groups of 5 to 8 children first, gearing up for larger scale tests involving a class of 30 to 60 children taught by their regular teacher.

The Playground 2 version of the language was tested using a group of 60 fourth and fifth graders during the spring of 1989. The children were taught in two groups of 30. Each group met twice a week for 4 weeks. Each session lasted 1 hour. Each session opened with 20 or 30 minutes of demonstration and discussion, followed by a "lab" period where pairs of children completed the assigned programming exercises.

The material was presented in the following sequence:

- How to run and quit the Playground program. Use of user interface to create and modify graphical objects. How to name objects and give them rules. The coordinate system and how to make an object move by writing a simple agent. How to run and freeze the Playfield.

- Create random motion of objects by changing their speed and heading. Construct agents that display the internal state of other objects. Change an object's costume. Assign properties to objects. Simple counting.

- Construct agents enabling a "Fish" object to detect food and move toward it when hunger has grown high enough. Detect when fish is over food and eat it, resetting a "hunger" counter. Use of "clone" command to create multiple instances.

- Construct "Plankton" and "Plant" objects and have grow, reproduce, and die. Enhance fish to follow a life cycle as well. Count birth and death statistics.

Unfortunately, the spring experiment was curtailed due to a system-wide teachers strike. If the experiment had not been halted, we would also have covered the following:

- Add a "Shark" predator to eat the fish. Add agents to the fish to notice sharks and evade them. Have fish weigh hunger against fear. Study the predator/prey balance and population ecology.

- Construct other simulations such as video games and animated stories using Playground's features.

Fortunately, the strike was settled in time to be able to debrief the children and teachers approximately 3 weeks after the experiment was halted.

The students remembered quite a lot about Playground, even after having been away from it for 3 weeks during the strike and its aftermath. The children generally enjoyed using Playground, and most succeeded in accomplishing their assigned tasks. They were naturally annoyed at the bugs, unnatural syntax conventions, the relatively low speed of the interpreted environment, and deficiencies in error handling and reporting.

One child astounded us by creating an elaborate aquarium that included two species of plankton, a whale, jellyfish, seaweed, rays, fish, and crabs, using features that were not explained in the workbook or by the teacher.

The Open School students has a long list of suggestions on how to improve the Playground. The following list is an excerpt from our notes:

Q. What improvements should we make to Playground?

A. Building video games. Add flip book animation. Speech synthesis. Speed it up. Put in a sound box with many sounds and the ability to add more. Proximity detector. FullPaint and HyperTalk painting tools. Mouths that move as objects talk. VCR-type control panel. Realistic movement. Grouping of objects. More commands. Directed animation (frog sticking out tongue). Path animation, More shapes, spelling checker, study box to remember mistakes. Speech recognition, clairvoyant typing, color mixing, get rid of typing coordinates. Better command keys for run and stop (Enter and Space were suggested). Rotation of objects. Make screen bigger. Linked Playfields like Hypercard's.

Q. What sorts of things would you like to be able to do with Playground?

A. Social Studies, Sports, Race Track, Gymnasium, Cartoons, Science Fiction, Olympics, Westerns, Murder stories, Chemistry, Treasure Hunt, Trigonometry, Games, Music, Comics, Car crash, Sound Effects, Commercials, RoboCop, Spiderman, record what you are doing. Make a movie. Give characters different voices. Make a playground, hide in holes, talk to it (using speech recognition), a soap opera, space station. Soccer. Buildings. Make faces.

CONCLUSION

Our experience with Playground has encouraged us to explore several areas for making the system more accessible to children, including expanding or altering the user interface.

INTERFACE

Comic books are well known for their popular appeal and offer a number of fruitful user intake ideas. For example, a sequence of operations can be expressed as a succession of panels. In addition, we could adopt a number of stylistic conventions for incorporating textual descriptions along with graphics. For example, the user could open a text editing balloon attached to a given object, and edit the text associated with it.

Another significant problem we face is enabling children to design pleasing animal forms with engaging modes of movement. One promising approach is guided evolution, pioneered by Dawns [Dawkins, 1986], in which a constructed genome controls the creation of form, the genome is randomly mutated in several ways, the user selecting among them.

OTHER USE COMMUNITIES

We hope to eventually create a general purpose language for personal computer users. We need to explore ways of applying the Playground programming style to desktop programming problems.

IMPLEMENTATION

We are convinced that the pulling-style control structure has significant advantages over message sending. We have yet to implement a version of pulling that is efficient enough to be the basis of all computation. We are exploring techniques used in artificial intelligence for dependency management, hoping to gain enough performance for our next round of experiments.

FINALLY

We envision a system in which a group of children sit around a large, central screen showing the composite view of the Vivarium, rendered in full color in three dimensions. Each child has an individual screen on which to view and modify the shared world.

Through three-dimensional input devices with feedback, they design the form and behavior of a group of animals are able to cooperate in building complicated individuals with sophisticated group behavior.

Perhaps the Central Intelligence Agency could use Playground to build a comprehensive simulation of the Soviet railway system that puts Lionel to shame. In any case, we look forward to being astounded with what the children of the world do with our system.

ACKNOWLEDGMENTS

Alan Kay and Ann Marion deserve credit as codesigners of Playground, along with Kent Beck and Scott Wallace. Thanks are due to Mike Travers for suggesting the gated agent rule approach. George Bosworth contributed insights and code, Ted Kaehler, Steve DeWitt, and members of our illustrious advisory board have made their contributions to Playgrounds design. Erfert Fenton helped edit this paper. David Mintz and B.J. Allen taught P to our kids, who themselves deserve honor for their pioneering spirit.

REFERENCES

Becker, Joseph D. June 1975. *The Phrasal Lexicon,* Bolt, Beranek, and Newman Report, No. 3081.

Borin, Alan H. November 1986. *Classes Versus Prototypes in Object Oriented Languages,* Proceedings of the ACM/IEEE Fall Joint Computer Conference.

Dawkins, Richard. 1986. *The Blind Watchmaker,* W.W. Norton & Company.

Digitalk. 1998. *SmallTalk/V Mac Tutorial and Programming Handbook,* Los Angeles.

Fauconnier, Giles. 1985. *Mental Spaces,* MIT Press.

Gardin, Francesco and Bernard Meltzer. 1989. *Analogical Representations of Naive Physics,* Artificial Intelligence 38, pg. 139-159.

Grier, James W. 1984. *Biology of Animal Behavior,* Times Mirror/Mosby College Publishing, St. Louis.

Ingalls, Dan, Scott Wallace, Yu-Ying Chow, Frank Ludolph, Ken Doyle. 1998. *Fabrik— A Visual Programming Environment,* OOPSLA 88 Proceedings, San Diego, pg. 176-190.

Lakoff, George. 1987. *Women, Fire, And Dangerous Things,* The University of Chicago Press, Chicago.

Minsky, Marvin. 1985. *The Society of Mind,* Simon and Schuster, New York.

Papert, Seymour. 1980. *Mindstorms: Children, Computers, and Powerful Ideas,* Basic Books, New York.

Smith, Randall B. June 1986. *The Alternate Reality Kit: An Animated Environment of Creating Interactive Simulations,* Proceedings of the 1986 IEEE Computer Society Workshop Visual Languages, Dallas TX, pg. 99-106.

Tinbergen, Niko. 1951. *The Study of Instinct,* Oxford University Press.

Travers, Mike. 1988. *Agar: An Animated Construction Kit,* Unpublished masters thesis, M.I.T. media lab.

Ungar, David and Randall B. Smith. 1987. *Self: The Power of Simplicity,* OOPSLA ë87 Conference Proceedings, pg. 227-242.

Wilensky, R. *Some Problems and Proposal for Knowledge Representation,* Computer Science Division, University of California- Berkeley, Report No. UCB/CSD 87/351.

Abridged Playground 3 Vocabulary

set NAME to VALUE—set value to a slot.

    set curiosity to 30.

angle; set angle to VALUE—controls the direction an object will travel. Angles are in degrees following the compass rose.

    set Angle to 90. ìgets player going eastî

bearing from VALUE {to VALUE}—the degrees to the object or point given as an argument.

    display bearing from 200 @ 100 to Sam.

bounds—gives the bounding rectangle
The boundaries of an object can be referred to by phrases like these:

    my top right corner
    my center
    the bottom right corner of VALUE and so on.

Each of the above can also be used in the set command for, example:

    set my top right corner to the center of cactus.

clock—how many ticks of the Playground world have gone by.

clone yourself—make an exact copy of this object and give it an independent existence in this world.

change costume to VALUE—set the way an objects looks.
set the costume to black rectangle.

depth, set depth to VALUE—change depth coordinate to new value given.

display VALUE—change my costume to display the number or name given as an argument.

distance from Object {to OBJECT}—calculate the distance from one object to another.

NAME from VALUE—returns the value of a property from another object.

go forward VALUE steps—move current object forward the number of units requested.

go to POINT—move object towards a specific point at the current speed.
go to 100 @ 150.

grow by VALUE—change size by factor given.

if VALUE then STATEMENT—execute STATEMENT only when VALUE is true.
if bozo < 12 then display "that's a bozo no no!".

make sound from file STRING—trigger playing sound with name given.
make sound from file 'monkey'. The quote marks are required.

move by XYAMOUNT—move the object by an amount on both x and y axis.
move by -20 @ -2. (move 20 to the left, 2 up)

move to LOCATION—move to the location given.
move to 100 @ 200.

nearest object with property NAME—returns nearest
object which has the property requested.
go to (nearest object with property green) center.

notice CONDITION—introduces the condition part of an
agent rule.

number—retrieve the value of the costume as a number.
display number * 2. "double each tick of the world"

over OBJECT—returns true when one object overlaps
another.

over somebody with property NAME—sets true if one
object overlaps another object which has a certain property.
notice over somebody with property food.

VALUE random—returns a random number between 0 and
1 less than VALUE.

remove yourself—removes this object from the world forever.

set result to VALUE—set result cell to value given.
return VALUE—return value as result for this agent.

my result—return result for this agent.
result for NAME—return result for another agent in this
object.
result for NAME {in VALUE}—return result for another
object.

speed, set speed to VALUE—sets the speed that an object should move in pixels per second.

wait VALUE ticks—cause THIS AGENT to wait the requested time interval before continuing execution.

who i am over {with property NAME}—returns a pointer to whatever object I am over that has the property requested, if any.

4

A LABORATORY FOR TEACHING OBJECT-ORIENTED THINKING

WITH WARD CUNNINGHAM
OOPSLA '89 Proceedings

This is the biggie, the paper that made my name (and to a lesser extent Ward's, since he was already a little famous). I got my name first on the paper because of our rule that whoever wrote the first draft of a paper got to put his name first. This has caused considered confusion since then, with people crediting me as the inventor of CRC, or telling Ward how exciting it must have been for him to work with me.

There are a couple of stories about this paper. First, the title. Ward and I wanted to be very careful not to claim more for CRC than we could prove. We knew it was good for teaching "object-think," so that's the approach we took in the paper, the one single point we pushed. We deliberately understated what we thought the impact would be, leaving it to our readers to extrapolate to making CRC cards into a design or analysis technique. We spent at least an hour on the phone polishing the title, and the result pleases me as much now as it did then.

Another story- I missed OOPSLA '89, waiting for the arrival of Lincoln Curtis, child number two. I had no idea of the impact of this paper. Then I attended OOPSLA '90 in Ottawa. I was in a "Design and Analysis" BOF. The biggies were all there: Booch, Constantine, Yourdon. We were fumbling for a place to start, so someone said, "Well, who here has tried CRC cards in the last year?" Every hand went up. I was absolutely floored. The discussion then went on to the extensions of CRC and how they differed from the classical or traditional style (remember, this is one year later). I was a guru. Yikes!

I T IS DIFFICULT TO INTRODUCE both novice and experienced procedural programmers to the anthropomorphic perspective necessary for object-oriented design. We introduce CRC cards, which characterize objects by class name, responsibilities, and collaborators, as a way of giving learners a direct experience of objects. We have found this approach successful in teaching novice programmers the concepts of objects, and in introducing experienced programmers to complicated existing designs.

Problem

The most difficult problem in teaching object-oriented programming is getting the learner to give up the global knowledge of control that is possible with procedural programs, and rely on the local knowledge of objects to accomplish their tasks. Novice designs are littered with regressions to global thinking: gratuitous global variables, unnecessary pointers, and inappropriate reliance on the implementation of other objects.

Because learning about objects requires such a shift in overall approach, teaching objects reduces to teaching the design of objects. We focus on design whether we are teaching basic concepts to novices or the subtleties of a complicated design to experienced object programmers.

Rather than try to make object design as much like procedural design as possible, we have found that the most effective way of teaching the idiomatic way of thinking with objects is to immerse the learner in the "object-ness" of the material. To do this we must remove as much familiar material as possible, expecting that details such as syntax and programming environment operation will be picked up quickly enough once the fundamentals have been thoroughly understood.

It is in this context that we will describe our perspective on object design, its concrete manifestation, CRC (for Class, Responsibility, and Collaboration) cards, and our experience using these cards to teach both the fundamentals and subtleties of thinking with objects.

PERSPECTIVE

Procedural designs can be characterized at an abstract level as having processes, data flows, and data stores[1], regardless of implementation language or operating environment. We wished to come up with a similar set of fundamental principles for object designs. We settled on three dimensions which identify the role of an object in a design: class name, responsibilities, and collaborators.

The class name of an object creates a vocabulary for discussing a design. Indeed, many people have remarked that object design has more in common with language design than with procedural program design. We urge learners (and spend considerable time ourselves while designing) to find just the right set of words to describe our objects, a set that is internally consistent and evocative in the context of the larger design environment.

Responsibilities identify problems to be solved. The solutions will exist in many versions and refinements. A responsibility serves as a handle for discussing potential solutions. The responsibilities of an object are expressed by a handful of short verb phrases, each containing an active verb. The more that can be expressed by these phrases, the more powerful and concise the design. Again, searching for just the right words is a valuable use of time while designing.

One of the distinguishing features of object design is that no object is an island. All objects stand in relationship to others, on whom they rely for services and control. The last dimension we use in characterizing object designs is the collaborators of an object. We name as collaborators objects which will send or be sent messages in the course of satisfying responsibilities. Collaboration is not necessarily a symmetric relation. For example in Smalltalk-80[2], View and Controller operate as near equals (see example below) while Ordered-Collection offers a service with little regard or even awareness of its client.

Throughout this paper we deliberately blur the distinction between classes and instances. This informality is not as confusing as it might seem because the concreteness of our method substitutes for naming of instances. This also makes our method for teaching independent of whether a class or prototype-based language is used.

CRC Cards

The second author invented CRC cards in response to a need to document collaborative design decisions. The cards started as a Hypercard[3] stack which provided automatic indexing to collaborators, but were moved to their current form to address problems of portability and system independence.

Like our earlier work in documenting the collaboration of objects[4], CRC cards explicitly represent multiple objects simultaneously. However, rather than simply tracing the details of a collaboration in the form of message sending, CRC cards place the designer s focus on the motivation for collaboration by representing (potentially) many messages as a phrase of English text.

As we currently use them, all the information for an object is written on a 4" x 6" index card. These have the advantages that they are cheap, portable, readily available, and familiar. Figure 4-1 shows an idealized card. The class name appears underlined in the upper-left hand corner, a bullet-list of responsibilities appears under it in the left two-thirds of the card, and the list of collaborators appears in the right third.

Figure 2 shows an example taken from the Smalltalk-80 image, the much-misunderstood model-view-controller user interface framework. We have deliberately shown only a portion of the responsibilities each of these objects assumes for clarity of exposition. Note that the cards are placed such that View and Controller are overlapping (implying close collaboration) and placed above Model (implying supervision). We find these and other informal groupings aid in comprehending a design. Parts, for example, are often arranged below the whole. Likewise, refinements of an abstraction can be collected and handled as a single pile of cards with the most abstract card on top where it can represent the rest.

The ability to quickly organize and spatially address index cards proves most valuable when a design is incomplete or poorly understood. We have watched designers repeatedly refer to a card they intended to write by pointing to where they will put it when completed.

Design with the cards tends to progress from knowns to unknowns, as opposed to top-down or bottom up. We have observed two teams arriving at essentially the same design through nearly opposite sequences, one starting with device drivers, the other with high-level models. The problem demanded a certain set of capabilities which both teams discovered in the course of fulfilling the requirements of the design.

We suggest driving a design toward completion with the aid of execution

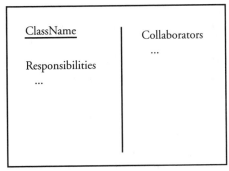

Figure 4-1 A Class-Responsibility-Collaborator (CRC) index card.

scenarios. We start with only one or two obvious cards and start playing "what-if". If the situation calls for a responsibility not already covered by one of the objects we either add the responsibility to one of the objects or create a new object to address that responsibility. If one of the object becomes too cluttered during this process we copy the information on its card to a new card, searching for more concise and powerful ways of saying what the object does. If it is not possible to shrink the information further, but the ob-

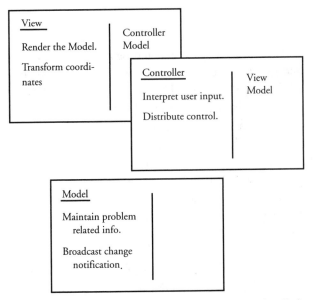

Figure 4-2 CRC-cards describing the responsibilities and collaborations of Smalltalk's Model, View and Controller.

ject is still too complex, we create a new object to assume some of the responsibilities.

We encourage learners to pick up the card whose role they are assuming while "executing" a scenario. It is not unusual to see a designer with a card in each hand, waving them about, making a strong identification with the objects while describing their collaboration.

We stress the importance of creating objects not to meet mythical future needs, but only under the demands of the moment. This ensures that a design contains only as much information as the designer has directly experienced, and avoids premature complexity. Working in teams helps here because a concerned designer can influence team members by suggesting scenarios aimed specifically at suspected weaknesses or omissions.

EXPERIENCE

One of the contexts in which we have used CRC cards is a three-hour class entitled "Thinking with Objects," which is intended for computing professionals who have programmed, but whose jobs do not necessarily involve programming every day. The class proceeds by introducing a data flow example (a school, with processes for teaching and administration) which is then recast in terms of objects with responsibilities and collaborators (such as Teacher, Janitor, and Principal). The class then pairs off and spends an hour designing the objects in an automatic banking machine, an exercise chosen because of everyone's familiarity with the application and its ready breakdown into objects to control the devices, communicate with the central bank database, and control the user interface. (See the appendix for a sample solution.) The exercise is followed by a definition of the terms "class", "instance", "method", and "message", and the class concludes with a brief discussion of the history and features of a variety of object-oriented programming languages.

In teaching over a hundred students this course we have encountered no one who was unable to complete the exercise unaided, although one pair in each class usually needs a few hints to get started. Although we have done no follow-up studies, the class is considered a valuable resource in the company and is still well attended with a long waiting list almost a year after its inception.

We have also asked skilled object programmers to try using CRC cards. Our personal experience suggests a role for cards in software engineering though we cannot yet claim a complete methodology (others[5], [6] have more fully developed methodologies that can take advantage of CRC methods). We know of one case where finished cards were delivered to a client as (partial) design documentation. Although the team that produced the cards was quite happy with the design, the recipient was unable to make sense of the cards out of context.

Another experiment illustrates the importance of the context established by the handling and discussing of cards. We had videotaped experienced designers working out a problem similar to the bank machine. Our camera placement made cards and the designers' hands visible but not the writing on the cards. Viewers of the tape had no trouble following the development and often asked that the tape be stopped so that they could express their opinions. the most telling moments came when a viewer's explanation required that he point to a blurry card in the frozen image on the screen.

Finally, we have used CRC cards to advantage in explaining complex designs. A few minutes of introduction is sufficient to prepare an audience for a card based presentation. Cards can be made out in advance or written on the spot. The latter allows the complexity in a design to be revealed slowly, a process related to Dave Thomas' "lie management". The cards are being used as props to aid the telling of a story of computation. The cards allow its telling without recourse to programming language syntax or idiom.

CONCLUSION

Taking our perspective as a base we give novices and experienced programmers a learning experience which teaches them something valuable about objects. CRC cards give the learner who has never encountered objects a physical understanding of object-ness, and prepares them to understand the vocabulary and details of particular languages. CRC cards also give useful and convincing experience with objects to those who has learned the mechanisms of objects but do not yet see their value.

Ragu Raghavan[7] has said that in the switch to objects strong programmers become stronger, but weaker programmers are left behind. Using the cards in group settings we found that even weaker programmers, without a deep understanding of objects, could contribute to object designs. We speculate that because the designs are so much more concrete, and the logical relationship between objects explicit, it is easier to understand, evaluate, and modify a design.

We were surprised at the value of physically moving the cards around. When learners pick up an object they seem to more readily identify with it, and are prepared to deal with the remainder of the design from its perspective. It is the value of this physical interaction that has led us to resist a computerization of the cards.

It is just this problem-integrating the cards with larger design methodologies and with particular language environments, that we feel holds the most promise for the future. The need to retain the value of physical interaction points to the need for a new kind of user interface and programming environment as far beyond what we have today as our current systems are beyond the tool-oriented environments of the past.

REFERENCES

DeMarco, T.: Structured Analysis and System Specification, Yourdon, 1978.

Smalltalk-80 image, Xerox Corp, 1983.

Hypercard manual, Apple Computer, Inc.

Cunningham, W. and Beck, K.: "A Diagram for Object-Oriented Programs," in Proceedings of OOPSLA-86, October 1986.

Wirfs-Brock, R. and Wilkerson, B. "Object-Oriented Design: a Responsibility-Driven Approach," submitted to OOPSLA '89.

Reenskaug, T.: "A Methodology for the Design and Description of Complex, object-oriented Systems," technical report, Center for Industrial Research, Oslo, Norway, November 1988.

Raghavan, R.: "Panel: Experiences with Reusability," in the Proceedings of OOPSLA '88, October, 1988.

APPENDIX

Here we provide a sample solution to the banking machine problem discussed in section 4.

Account and Transaction provide the banking model. Note that Transaction assumes an active role while money is being dispensed and a passive role thereafter.

Transactions meet their responsibilities with the aid of several objects that serve as device drivers. The Dispenser object, for example, ultimately operates the dispensing device.

The CardReader object reads and decodes the information on the bank card's magnetic strip. A common mistake would be to itemize all of the information stored on the bank card. Card encoding formats must certainly be well thought out and documented. However, for the purpose of designing the objects, we need only identify where that knowledge will be placed in the program

The RemoteDataBase drives the communication lines and inter-

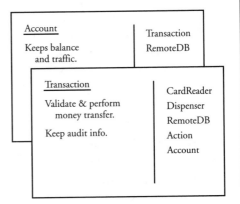

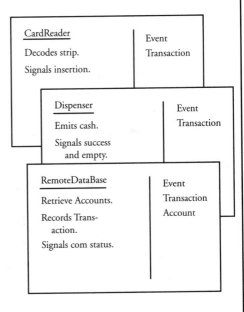

prets data transmitted across them. It creates Account objects and consumes Transaction objects.

The device drivers signal exceptional or asynchronous events by adding Event objects to a shared queue.

Events drive the human interface by triggering Actions that sequence through Screens. The actual format and sequence of screens will be determined by the user-interface design and will probably vary from bank to bank. We offer objects from which state-machine like interfaces can be built.

Screen objects correspond to the states and Action objects correspond to the transitions. Screens may vary in how they dispatch Actions. Actions themselves will vary in how they process events. Actions ultimately construct Transactions to which they delegate the further operating of the bank machine.

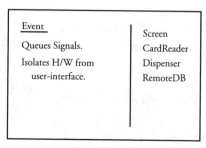

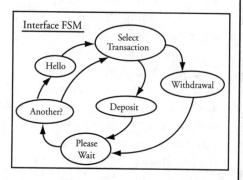

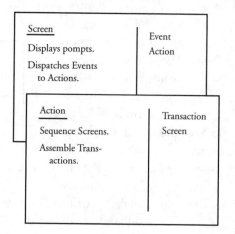

5

THINK LIKE AN OBJECT

Unix Review, OCTOBER, 1991

This was the first article I wrote after the big splash. I was asked to write the article for a special issue on objects, "something about CRC cards." I remember re-reading the "Laboratory..." article and thinking, "I can't do anything better than that. That article says it all."

After a brief pause for a personal crisis, I thought, "What the hell. I'll just write the same stuff with different words." What came out, though, was very different. The original CRC article convinced bright people that CRC was a good idea. This one convinces regular engineers that they, too, can get started with objects.

Ward's goal when we wrote together was to write prose that fairly dripped with meaning. You could read the same sentence every six months and get new meaning out of it. The result is complex, dense, evocative, and sometimes hard to read.

This article is the first time I found my own voice. My writing voice is much plainer than Ward's. I write like I speak: plain and direct (although I generally use fewer expletives when I write). Both Ward's style and mine are directly at odds with my academic training, which was to layer any possible meaning behind layers of jargon, notation, and convoluted sentence structure. I suppose it's no wonder it took me a while to get over that.

The opening sentence of this article came to me whole, and the rest of the article kind of took care of itself. To write the article, I put myself in the place of someone who had heard about objects but was kind of afraid to get started, and told him or here what to do to get over that hump.

I was shocked when I was done. The article sounded like nothing I had ever written before, but I really liked it. Looking at it again, I still wiggle my shoulders proudly. This is decent advice today for someone who wants to get started with objects.

TOSS OUT SOME OLD IDEAS, take an objective perspective, and shuffle some index cards. The CRC method makes object-oriented design approachable.

You may have been reading about objects for a long time but never actually tried making any of your own. Learning to design good objects requires a shift from thinking globally about the system to taking the perspective of each object in turn. This article explains how you can begin to design objects in a few hours with ordinary office supplies.

When I learned about object-oriented programming using Smalltalk, I was preoccupied by the picayune details of the language. I spent the first six months understanding the subtleties of the syntax, learning the class libraries, studying the language semantics and implementation, and mastering the programming environment. At the end of that first half year, I had a solid grasp on all the little issues of an object language, but I still knew nothing about objects.

I had been reimmersing myself in issues familiar to time from my days as a procedural programmer. I focused on the non-object-oriented aspects of my object-oriented language to avoid the uncomfortable feeling that I didn't know what was going on. By clinging to my old ways of thinking, like a nervous swimmer to the side of the pool, I was preventing myself from reinventing my perspective. It was only through patient and expert tutelage that I was able to break free to my old habits and begin to make use of the power in objects.

I now know that learning objects needn't be frightening or confusing. By appropriately focusing on purely object issues and ignoring more familiar but confusing topics, I have helped hundreds of procedural programmers, managers, quality engineers, and educators obtain the experience of object-oriented design in a three-hour class. Others who teach this approach have introduced thousands more to objects. If you're willing to trust yourself to learn the syntax and programming environment later (after all, you've probably learned several of each already), you can be doing objects in a few hours, too.

The rest of this article explains a perspective on objects that reduces objects to their essence and describes an example object-oriented design in terms of this perspective. Then I'll discuss how you can use this view of objects to do your own designs, and I'll conclude with some tips for evaluating object designs.

THE CRC PERSPECTIVE

If you are going to quickly learn about designing objects you can't possibly focus on everything at once. The approach described here focuses on deciding which object will do which part of the computation. Only when the right objects are doing the right jobs is it appropriate to move on to other issues, such as how the objects will be represented and how they will use inheritance.

Procedural programming fosters a global perspective. In any given subroutine in a procedural program you know where you came from and where you are going. On the other hand, each object in an object-oriented program has a strictly local perspective. It is the collective effect of the community of objects working together that accomplishes the computation. Learning object-oriented design requires a shift from relying on overall knowledge to make design decisions to taking on a multiplicity of local views.

Designing objects requires many small decisions, giving parts of the computation to different objects. Ward Cunningham recognized this "distribution of responsibility" as the fundamental design decision to which all others are secondary. He devised a method called Class-Responsibility- Collaborator (CRC) that helps designers distribute responsibilities without worrying about issues properly left until later in the design. The CRC method characterizes objects along three dimensions:

- *Class name.* Naming objects creates a vocabulary that will be used to discuss the design, implementation, and user's model. Carefully choosing names early in design clarifies the designers' collective understanding of the system and sets the stage for correctly making later design decisions.

- *Responsibilities.* Each object fulfills a purpose in the design. It implements some small portion of the overall behavior of the system. These responsibilities are described by short phrases using active verbs. As with object naming, refining the words used to describe responsibilities is a valuable design activity.

- *Collaborators.* Each object relies on others to fulfill its responsibilities. The set of helper objects an object needs is called its collaborators. Nothing collaboration helps refine the designers' understanding of how re-sponsibilities are distributed across the system.

The CRC design perspective explicitly defers decisions about inheritance until later in the design (or even implementation). Novice object designers who are allowed to think about inheritance first will spend far too much time ar-riving at a perfectly factored class hierarchy that ignores the needs of users and the realities of the implementation. The CRC view places the valuable resource of inheritance firmly in the hands of the implementor, where it can be used to pragmatically reduce the number of lines of code written and maintained.

Inheritance has other valid uses, such as protocol specification or object classification. Regardless of inheritance decisions until after you have fac-tored the behavior in your system into objects will ensure that you make the best use of inheritance.

CRC also ignores issues of object representation. At some point repre-sentation decisions become critical: embedded vs. pointed-to, stack vs. heap-allocated, and object types vs. build-in language types. Having a solid distribution of responsibility will make these decisions easier because you will know what each object has to do with the information it stores.

An Example

The following example will show how objects are represented in the CRC model, how responsibilities are discovered, and how responsibilities shift from object to object during design.

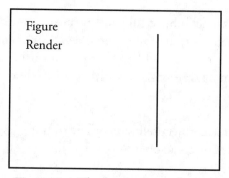

Figure 5-1 The beginnings of a Figure.

Let's say we want a simple drawing editor that manipulates a collection of rectangles in a window. The fundamental object—the rectangle on the screen—we will call a *Figure*.

As yet, *Figures* only have the responsibility of rendering themselves. Rendering implies that the Figure knows where and how big it is, but having noted the need to represent this information we will ignore it, trusting that the correct representation will be more clear after the design has taken shape.

Figures do not stand alone; they exist in relation to other *Figures*. Here we come to our first distribution-of-responsibility decision: do *Figures* have the responsibility of ordering themselves front to back (for example, in a linked list) or does some other object order them? Ordering seems to be so different a responsibility from rendering that we put it in a separate object, the *Drawing*.

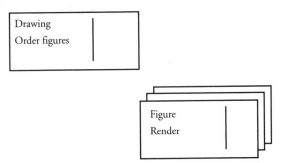

Figure 5-2 Drawing a Figure.

We can imagine putting messages like "bring to front" and "send to back" in the *Drawing,* while the *Figures* would never know they were being shuffled about. This simple thought experiment helps convince us that we are on the right track.

To complete the display portion of our drawing editor, we must add to the system the responsibility of displaying the drawing clipped to a window on the screen. Since this responsibility seems foreign to the objects we have so far, we create a third object, *DrawingWindow*.

First, notice we added *Drawing* as a collaborator of *DrawingWindow*. The *DrawingWindow* cannot discharge its responsibility of rendering without help from the *Drawing*. Second the *DrawingWindow* is protected from the knowledge that its *Drawing* is really an ordered sequence of *Figures* by pushing most of the work of rendering off on the *Drawing*. This way, if we had a drawing that was nothing more than a bitmapped picture we could still use *DrawingWindow* unchanged. Again, a thought experiment that stresses the design convinces us we are making progress.

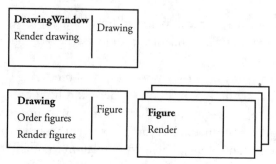

Figure 5-3 A Drawing in a Window.

Now we want to let users interact with the *Figures*. If we assume this editor will run in an environment where windows are delivered user-interface events (such as "the mouse button just went down"), we can add the responsibility for interpreting events to *DrawingWindow*.

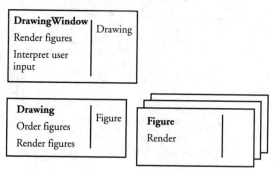

Figure 5-4 A Window begins to edit.

The interaction is not complete, since the *DrawingWindow* does not know which *Figure* to modify. The *Drawing* and *Figures* will have to collaborate to tell the *DrawingWindow* which *Figure* is being pointed at, since only the *Drawing* knows *Figures* is in front (the search will proceed front to back) and only the *Figure* knows where and big it is.

To complete our simple scenario we need to be able to move a *Figure* once it has been identified by the *DrawingWindow*. A simple implementation has the *DrawingWindow* get a *Figure* from the *Drawing* geographically, note the *Figure*'s outline, move the *Figure*, and redraw the area in the union of the old and new outlines.

This design has the virtue of simplicity, but it gives the *DrawingWindow*

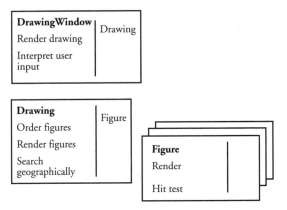

Figure 5-5 Finding a Figure.

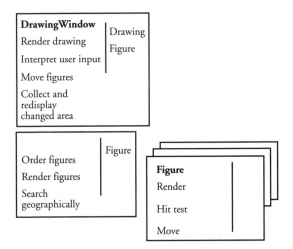

Figure 5-6 Moving A Figure.

a new collaborator and violates the valuable property noted previously that the *DrawingWindow* doesn't know that its *Drawing* is a list of *Figures*.

Another approach that simplifies our design is to have the *DrawingWindow* defer responsibility for moving *Figures* and collecting changes to the *Drawing*, and keep for itself only the responsibility for redisplaying the changed area.

The resulting design is beginning to show a bit of strain on the *Drawing* as it collects more responsibilities. If we were going to continue to refine the design, we might find other objects to accept some of the *Drawing*'s responsibilities or find a way to express them more concisely.

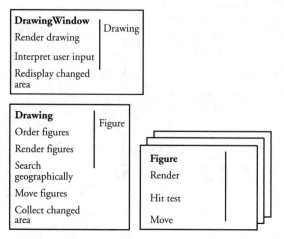

Figure 5-7 Redistributed responsibilities.

In summary, we have seen a design grow from a single object with a single responsibility to a community of objects in which responsibilities have shifted as the complexity of the design reveals itself.

DESIGNING WITH CRC

I use the CRC perspective with simple 3" x 5" index cards to design objects. I lay out the cards as shown in the example above. The class name goes in the upper left corner, responsibilities down the left edge, and collaborators down the right side. Although the temptation to computerize the cards is strong, current user-interface technology doesn't provide many of the benefits of index cards:

- *Cheap.* You can design hundreds of objects per dollar.

- *Approachable.* No one is intimidated by the user-interface. New designers can focus exclusively on the design itself, without also having to think about which mouse button to use or which menu contains the item they are looking for.

- *Physical.* When you pick up an object you are encouraged to look at the rest of the design from the object's perspective, knowing no more than that objects knows. Choosing to temporarily ignore global design knowledge and take a strictly object-centered view is the first step in learning to "think like an object."

- *Portable.* Anyone can carry a stack of cards around, so the design medium is available wherever and whenever it is needed.

This is not to say that computers are not an appropriate medium for CRC-based designs; they just have a long way to go before they can match the advantages of using simple scraps of paper.

When I design with CRC cards, I start with one or two objects. Designers who start by creating all the objects they're "just sure" they'll need usually throw them away by the end of the design phase. Save yourself the trouble and start small, with something you're sure you understand.

I drive the development of the design from concrete scenarios. We will be in the middle of designing and one of the team will say, "Yeah, but what about this?" Off we go, simulating the execution of the objects by waving them around, until we discover a responsibility we have missed. Designs tend to come to a closure when everyone has run out of scenarios. That is the time to move on to the next level of design (or even implementation).

I have mentioned several times the value of picking the cards up and moving them around. Perhaps it is because most office activities are physically passive, but when designers (whether they are managers, users, or programmers) are given permission to "get physical" amazing things happen. In an incident reported by Sam Adams of Knowledge systems Corp., a supposedly staid banker ended up jumping around the room with a card clutched to her chest yelling, "Okay, I'm this object, what do I do now?" Designers who identify this strongly with an object are showing clear signs that "object think" is beginning to set in. Sometimes, just reminding confused students to pick up the cards they are talking about rather than just point at them can bring about a remarkable transformation.

I like to design in groups. Although the sociological reasons are not yet clear, the cards actually encourage group interactions. When using CRC cards in a group, make sure all the participants understand every design decision as you go along. The process of explaining what has already been decided will help everyone refine their understanding of the design.

The spatial relationships of the cards convey valuable, if ephemeral, information. I like to design sitting around a large table, or better yet, seated on a padded floor. That way I don't feel constrained to line the cards up carefully. I might make a stack of objects for each group involved in the implementation and run a few scenarios to see if two stacks are unduly connected. or I might stack all of the cards in a design, shuffle them and deal them out at random to see what new perspectives I can gain.

Lastly, I cannot stress enough the value of choosing words carefully. I always have a dictionary and thesaurus handy when I design. When a group of designers has been struggling to find a word to describe and object or responsibility, the members will lean forward over the cards. When someone finally discovers just the right word, they collectively heave a sigh of relief and sit back, confident that the important concept they have all understood is now encoded in the design. The words you use to describe your objects will live on for years in the lexicons of developers, maintainers, and even users. Poorly chosen words can hinder the acceptance and understanding of a product, while the right words can make your design much easier to explain.

WHAT'S A GOOD OBJECT?

Since new designers always want to know, "Have I done good?" here are a few rules of thumb I use to evaluate a design. Formal metrics for object-oriented designs are largely unexplored, so evaluating these criteria requires human taste and judgment. This list is by no means comprehensive, and I don't claim that all expert designers would agree to all of the items, but I find them helpful.

BETTER CRC OBJECTS

- Have a consistent set of names, often taken from a physical metaphor. For instance, if you were designing an object-oriented graphics model you might choose the metaphor of painting on canvas. The names of your classes would be taken from common words painters use. You wouldn't call one kind of paint "Paint" and another "ColorValue."

- Have terse, strongly worded responsibilities. As your object designing matures, your objects will add behavior to your designs and not just act as holders behavior to your designs and not just act as holders of data for other objects to manipulate.

- Have a small, sensible set of collaborators. "Indispensable" objects that talk to everyone in the world are a sign of global, procedural thinking. Break up such objects, with by distributing their responsibilities to existing objects or creating several new objects to take their place.

- Fit comfortably on an index card. If a card is crowded, find a more concise way of stating the object's responsibilities. Failing that, the object is doing too much. Find or create other objects to take on some of its tasks.

WORSE CRC OBJECTS

- Don't have any responsibilities. It's fine to create an object with a name but no responsibilities, trusting that its behavior will become clear as the design progresses. Once a design is finished, however, discard any object that doesn't carry its share of the computational load.

- Have the word "Manager" in their name. Words like "Manager," "Object," or "Thing" add nothing to the meaning of the object's name. If you can't just eliminate the offending "noise" word, find a better word from the metaphor domain or substitute a word that tells what the object is doing. For example, use ProcessScheduler rather than ProcessManager or Figure rather than DrawingObject.

- Use the words "has," "holds," or "uses" in their responsibilities. These words suggest representation but not behavior. Replace the responsibility with one that explains why the other object is held. For example, in a Bitmap object you might list as one of its responsibilities "Holds width and height." You can rewrite it more actively by saying "Shapes bits into a rectangle."

- Have large, highly connected clumps. If an object takes care of a limited part of the computation it can't need to talk to lots of other objects. Good designs have small clusters of objects with limited connections between them. Shuffle responsibilities to achieve this kind of interconnection pattern.

Doing objects isn't hard, but trying to learn all the peripheral issues at the same time you're learning to design objects makes it difficult. The CRC perspective, with its focus on what objects are called and what they do, can help you experience the essence of object-oriented programming. CRC cards make object-oriented design approachable.

A CRC design can also form the basis of a more detailed design. Rebecca Wirfs-Brock and Brian Wilkerson have created a design methodology, called responsibility driven design, based on CRC.2 Other object-oriented design and analysis techniques have also been influenced by CRC.3

Completing the transition to OOP requires experience at all levels:

- Mastering the new resources the languages provide at an implementation level

- Understanding the appropriate use of available class libraries

- Observing the relationship of design decisions to the implementation

- Refactoring an existing implementation for greater reusability.

Learning to distribute responsibilities among objects is an important first step in beginning to "think like an object."

References

Beck, Kent and Ward Cunningham. "A Laboratory for Teaching Object-Oriented Thinking," *OOPSLA-89 Proceedings*.

Wirfs-Brook, Rebecca, Brian Wilkenson, and Lauren Wiener. *Designing Object-Oriented Software*. Englewood Cliffs, NJ: Prentice-Hall, 1990.

Coad, Peter and Edward Yourdon. *Object-Oriented Analysis*, 2nd ed. Englewood Cliffs, NJ: Yourdon Press, 1991.

6

Why Study Smalltalk Idioms?

Smalltalk Report, May, 1992

This was my first column in The Smalltalk Report.

The Smalltalk Report *occupies an important position in legitimizing Smalltalk. While it has in the past seemed the ugly stepchild of the SIGS family, the mere fact of its existence has gone far towards convincing reluctant decision makers that Smalltalk is worth betting on.*

When I started writing for The Smalltalk Report, *I had already made something of a name for myself in the Smalltalk world. The CRC paper was out and making its splash, I had been working on Smalltalk in various guises for eight years, and I was well into my tenure at MasPar.*

My life in a startup cloister was a big part of my decision to begin writing the column. Startups are great fun, but you don't join one to see the world and become famous (if you're not in sales, anyway). Writing the column kept me in touch with my friends.

In the end, the benefits of writing the column were much greater than I had imagined, as were the pains. It always seemed that the next deadline hit just after I'd finished the last column. Dragging fingers to keyboard when a paying customer was already waiting for code was tough. However, I got much more from the column than I put into it. First, I learned to write. You will see a distinct change in my writing style from the first columns to the last. I learned to write plainly and familiarly, which is not nearly as easy as it might seem. Second, I got tremendous visibility in the Smalltalk community.

MY DICTIONARY DEFINES an idiom as "a phrase whose meaning cannot be predicted from its words." While learning Smalltalk (a task that continues daily), I have often been puzzled by a fragment of code. Only upon reflection do I understand the author's intent. About a year ago, I began collecting examples of idioms I encountered and asked my friends to tell me about ones they found. This article is an introduction to the material I have collected.

Many programmers new to Smalltalk spend most of their time just reading code. Studying idioms can accelerate this process. Knowing what to expect, or at least having somewhere to turn when you are baffled by a piece of code, is important to new Smalltalkers.

Another meaning for idiom is "a style of speaking of a group of people." As with spoken language, Smalltalk has several dialects. The two most prominent are the Digitalk and ParcPlace dialects. There were also two distinct Tektronix dialects, easily distinguished from one another. Xerox Special Information Systems (the Analyst folks) also had their own distinctive style. New offshoots arise anywhere Smalltalk has taken root for several years.

Being conscious of the collective idiom of a body of code can also help more advanced programmers. Code that adheres to a shared idiom is easier to maintain, because there are fewer gratuitous surprises for new readers. Idioms also speed development through a kind of pattern-matching process. Once you have identified a circumstance in which an idiom is applicable, coding proceeds much faster than if you always have to invent new mechanisms from scratch. Standing on the brink of a new column, I look forward to exploring the range of idioms available to Smalltalk programmers. From time to time I'll be joined by prominent Smalltalkers who will describe their favorite idioms. We will also explore the subtle differences between the Digitalk and ParcPlace schools.

This column will present idioms at many levels of complexity and scope. Rather than present all 50 or so of the idioms I have identified so far, I have chosen a smattering to get things going. The first few are small in scale and likely to trip up programmers new to Smalltalk. The concluding design idioms are more likely to interest more advanced programmers.

CONDITIONALS AS EXPRESSIONS

In most procedural languages, conditional statements do not return values. In Smalltalk, however, the result of sending ifTrue:ifFalse: to the Boolean "true", for example, is the value of the last expression in the block, which is the first argument. This fact can be used to advantage to simplify some methods considerably. While you could write:

```
| result |
foo isNil
   ifTrue: [result := 5]
   ifFalse: [result := 7].
^result
```

it is shorter (and, after you get used to it, easier) to write:

```
| result |
result := foo isNil
   ifTrue: [5]
   ifFalse: [7].
^result
```

Once you've gone that far, you can get rid of the temporary variable entirely and simply write:

```
^foo isNil
   ifTrue: [5]
   ifFalse: [7]
```

and: AND or: VERSUS & AND |

There are two methods each for conjunction and disjunction in Smalltalk. and: and & both return true only if both the receiver *and* the argument are true, and or: and | both return true if either the receiver *or* the argument are true. The difference is that the keyword versions (and: and or:) take a block as an argument rather than a Boolean. The block is evaluated only if the result of the message is not determined by the receiver. For instance, you should use the keyword version of conjunction if evaluating the argument would cause an error if the receiver was false. For instance, if you wrote:

```
anArray size >= 10 & (anArray at: 10) isNil
```

you would get an error if **anArray** held less than ten elements. In this case you would use the keyword version:

anArray size >= 10 and: [(anArray at: 10) isNil]

This way the at: message is not sent if **anArray** is too small. The Object-works\
Smalltalk Release 4 image uses or: to determine if operating system resources (such as pixmaps) that do not survive over snapshots need to be reinitialized. It is common to see code like this:

(pixmap isNil or: [pixmap isOpen not]) ifTrue: [pixmap := Pixmap extent...

The other reason to use the keyword versions is for optimization. If the second part of a conjunction is expensive and the receiver is often false, using and: instead of & can result in a considerable savings. Why would anyone ever use the binary message versions of conjunction and disjunction? Style, baby. The keyword versions often introduce extra parentheses (as in the pixmap example above). They use far more characters. And since they are a little unusual, they require a moment of thought every time you encounter them.

DEFAULT PARAMETERS

Many programming languages provide the ability to not specify certain parameters for a procedure call and have them set to a default value. Smalltalk provides this facility through a programming idiom. A displayable object, for instance, might implement a message display as follows:

display
    self displayOn: Display

which in turn is implemented as

```
displayOn: aDisplayMedium
    self displayOn: aDisplayMedium at: 0@0
```

and so on, until all the parameters needed to display the object have been collected. As the user of this object, you can specify as many or as few parameters as you need to get the job done.

The downside of implementing default parameters this way is the combinatorial explosion in the number of methods that can result. If you are creating default parameters for a method that has five parameters you could potentially create 5! = 120 different methods. If you write all the possible combinations, you obscure the purpose of the original method. If you don't write them all, you run the risk of not providing the combination that someone needs.

A common idiom for organizing default parameters is to choose a priority order. Create one method that defaults the most important parameter, another which specifies that parameter but defaults the next most important, and so on until you specify all parameters. In the example above, the destination for display is the most important parameter and the location, the next most important. This approach limits the number of methods but ensures that the most commonly used combinations are available.

ABSTRACT SUPERCLASSES

Some classes are not meant to be instantiated. They exist only as repositories for interesting related bits of behavior. The most powerful of these abstract superclasses reduce a set of related messages to one or two methods that each concrete subclass is required to implement. Both Smalltalks provide Collection as a good example. If you create a subclass of Collection, you need only implement do:. You get the rest of the enumeration methods without further effort.

Identifying candidates for abstraction is not easy. I got the following strategy for using this idiom from Ken Auer of Knowledge Systems. If reusability is ever going to be an issue for a class divide it into two parts at the beginning: an abstract part that contains only methods and few or no variables, and a concrete part that holds the state necessary to actually compute. The example he used had an abstract **FinancialInstrument** and a concrete **Bond**. As you go along, only allow state to move into the superclass if you can't reasonably put it in the subclass. By pushing implementation decisions (state) down to the concrete class, you have a better chance of finding what is truly common to the implementation of all such objects by examining what is left in the abstract superclass.

Another strategy for finding abstract superclasses comes from Ward Cunningham. He suggests beginning an implementation without using inheritance at all. Only when you get tired of manually copying and pasting methods from one class to another do you factor their commonality into a superclass for both. This strategy has the advantage that it identifies commonality from concrete examples. The best use of inheritance for code sharing is often not apparent until far into the design.

Values Masquerading as Objects

One of the glories of objects is the ease with which they can be passed around. But this easy mobility can become a nightmare if you have passed off an object and it begins to change without your knowledge. There is a suite of idioms for dealing with these aliasing problems. The one described here is the simplest, but it can have the greatest performance impact. If once you have created an object you never change its state, you cannot possibly have aliasing. I call objects used in this way "values" because of their similarity to numbers. In fact, numbers in Smalltalk are implemented in just this way. If you have the object 10 and you add 5 to it, you don't change 10, you get a new object, 15, instead. You don't have to worry about giving away your 10 and having it turn into a 15 behind your back.

Points and Rectangles are implemented in much the same way. After you have created a **Point** with **Number>>@**, all other operations (+, *, translateBy:) return new **Points**. Unfortunately, **Points** can have their coordinates changed directly via **x:** and **y:**, and **Rectangles** also offer methods for directly changing their values.

The simplicity of value objects comes at a price. Their indiscriminate use can result in excessive memory allocation. If you must side-effect an otherwise functional object, do so only with a freshly allocated one in a small, well-defined scope (preferably a single method). As with all optimizations, pillaging a value object for speed should only be done when the performance of the finished applications is a problem for real users, never on mere speculation.

CONCLUSION

A good grasp of Smalltalk's many idioms can speed assimilation of the language and its class libraries, improve the productivity of new development, and accelerate understanding of legacy code. This article has only scratched the surface of known Smalltalk idioms, all of which were present in Smalltalk-80 as it escaped from Xerox. The dispersion of Smalltalk will fuel the growth of many new idioms.

I am still collecting idioms. If you identify one you would like to share, contact me.

7

THE DREADED SUPER

Smalltalk Report, JUNE, 1992

This is a bit of work I am particularly proud of. I wrote a little workspace that got me a method list browser on all the methods in the image that use "super" (that in itself was fun). Then I went through them trying to categorize each one. I felt like a real scientist there for a minute- taking samples, making hypotheses, testing them in the "real world." The result is a "theory of super," which is much simpler than the language feature (and perhaps not coincidentally quite similar to the "inner" feature of Simula, from which super was derived).

WHAT IS IT with this super thing, anyway? The pseudo-variable super is a curious wart on the otherwise unblemished Smalltalk language design. Ordinary messages are sufficient to capture composition, conditionals, and looping. The three components of structured programming thus become unified in Smalltalk. Yes, but....

The exception is super. It means the same object as self, but when you send it a message the difference is revealed. When you send an ordinary message the class of the receiver of the message is examined for an implementation of that message. If one is not found the superclass is searched, then its superclass, and so on until a method is found. Super circumvents normal message lookup. When you send a message to super the search begins in the superclass of the class in which the executing method was found.

Super is pretty benign as warts go. It makes no reference to explicit class names, so methods still contain no assumptions about what other classes are called. You cannot affect method lookup in other objects by using super, only the one currently executing. The only assumption introduced by using super is that some superclass of the current class contains an implementation of a method.

A variety of idioms, some useful and necessary, some gratuitous, have grown up around super. For example, I found that about 7% (28 out of 381) of the methods which use super in the Objectworks\Smalltalk Release 4 image could use sends to self without changing their meaning. In this article, we'll examine the uses and abuses of super. Where is super appropriate? What does it cost? What should you avoid when using it?

The code quoted in this article was taken from ParcPlace Systems Objectworks\Smalltalk Release 4. ParcPlace owns all the copyrights. In places, I have simplified the code for purposes of presentation.

ORTHODOX USE

The usual use of super is to invoke a superclass's implementation of the currently executing method. One example from Objectworks\Smalltalk is the initialization of subclasses of ValueModel. ValueModel>>initialize sets its instance variable accepted to false.

```
initialize
    accepted := false
```

The subclass ValueHolder first invokes super initialize, then sets its instance variable active to true.

```
initialize
    super initialize.
    active := true
```

This use of super segments behavior across several classes. The subclass's method depends on nothing that the superclass does. The subclass only assumes that the superclass has something useful to say about the message and makes sure it gets invoked. The "meaning" of the message in the context of the receiver is spread disjointedly across several classes.

Initialization is a common situation in which several methods which have nothing to do with one another except that they are all executing on behalf of the same object may be invoked by means of super. PostCopy, the message which cleans up a copy of an object, is another case where instance variables are manipulated without many messages, and which fits the description of segmented behavior. Using super to segment behavior across classes does not create much risk of cross-class dependencies. Even if the superclass changes, the subclass should not have to change.

A use of super that involves slightly more risk is the modification of a superclass's behavior. ChangeListView>>displayOn: is a good example.

```
displayOn: aGraphicsContext
    super displayOn: aGraphicsContext.
    self displayRemovedOn: aGraphicsContext
```

It operates by first invoking super displayOn: (which is implemented in ListView) to draw the list elements, and then drawing a line through all the list elements which have been removed. The dependency is that should ListView dramatically change its presentation of items (such as by displaying them as file folder tabs), ChangeListView displayOn: would also have to change.

Another kind of modification of superclass behavior is invoking general-purpose algorithms only when special purpose one fail. For example, Byte-EncodedString>>at: is implemented by grabbing the raw byte at an index and then encoding it.

```
at: index
    ^self stringEncoding decode: (self byteAt: index)
```

ByteString, the optimized subclass, implements at: primitively.

```
at: index
    <primitive: 63>
    ^super at: index
```

Should anything occur that the primitive is not prepared to handle (for example an unknown character or an index out of range) it will fail. The Smalltalk implementation of **ByteString>>at:** returns the result of **super at:**. Thus, the special case gains a speedup most of the time, but under normal circumstances it is prepared to invoke the full available generality.

    Array>>storeOn: is another example of using **super** to implement a specialized algorithm that is prepared to devolve into a more general one.

```
storeOn: aStream
    self isLiteral
        ifTrue: [self storeLiteralOn: aStream]
        ifFalse: [super storeOn: aStream]
```

Arrays of literals are treated specially by the compiler and can thus be printed more compactly than arrays of general objects. If the receiver is not literal (meaning some of its elements are not literals), **Array>>storeOn:** invokes **super storeOn:** so as to use the general collection storing method.

    Otherwise, the receiver is printed so that the compiler can recreate the array while parsing the printed string.

DISINHERITANCE IN THE FACE OF SUPER

Using **super** involves a more direct reference to a superclass than a regular message send. You can get into situations where you will feel trapped by the use of **super**. One common pitfall is the need for disinheritance. For example, suppose we create an abstract communication object, **Communicator**, which sets up important state in its initialize method.

```
initialize
    "Set up important state..."
```

We then create a concrete subclass, **SocketCommunicator**, which uses a socket for communication. Its initialize method will send **super initialize** and then create the socket.

```
initialize
    super initialize.
```

```
socket := Socket new
```

Finally we create a subclass of SocketCommunicator, TestCommunicator, which is used for testing. It reads its input from a file. Its initialize method needs the behavior in Communicator>>initialize, but it can't just send super initialize without accidentally creating a socket.

The solution is to factor the initialization of the communication channel of SocketCommunicator out of the initialize method into its own method, initializeChannel.

```
initialize
    super initialize.
    self initializeChannel

initializeChannel
    socket := Socket new
```

Then TestCommunicator can override initializeChannel directly.

```
initializeChannel
    socket := Filename fromUser
```

TestCommunicator may not even need to override initialize at all.

In general, the need for disinheritance points out opportunities for you to factor your code better. Remember that as you break a class down into smaller methods you make it easier to subclass later. If each method does one and only one thing, when you want your subclass to do one thing differently you will find exactly the right method to override.

EXCEPTIONS

So far the uses of super have been limited to invoking a method in a superclass which has the same name as the one currently executing. Because the names are the same, any violation of encapsulation between the subclass and superclass is limited. After all, if a message makes sense to the subclass it probably should make sense to the superclass as well. However, there are legitimate reasons to use super with a different selector than the currently executing method.

One reason to invoke super with other than the current method's selector is to avoid looping in mutually recursive methods. One example is ControllerWithMenu. In controlActivity it checks to see if the red mouse button is pressed, and if so sends itself redButtonActivity.

```
controlActivity
    self sensor redButtonPressed & self viewHasCursor
        ifTrue: [^self redButtonActivity].
    super controlActivity
```

ControllerWithMenu>>redButtonActivity wants to invoke the superclass's controlActivity as its default behavior.

```
redButtonActivity
    super controlActivity
```

If the send were to self an infinite loop would result. Instead, redButtonActivity sends controlActivity to super, thus avoiding the loop.

Another reason for this kind of send to super is to avoid duplicating effort. For instance, ComposedText class>>new initializes the new instance with a new Text.

```
new
    ^self withText: '' asText
```

ComposedText also has an instance creation method which takes a Text as an argument, withText:style:. If it sent new to self the new instance would be initialized twice, once with a new Text and once with the Text passed in as an argument. To avoid this duplication ComposedText>>withText:style: sends new to super.

```
withText: aText style: aTextStyle
    ^super new
        text: aText
        style: aTextStyle
```

A final reason for invoking super with a different selector is if the subclass has different external protocol than the superclass but is implemented using the superclass's behavior. An example of this is Dictionary, which is a subclass of Set although its external protocol is much more like SequenceableCollection. Dictionary>>includesAssociation: wants to use includes: except that Dictionary overrides includes: to look only at the values, not the whole Association. IncludesAssociation: sends includes: to super to invoke the correct method.

```
includesAssociation: anAssociation
    ^super includes: anAssociation
```

This last exception is probably the least defensible of the three listed here, as subclassing solely for implementation sharing where there is little commonality in external protocol is generally a bad idea.

All of these sends to super where the selector is different than that of the current method are suspect, as they introduce the possibility of unnecessarily using super. If a message is sent to super and the class does not implement that method the message could just as well be sent to self. If at a later date you decide to override the message, you can spend many frustrating hours trying to find out why the new method is not being invoked. If you find an unnecessary super don't worry. As I noted at the beginning of the article, 28 out of the 381 uses of super in the Objectworks\Smalltalk Release 4 image are unnecessary (see the sidebar for the code I used to find these numbers).

Joel Spiegel came up with the only plausible reason for using super where self would do. You might use super if you were absolutely certain that a superclass's implementation of a method had to be invoked and you didn't want to give future subclasses any opportunity to interfere. I would be interested in any legitimate examples of this kind of "prophylactic" use of super.

CONCLUSION

Super must be used carefully. It introduces a dependency between the subclass and superclass. Also, as an exception to the otherwise remarkably consistent control flow of Smalltalk, it will make your code harder to read. Correct use can significantly enhance your ability to partition behavior between classes. It can also make it easier to incrementally modify the behavior of subclasses.

ANALYZING USES OF SUPER

—

The standard image does not contain much support for searching the image for uses of super. During the preparation of this column I had to extend the system to let me flexibly search for uses of super. Here is the code I created, working from the bottom up.

InstructionStream, the object which simulates execution of Smalltalk bytecodes, has support for decoding message sends, but not sends to super in particular. I added peekForSuper, which returns nil if the method being interpreted is not about to send to super and the selector which is to be sent if it is. It is modeled after InstructionStream>>peekForSelector.

```
peekForSuper
    "If this instruction is a send to super, answer its selector,
    otherwise answer nil."
    | byte x1 x2 |
    byte := method byteAt: pc.
    byte = OpXSuper
        ifTrue:
            [x1 := method byteAt: pc + 1.
            ^method literalAt: (x1 bitAnd: 31) + 1]
    byte = OpXXSend
        ifTrue:
            [x2 := method byteAt: pc + 2.
            ^method literalAt: x2 + 1].
    ^nil
```

Next, I implemented a CompiledCode method to test whether the code sends a message to super by using InstructionStream>>peekForSuper. It is similar to CompiledCode>>sendsSpecialSelector:.

```
sendsSuper
    "Answer whether the receiver sends to super."
```

```
| scanner |
self withAllBlockMethodsDo:
   [:meth |
   "Make a quick check"
   ((meth bytesIncludes: OpXSuper)
      or: [meth bytesIncludes: OpXXSuper])
   ifTrue:
      [scanner := InstructionStream on: meth.
      (scanner scanFor: [:byte |
      scanner peekForSuper notNil])
         ifTrue: [^true]]].
^false
```

SystemDictionary>>allSelect: iterates through all the Compiled-Methods in the system. Now I could find out how many methods in the system send super by executing

```
(Smalltalk allSelect: [:each | each sendsSuper]) size
```

or open a browser on all of the methods by executing:

```
Smalltalk browseAllSelect: [:each | each sendsSuper]
```

To do more sophisticated analysis of sends to super I needed more objects than just the CompiledMethod. I invented a protocol similar to SystemDictionary>>allSelect: which I called allMethods:. The Block argument to allMethods: takes three parameters instead of one: the class of the method, the selector of the method, and the method itself.

```
allMethods: aBlock
   "Answer a SortedCollection of each method that, when
      used with its class and selector as the arguments to
      aBlock, gives a true result."  |
   aCollection |
```

```
aCollection := OrderedCollection new.
Cursor execute showWhile:
  [self allBehaviorsDo:
    [:eachClass |
    eachClass selectors do:
      [:eachSelector |
      (aBlock
        value: eachClass
          value: eachSelector
            value: (eachClass compiledMethodAt:
            eachSelector))
      ifTrue: [aCollection add:
        eachClass name , ' ' , eachSelector]]]].
  ^aCollection asSortedCollection
```

To complete the analysis I also needed the selector sent to super, not just a Boolean telling me whether a send took place or not. I implemented CompiledCode>>selectorSentToSuper to provide the selector.

```
selectorSentToSuper
  "Answer the selector the receiver sends to super or nil."
  | scanner |
  self withAllBlockMethodsDo:
    [:meth |
    "Make a quick check"
    ((meth bytesIncludes: OpXSuper) or: [meth
    bytesIncludes: OpXXSuper])
      ifTrue:
        [scanner := InstructionStream on: meth.
        scanner scanFor:
          [:byte || selector |
          selector := scanner peekForSuper.
          selector notNil ifTrue: [^selector].
          false]]].
```

```
^nil
```

Now I could find all of the methods which sent super with a different selector by executing:

```
Smalltalk allMethods:
  [:class :selector :method II superSelector I
  superSelector := method selectorSentToSuper.
  superSelector notNil & (superSelector ~= selector)]
```

Or the methods in which sends to super could be changed to sends to self by executing

```
Smalltalk allMethods:
  [:class :selector :method II superSelector I
  superSelector := method selectorSentToSuper.
      superSelector notNil and: [class includesSelector:
      superSelector)
  not]]
```

I find the creation of this kind of quick analysis tools one of the most fun things about Objectworks\Smalltalk. When I program in Smalltalk/V, with its limitations on access to system internals, I always miss the ability to quickly answer complex questions about the system.

8

ABSTRACT CONTROL IDIOMS

Smalltalk Report, JULY–AUGUST, 1992

Notice that I am still calling what I am doing "idioms." What I am describing are really patterns, even if they are small-scale patterns. I figured it was better to bring my audience along a bit, prove myself useful, and then spring the bigger idea of which this is all a part.

I wouldn't do this again. Better to just say what you mean, and if you lose some people, so be it. I have a real tendency to try to please everybody, so this approach kind of goes against the grain.

The tension between evolutionary and revolutionary change is something I struggle with constantly. On consulting gigs, it is always a temptation to just say, "Throw the bastards out," to start fresh. Often this will produce the best results the quickest. However, it requires courage and a lack of ego to "toss out" hard work. On the other hand, I'm always worried that if I were a little smarter, I'd be able to deal with the situation as it is.

The column is a good example of a technique I learned from Dave Thomas that he calls "lie management." You present an over-simplified but essentially correct view of the world, then you fix it. The engineer in me recoils at this—I will go to ridiculous lengths to understand things completely, and everyone must be like me, right? Right? Thinking like a teacher and not an engineer, though, it is more important that you make sure readers have some concrete understanding that they can grow from rather than risk them ignoring you as you try to explain every last detail.

I STARTED WRITING ABOUT the new **ValueModel** style used in ParcPlace's Objectworks\Smalltalk Release 4 as promised, but soon discovered that I need to cover some preliminary material about the "traditional" style first. I split the column into two parts. This one talks about how abstract control has been used to date. Next issue's will cover the new possibilities available with the advent of **ValueModels**.

Messages Limit Reuse

Reuse is the name of the game. Headlines shout. Marketing literature trumpets. Salesmen ooze. Objects will solve your reuse problems. Not true, of course. Programmers solve reuse problems. It is possible to reuse procedural code, and it can be impossible to reuse objects. If the mere presence of objects doesn't enable reuse, what is it that makes reuse happen, technically?

Whenever I am able to reuse a piece of code, either by design or through serendipity, it is because the code makes few assumptions about what the rest of the world looks like. A graphics model that assumes all coordinates are integers is significantly harder to use than one that is prepared to take any kind of number. What does this have to do with messages limiting reuse?

Every time you send a message you build into your code the assumption that one and only one action will be invoked. What happens when you later decide you need two things to happen? Or sometimes none and sometimes many? You have to change the original code.

I can think of three levels of code reuse. By far the simplest is reuse by *instantiation*. You create an object, send it some messages, and good things happen. Far more complicated is reuse by *refinement*. To subclass you have to understand the inner workings of the superclass to know what messages to intercept and how to compatibly extend the representation. By far the most expensive reuse in terms of downstream costs is reuse by *tweaking*. Somehow the original author never factors the methods enough, but by a little judicious editing you can create an object you can subclass for your purposes.

Tweaking is becoming infeasible as a production programming strategy. As Smalltalk programs grow, it becomes increasingly desirable to treat code from outside sources as immutable. I have enough trouble keeping up with changes to my own objects, much less trying to track what several vendors have done with code I have modified. If we had a mechanism that was like message sending, but was extensible without modifying the original code, we could gain reusability for our libraries of objects.

The Smalltalk Solution: Update/Changed

Update/changed, also known as *change propagation* or *dependency*, is the Smalltalk solution to a "more abstract message send." It is more abstract in the sense that zero or more receivers can be activated by one action in the sender; the number and identity of the receivers is determined at runtime and can easily be changed by code that is otherwise unrelated to the sender; and the receiver has much more choice in responding to the changed message than an ordinary message send. On the other hand, because it is not implemented by the Smalltalk virtual machine, it is not as efficient as ordinary message sending.

I talked to Diana Merry-Shapiro (one of the long-time members of the original Smalltalk team) about the evolution of the dependency mechanism. The early Smalltalkers took as their benchmark problem a model consisting of a collection of numbers and two views, one a pie chart and the other a bar chart. The problem was to keep both charts consistent with the model while leaving the model as ignorant of the fact that it was being viewed as possible. According to Diana, it was Dan Ingalls who finally implemented the dependency mechanism as we know it.

Here is a quick review of the fundamentals of dependency. The system associates with each object a collection of dependents, other objects to be notified when it changes. Here is a simplified implementation:

```
Object>>addDependent: anObject
    Dependents "a class variable in Object" isNil
        ifTrue: [Dependents := IdentityDictionary new].
    (Dependents includesKey: self)
        ifFalse: [Dependents at: self put: Set new].
    (Dependents at: self) add: anObject

Object>>removeDependent: anObject
    Dependents isNil ifTrue: [^self].
    (Dependents at: self ifAbsent: [^self])
        remove: anObject
        ifAbsent: [^self].
    (Dependents at: self) isEmpty
        ifTrue: [Dependents removeKey: self]
```

Most objects don't have any dependents, and there is no space cost for non-participants, so the memory overhead of dependency is not high.

When an object changes its state in a way that it thinks dependents might be interested in, it sends itself the message **changed**, which causes all of the dependents to be sent the message update. Each dependent then takes whatever action is necessary to reconcile it with the new state.

```
Object>>dependents
    Dependents isNil ifTrue: [^#()].
    ^(Dependents at: self) ifAbsent: [#()]

Object>>changed
    self dependents do: [:each | each update]

Object>>update
    ^self "Do nothing by default"
```

The solution to the benchmark problem mentioned above is to make the pie chart and the bar chart dependent on the list of numbers. Every time the list changes, adds, or deletes a value, it sends itself a changed message. Both of the views in their update methods simply redisplay, and the consistency problem is solved. The solution has the additional attraction that new kinds of views can be added, and as long as they are registered to the model they will operate without any changes to the model. Finally, the model works in the absence of a user interface just as well as it does interactively. Because all communication with the user interface is through dependency, its presence or absence makes no difference to the model.

The first problem that becomes apparent with this simple dependency mechanism is that not every dependent is interested in every change. The most common form of changed message adds a parameter, a symbol by convention, which suggests the kind of change taking place. The parameter is passed along to the dependent. Notice that the generic update gets sent if update: is not overridden.

```
Object>>changed: aSymbol
    self dependents do: [:each | each update: aSymbol]

Object>>update: aSymbol
    self update
```

Most applications that need dependency can be coded with no more complexity than this.

DEPENDENCY IDIOMS

For consumers of update messages, the primary idiom is to override update: and switch on the parameter. Here is ListView>>update:

```
update: aSymbol
    aSymbol == #list
        ifTrue: [^self setNewList].
    aSymbol == #listIndex
        ifTrue: [^self setNewSelection]
```

I have found it good practice to have only a single send to self for each case. When I am tempted to put several statements in the block, I invariably end up creating a method later which is exactly along those lines. Also, the code is simpler to read if each implementation of update: has the same form.

What if you want several views on the same model, but you want each to respond to different updates? The old license Version 2 image introduced pluggable views to solve this problem. Rather than create a subclass for each slight variant, each of which would override update:, a pluggable view stores the pattern against which update messages are matched in an instance variable. Here is SelectionInListView, the pluggable variant of ListView.

```
update: aSymbol
    aSymbol == partMsg
        ifTrue: [^self setNewList].
    aSymbol == initialSelectionMsg
        ifTrue: [^self setNewSelection]
```

The instance variables are set when a list is created with the SelectionInListView>>on:aspect:blah:blah: message. Each list also needs to send a different message to the model to get the contents and set the selection. The symbols used for checking updates double as messages that are sent to the model via **perform:**. I have always thought this was kind of sleazy, but in practice it works quite well.

The other commonly used pluggable view is **TextView**. **SelectionIn-ListView** uses one symbol to check to see whether to update the list contents and another as the message to send to the model to get the list. **TextView** uses the same symbol for both (the **aspect:** parameter of the instance creation message).

A final note about implementing **update:**—remember to send "**super update: aSymbol**" if the current method hasn't consumed the update message. That way your classes will fit more neatly into hierarchies.

I looked through all senders of **changed:** to see if I could find any pattern to the symbols that are used as the parameter, and I wasn't able to discover anything profound. The parameter should, of course, have some relation to the change taking place in the model. Other than that there doesn't seem to be much of a pattern to how the symbols are selected.

Deciding to Use Dependency

If dependency is so cool, why not use it all the time? Playground, a language I worked on at Alan Kay's Vivarium project, was an attempt to do just that. It used dependency as its only control abstraction. Because Playground was a pure abstract control language, it threw the two biggest drawbacks of dependency into high relief: debugging and performance.

There are two problems with debugging update messages. The first is in the debugger. It takes a long time to single-step through code that does an update. You have to go through all the intermediate steps of the implementation for each dependent. (The real implementation is considerably more complicated than the one outlined above. See the section called Gory Details for the, well, you know.) If you have lots of dependents and only one of them is interesting, this can be tedious and frustrating.

The browser also does little to help debug dependency. If you have symbols built in to your implementations of **update:**, you can at least use senders (from the Launcher window) to find out where they are used as parameters to **changed:**. If you are implementing a pluggable view, however, the symbol will only show up in the user interface code that creates the view.

From this it is often hard to see how an update will be triggered. A trick I use is to add "Transcript cr; show: aSymbol" as the first line of the update: method I am interested in. I can then see all the update messages and the order in which they arrive.

A less compelling, but occasionally fatal, drawback of dependency is performance. Unlike a message send, which every part of the Smalltalk implementation is tuned to make efficient, changed messages have to go through several layers of invocation to get to their recipient. If you have lots of dependents, most of whom aren't interested in most updates, you can spend enormous amounts of effort creating a little activity. A related minor annoyance is that all those layers of invocation tend to clutter performance profiles, especially if you have several layers of updates happening.

Since dependency has significant costs associated with it, when is it worth using? The one clear case is when you are implementing new views or models. You need dependency so your code fits well with the rest of the system. Also, dependency makes your models more reusable by insulating them from the precise details of the interface or interfaces that are viewing them.

Other than models and views in the traditional sense, you should use dependency anywhere you want an object to be thoroughly insulated from the environment in which it operates. Any object that you know will be used in a variety of ways and that you want to keep clean is a candidate for dependency.

When is dependency being abused? Here are some signals that you have gone too far:

- An action spawns several updates and their order matters.

- You forget which symbols mean what.

- Your update messages create an infinite loop.

- You find update messages that aren't handled by anyone.

When your code begins exhibiting any of these symptoms, it is time to revisit the decision to use dependency. You may discover that one of the connections you are making always works out to use exactly one object, in which case you can replace the dependency with a direct reference and message sends. Or you may have a collection of objects that all respond to the same messages, so you can store a collection and use direct messages.

The Gory Details

The dependency implementation in Objectworks\Smalltalk Release 4 is more complicated than the one outlined above. There is a variant of the update method that takes three parameters: an aspect, an optional parameter, and the changing object. Changed: sends changed:with:, which sends update:with:from:, which by default sends update:with:, which sends update:. All of these intermediate steps add greatly to the functionality and complexity of dependency. However, in my opinion, if you use all the available generality of the three-parameter version of update:, you are stressing what was intended to be a very simple mechanism, and you are likely to run into trouble.

The implementations of addDependent: and removeDependent: in Object are much like the ones above. They have a serious flaw. If an object has been registered as a dependent and it fails to remove itself, or if an object gains dependents that are not removed, it cannot be garbage collected because it is referred to from a global variable. To deal with this problem, there is a subclass of Object called Model that adds an instance variable and dependents and that overrides addDependent: and removeDependent:. Since the model is not referred to globally, it is easier to get it garbage collected; once it has been collected, it no longer refers to its dependents, so they become candidates for collection.

A final nuance of the implementation of dependency is the use of DependentsCollection, a subclass of Array. If a Model has only a single dependent, the value of its instance variable dependents is that dependent. Object>> changed:with: sends update:with:from: and off to that dependent and everything works. If there is more than one dependent, then dependents is a DependentsCollection, which overrides update:with:from: to forward the message to each of its elements. This little trick saves an additional object when there is only one dependent.

Conclusion

We have seen how abstract control structures, implemented by Smalltalk dependency mechanism, can reduce the strength of the connection between two objects. This can lead to enhanced reusability. Because it is outside the language and is not directly supported by the programming environment, excessive use of dependents can make programs hard to read and debug and can lead to performance problems.

9

VALUEMODEL IDIOMS

Smalltalk Report, SEPTEMBER, 1992

Notice the connection between the last column and this. The biggest difference between writing an article and writing a column is that an article has to tell a whole story, while a column ought to tell a story, but also provide hooks to the future and the past. I think this was the first time I began to exploit the serial nature of columns on such a large scale. Earlier, all I had done was drop one-or two-word hints of future topics.

This column is another piece of science, like the earlier column on super. I found the material by going through the VisualWorks image and finding all the ways the (then new) ValueModel framework was being used.

MY LAST COLUMN outlined ways of using dependency as embodied in Smalltalk's update and changed messages. ParcPlace's release 4 of Objectworks\Smalltalk introduced a significant refinement of dependency called ValueModel, which addresses some of the shortcomings of the classic style of dependency management.

CLASSIC SMALLTALK STYLE

Here is another example of the classic style of Smalltalk change propagation. A Mandelbrot renders a portion of the Mandelbrot set while it measures performance.

Mandelbrot
  superclass: Model

instance variables: region flops

A Mandelbrot object renders the portion of the Mandelbrot set in region (a Rectangle with floating point coordinates) on an Image when sent displayOn:. Assume we have implemented a primitive rendering method that returns the number of floating point operations it initiates as it displays. The DisplayOn: method divides the number of operations by the rendering time to compute the number of floating point operations per second, which will be stored in flops.

```
displayOn: anImage
    | time ops |
    time:= Time millisecondsToRun:
        [ops := self primDisplayOn:anImage].
    self flops: ops / time / 1000
```

The model responds to openflops by creating a window that displays the value of flops.

```
openflops
    | window |
    window:= ScheduledWindow new.
    window addChild: (TextView on: self aspect: #flopsString
        change:nil menu: nil)
    window open
```

Some users complain that putting an open method in the model allows too much of the interface to leak through. But in my opinion one is free to open any kind of window, and if the model offers a default way, so much the better. Putting open in the model keeps the code together; if more flexibility is needed later it can always be moved.

TextView's symbol flopsString is used by the view both to recognize an interesting broadcast and as a message to the model to return a string suitable for viewing. The model thus needs to respond to flopsString.

```
flopsString
    ^self flops printString, 'flops'
```

Now all that remains to update the view is to propagate a change whenever the flops change.

```
flops: aNumber
    flops:= aNumber.
    self changed: #flopsString
```

Already the interface is beginning to leak into the model. Because the example interface uses the symbol #flopsString, the model must have this particular symbol built in. Other interfaces viewing other aspects of the model dependent on the measured flops will require additional broadcasts when the flops change. The model is no longer insulated from changes to the interface.

Let's refine the model a bit to see where this style of change propagation begins to fall apart. What if instead of displaying the last value of flops we want to display the average of recent values? flops holds an OrderedCollection instead of a Number.

```
initialize
    flops := OrderedCollection new
```

The setting method adds to the collection instead of changing the instance variable.

```
flops: aNumber
    flops adLast: aNumber.
    self changed: #flopsString
```

The accessing method has to compute the average instead of just returning the value.

```
flops
    flops isEmpty ifTrue: [^float zero].
    ^(flops inject: float zero into: [:sum :each | sum + each])
        / flops size
```

The above code is still fairly clean from an implementation perspective. From a design standpoint, though, it is a dangerous path.

The first problem is that the needs of the interface influence our implementation of the model. Conversely, our concept of an interface is constrained by the way we have implemented the model. The separation of model from interface, supported at the implementation level by broadcasting changes, merely reappears as a design problem. In other words, the letter of "separate model and interface" is satisfied because the model makes no direct reference to the interface, but the spirit is violated because interface decisions have caused us to change a model that should be oblivious to such concerns.

Other views with other aspects require inserting more hardwired broadcast messages. In large projects, this process of broadcast accretion leads to a bewildering profusion of broadcasts, often with intricate time dependencies.

Another problem is that this style of programming discourages reuse. Each instance variable is a special case, to be handled by special case code. For example, suppose we are working in a multiprocessor environment and want to view a running average of the number of processors active during rendering. We could add an instance variable, utilization, with accessing and setting methods that are copies of the respective messages for flops, but we could do no better at reuse than copy and paste.

This last point suggests that state change and change propagation somehow must be folded together into a new object. This object will be used instead of a bare instance variable as a model for views. We can create a family of these objects to model the different ways of viewing state changes over time. By using various kinds of objects in varying circumstances we can change the interaction supported by the model without changing the model itself.

The most common solution to these problems is to separate the model into a "browser" object and a clean underlying model without broadcasts (see Figure 9-1). The browser mediates between the user interface and the "real"

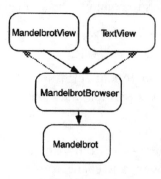

Figure 9-1

model, translating user requests into messages to the model and propagating changes back to the interface. Although fairly simple conceptually, this style of programming introduces another layer of objects between the user and the model without addressing the problem of multiple browsers on the same model (for example, the problem of updating the source code of a method appearing in more than one Browser).

VALUEMODEL STYLE

ValueModels in Objectworks\Smalltalk Release 4 fill the role of an interaction model. Rather than appearing between the domain model and the interface, ValueModels are placed "beneath" the domain model. This allows the view to interact directly with the state of the domain model and does not clutter the model itself with interaction concerns.

Here's how an ideal implementation can be applied to our example:

```
initialize
    value := OrderedCollection new
value
    value isEmpty ifTrue: [^Float zero].
    ^(value inject: Float zero into: [:sum :each I sum + each])
        / value size
value: anObject
    value addLast: anObject
```

We can install the new behavior by changing

```
Mandelbrot>>initialize.
    initialize
        flops := AveragingValueModel new
```

No other changes to the model are necessary. When we want to open a window on a running average of processor utilization we can create another AveragingValueModel. We do not need to duplicate any code.

The model has acquired a large measure of independence from changes mandated by the interface. For many interface changes we no longer need to touch code in the domain model beyond modifying the initiation. We instantiate a new kind of ValueModel, and the rest of the model remains unchanged.

THE REST OF THE STORY

The above code still doesn't quite work. The TextView expects a String or a Text from its model, and the ValueModel in this case returns a Number. The Release 4.1 solution is to interpose another object, called a PluggableAdaptor, between the model and the view. A PluggableAdaptor contains three blocks. The first is invoked when it receives the message value. The block takes one argument, the adaptor's model (in this case the ValueModel), and by default returns the result of sending value to the model. The block can be used to arbitrarily transform the value. In our case we want to create a string from the number:

```
openflops
    | window adaptor |
    window := ScheduledWindow new.
    adaptor := AspectAdaptor on: flops.
    adaptor getBlock: [:m | m value printString, 'flops'].
    window addChild: (TextView on: adaptor aspect: #value
        change: nil menu: nil).
    window open
```

The second block in a PluggableAdaptor is evaluated when the adaptor receives the value: message. The block is invoked with the model and the new value as arguments. By default it passes the message along to the model. This block translates the value from a form the view understands to one the model understands. If it were possible to change the flops rating, we might write something like this:

```
openflops
    | window adaptor |
```

```
window := ScheduledWindow new.
adaptor := AspectAdaptor on: flops.
adaptor getBlock: [:m | m value printString, 'flops'].
adaptor putBlock: [:m :v ]
    m value: (Number readFrom: v readStream)].
window addChild: (TextView on: adaptor aspect: #value
    change: nil menu: nil).
window open
```

The final PluggableAdaptor block is used to filter update messages. The block takes three arguments: the model, the aspect from the update: message, and the optional parameter from the update: message. The block evaluates to a boolean that is used to decide whether or not to forward the update. In our example we may not want to update the text if the flops rating is too low. We could change openflops as follows:

```
openflops
    | window adaptor |
    window := ScheduledWindow  new.
    adaptor := AspectAdaptor on: flops.
    adaptor getBlock: [:m | m value: printString, 'flops'].
    adaptor putBlock: [:m :v | m value. (Number readFrom: v
readStream)].
    adaptor updateBlock: [:m :a :p | m value > 1e6].
    window addChild: (TextView on: adaptor aspect: #value
        change: nil menu: nil).
    window open
```

When an object is dependent on two or more ValueModels it is often important to distinguish which one is generating the broadcast message. One solution is to take advantage of the full generality of the update message.

A cleaner solution is to use the update block of a pluggable adaptor to generate different updates for each ValueModel. The initiation would look like this:

```
initializeWith: model1 with: model2
    | adaptor1 adaptor2 |
    adaptor1 := PluggableAdaptor on: model1.
```

```
adaptor1 updateBlock: [:m :v :p | v == #value
    ifTrue: [adaptor1 changed: #value1]].
adaptor1 addDependent: self.
adaptor2 := PluggableAdaptor on: model2.
adaptor2 updateBlock [:m :v :p | v == #value
    iftrue: [adaptor1changed: #value2]].
adaptor2 addDependent: self
```

Then the update method can look like this:

```
ValueModel
    superclass: Model
    instance variables: value

value
    ^value

value: anObject
    value := anObject
    self changed: #value
```

We can recast **Mandelbrot** to use this simple **ValueModel**. First, the initialization method sets flops to a **ValueModel**.

```
initialize
    flops := ValueModel new
```

When accessing or setting the value you must remember to send messages to flops and not just use the instance variable. Religious use of accessing and setting methods, though, can hide this detail from the rest of the object.

```
flops
    ^flops value
```

Note that when tile value is set the **Mandelbrot** no longer needs to propagate changes.

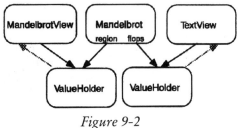

Figure 9-2

flops: aNumber
   flops value: aNumber

When making a view to display flops the ValueModel is the model of the TextView, not the Mandelbrot.

```
openflops
   | window |
   window := ScheduledWindow new.
   window addChild: (TextView on: flops aspect: #value
      change: nil menu: nil).
   window open
```

We now have a system with the same functionality as the simplest one described above. Figure 9-2 diagrams the relationships between the various components in the value model-style Mandelbrot.

The worth of ValueModels becomes apparent when we display a running average rather than a single value. The change is made creating a subclass of ValueModel called AveragingValueModel, which accumulates a history of values in response to value:messages.

```
AveragingValueModel
   superclass: ValueModel
   instance variables: none
update: aSymbol
      aSymbol == #value1 ifTrue: [self updateValue1].
      aSymbol == #value2 ifTrue: [self updateValue2]
```

The preceding information is written assuming ValueModel holds values. In the real system, though, ValueModel is an abstract superclass, and the subclass acting as ValueModel above is really called ValueHolder. PluggableAdaptor is also a subclass of ValueModel. Other subclasses (like AveragingValueModel) should arise as the full utility of the ValueModel style becomes apparent.

LAZY VIEWS

A final idiom that accompanies Objectworks\Smalltalk Release 4 and later is lazy updating of views. Back when dinosaurs ruled the earth and Smalltalk did its own window management, it was common to directly redisplay a view in response to an update:

```
update: aSymbol
    (self interestedIn: aSymbol) ifTrue: [self displayView]
```

A serious problem with this strategy is that the view will be redisplayed several times if multiple update messages come in. Multiple updates look bad and slow your programs down. This is especially true with the expanded use of broadcast messages in Release 4.

When you implement views in Release 4 and later, you should never directly redisplay the view. Instead the view should send itself an invalidate message:

```
Update: aSymbol
    (self interestedIn: aSymbol) ifTrue: [self invalidate]
```

These invalidations are pooled together. The next time a Controller sends itself poll (or someone explicitly sends checkForEvents to ScheduledControllers) all views with some invalid area will be asked to display. This ensures that if there is a change to a model causing several views to update they will display as simultaneously as possible.

CONCLUSION

The ValueModel style of coding manages complexity by strictly separating interface and model.

We have just begun to explore the range of possibilities inherent in the ValueModel style. You can expect to discover new uses as you begin using it yourself. If you find new ValueModels, or new uses for the existing ones, please drop me a line so I can publish them here.

10

COLLECTION IDIOMS:
STANDARD CLASSES

―――

Smalltalk Report, NOVEMBER–DECEMBER, 1992

If you have read The Smalltalk Best Practice Patterns, *you can see in this column the beginnings of the section in the book on collections. Once again, I mined the material from the image. Thinking back, I'm amazed at how important reading the image has been to me. I can remember being incredibly frustrated at having to spend all day looking for the method or class that I wanted, but then realizing at the end of the day that I had gotten more accomplished with six hours of reading and ten minutes of typing than I used to accomplish with ten hours of typing.*

We may underestimate the value of a shared body of literature (the image) in creating and sustaining the Smalltalk culture. Perhaps that's why the visual "wire-and-fire" front-ends failed to have much impact-there was no corpus of visual code that everyone routinely consulted.

O UR PREVIOUS COLUMN focused on enumeration methods and how to use all of them to advantage. This column covers the common collection classes, how they are implemented, when you should use them, and when you should be careful.

COLLECTION CLASSES

ARRAY

Use an Array if you know the size of the collection when you create it and if the indices into the elements (the first argument to at: and at:put:) are consecutive integers between one and the size of the array.

Arrays are implemented using the "indexable" part of objects. Recall that you can declare a class indexable. You can send new: anInteger to an indexable class and you will receive an instance with anInteger-indexable instance variables. The indexable variables are accessible through at: and at:put:. Array needs no more than the implementation of at: and at:put: in Object, and the implementation of new: in Class to operate.

Many people use OrderedCollections everywhere they need a collection. If you:

- want a dynamically sized collection without the OrderedCollection overhead (see below),

- are willing to make the referencing object a little less flexible, and

- don't often add or remove items, compared with how often you access the collection,

you can use arrays instead. Where you had:

```
initialize
    collection := OrderedCollection new
```

you have:

```
initialize
    collection := Array new "or even #()"
```

then you replace add: and remove: sent to collection with copyWith: and copyWithout: and reassign collection, then

```
foo
    collection add: #bar
```

becomes:

```
foo
    collection := collection copyWith: #bar
```

The disadvantage of this approach is that the referencing object now has built into it the knowledge that its collection isn't resizable. Your object has, in effect, accepted some of the collection's responsibility.

BYTEARRAY

ByteArrays store integers between 0 and 255 inclusive. If all the objects you need to store in an Array are in this range, you can save space by using a ByteArray. Whereas Arrays use 32-bit slots (i.e., soon-to-be-obsolete 32-bit processors) to store object references, ByteArrays only use 8 bits.

Besides the space savings, using ByteArrays can also make garbage collection faster. Byte-indexable objects (of which ByteArrays are one) are marked as not having any object references. The collector does not need to traverse them to determine which objects are still reachable.

As I mentioned in the last column, any class can be declared indexable. Instances are then allowed to have instance variables that are accessed by number (through at: and at:put:) rather than by name. Similarly, you can declare classes to be byte indexable. at: and at:put: for byte-indexable objects retrieve and store 1-byte integers instead of arbitrary objects. A significant limitation of byte-indexable objects is that they can't have any named instance variables. This is to preserve the garbage-collector simplification mentioned above.

If you want to create an object that is bit-pattern oriented but shouldn't respond to the whole range of collection messages, you should create a byte-indexable class. Such objects are particularly useful when passed to other languages because the bits used to encode the objects in a byte indexable object are the same as those used by, for instance, C, whereas a full-fledged Small-Integer has a different format than a C int.

DICTIONARY

Dictionaries are like dynamically sized arrays where the indices are not constrained to be consecutive integers. Dictionaries use hashing tables with linear probing to store and look up their elements (Figure 10-1). The key is sent "hash" and the answer modulo is the basic size of the Dictionary is used to begin searching for the key. The elements are stored as Associations.

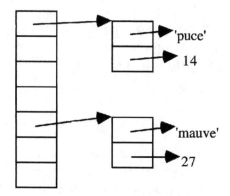

Figure 10-1 A typical Dictionary.

Dictionaries are rather schizophrenic. They can't decide whether they are arrays with arbitrary indices or unordered collections of associations with the accessing methods at: and at:put:. It doesn't help that Dictionary subclasses Set to inherit the implementation of hashed lookup. I treat them like arrays. If I want to think of them as associations, I use the message "associations" to get a set of associations I can operate on unambiguously.

When a Dictionary looks up a key, it uses = to determine if it has found a match. Thus, two strings that are not the same object but contain the same characters are considered to be the same key. This is why when you reimplement =, you must also reimplement hash. If two objects are =, they must have the same hash value.

If you read your Knuth, you will see that hashed lookup takes constant time—it is not sensitive to the number of elements in the collection. This mathematical result is subject to two pragmatic concerns, however hash quality and loading. When you send hash to the keys, you should get a random distribution. If many objects return a number that is the same modulo the basic size of the Dictionary, then linear probing degenerates to linear lookup. If most of the slots in the Dictionary are full, the hash is almost sure to return an index that is already taken and, again, you are into linear lookup. By randomizing the distribution of hash values and making sure the Dictionary never gets more than 60% full, you will avoid most of the potential performance problems.

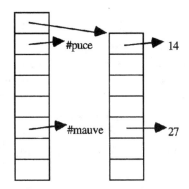

Figure 10-2 A typical Identity Dictionary.

IDENTITYDICTIONARY

IdentityDictionaries behave like Dictionaries except that they compare keys using == (are the two objects really the same object?). IdentityDictionaries are useful where you know that the keys are objects for which = is the same as == (e.g., Symbols, Characters, or SmallIntegers).

Instead of being implemented as a hash table of associations, Identity-Dictionaries are implemented as two parallel arrays. The first holds the keys, the second the values (Figure 10-2).

This implementation saves space because each association in a Dictionary takes 12 bytes of header + 8 bytes of object reference = 20 bytes. The total memory usage for a Dictionary is 12 bytes for the header of the Dictionary + 4 bytes times the basic size of the Dictionary + 20 bytes times the number of entries. The memory required for an IdentityDictionary is 24 bytes for the header of the object and the value collection + 8 bytes times the basic size.

For example, a 10,000-element Dictionary that has 5,000 entries free would take 12 + (4 * 15000) + (20 * 10000) = 260,012 bytes. You can see how the overhead of the Associations adds up. The same collection stored as an Identity-Dictionary would take 24 + (8 * 15000) = 120,024 bytes.

ORDEREDCOLLECTION

OrderedCollections are like Arrays in that their keys are consecutive integers. Unlike **Arrays**, they are dynamically sized. They respond to **add:** and **remove:**. OrderedCollections preserve the order in which elements are added. You can also send them **addFirst:**, **addLast:**, **removeFirst**, and **removeLast**.

Using these methods, it is possible to implement stacks and queues trivially. There are no **Stack** or **Queue** objects in Smalltalk because it is so easy to get their functionality with an OrderedCollection. To get a stack, you use **addLast:** for push, **last** for top, and **removeLast** for pop (you could also operate the stack off the front of the OrderedCollection). To implement a queue, you use **addFirst:** for add and **removeLast** for remove.

As an example of using an OrderedCollection for a queue, let's look at implementing level-order traversal. Given a tree of objects, we want to process all the nodes at one level before we move on to the next:

```
Tree>>levelOrderDo: aBlock
    | queue |
    queue := OrderedCollection with: self.
    [queue isEmpty] whileFalse:
        [| node |
        node := queue removeFirst.
        aBlock value: node.
        queue addAllLast: node children]
```

OrderedCollections keep around extra storage at the beginning and end of their indexable parts to make it possible to add and remove elements without having to change size (Figure 10-3).

Because OrderedCollections are dynamically sized they preallocate a number of slots when they are created in preparation for objects being added. If you are using lots of OrderedCollections and most are smaller than the ini-

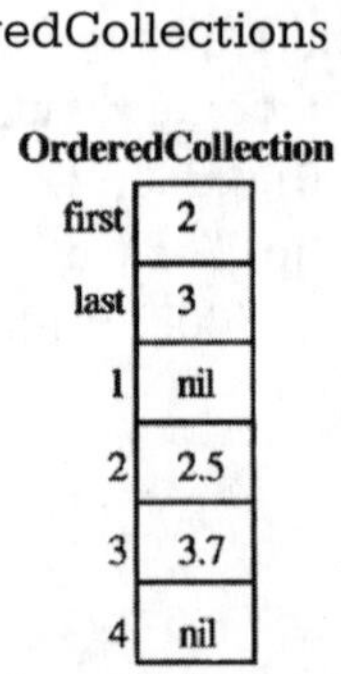

OrderedCollection

first	2
last	3
1	nil
2	2.5
3	3.7
4	nil

Figure 10-3 The result of (OrderedCollection new: 4) add: 2.5;
add: 3.7.

tial allocation, the space overhead and its effect on the storage manager can be significant. I have heard stories of programs speeding up by a factor of 60 just by replacing OrderedCollection new with OrderedCollection new: 1 at the right spot. Gather statistics on the number and loading of your OrderedCollections to determine if this optimization will help you.

Another performance implication of using OrderedCollections is the level of indirection required to access elements. at: as defined in Object just invokes a primitive to index into the receiver's indexed instance variables. To implement at: and at:put:, OrderedCollections have to first take into account:

```
OrderedCollection>>at: anInteger
    anInteger > self size ifTrue: [self error: 'Out of bounds']. ^
    super at: anInteger + first - 1
```

RunArray

RunArrays have the same external protocol as OrderedCollection, but they are optimized for storing collections in which the same object is added consecutively many times. Rather than just store the objects one after the other, RunArrays store two collections: one of the objects in the collection, the other the number of times the object appears (Figure 10-4).

Each entry in a RunArray requires two object references. RunArrays require storage related not to the number of elements in the collection but to

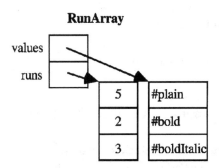

Figure 10-4 The result of RunArray new addAll: (plain plain plain plain plain bold bold boldItalic boldItalic boldItalic).

the number of times adjacent objects are different. In the worst case, RunArrays require twice as much storage as an OrderedCollection.

Indexing into a RunArray is potentially an expensive operation, requiring time proportional to the number of runs. Following is an implementation of at:.

```
RunArray>>at: anInteger
  | index |
  index := 0.
  1 to: runs size do:
    [:each |
    index + (runs at: each) >= anInteger
      ifTrue: [^values at: each].
    index := index + (runs at: each)]
```

This simple implementation makes code like

```
1 to: runArray size do: [:each | runArray at: each]
```

take time proportional to the number of runs multiplied by the number of elements in the collection. Because the access pattern for RunArrays usually marches along the collection from first element to last, RunArrays cache the beginning of the run in which the last index was found. Looking up the following index only requires checking to make sure that the new index is in the same run as the old one:

```
RunArray>>at: anInteger
  ^anInteger >= cachedIndex
    ifTrue: [self cachedAt: anInteger]
    ifFalse: [self lookUpAt: anInteger]

cachedAt: anInteger
  anInteger - cachedIndex > (runs at: cachedRun)
    ifTrue:
      [cachedIndex := cachedIndex + (runs at: cachedRun).
      cachedRun := cachedRun + 1].
  ^values at: cachedRun
```

```
lookUpAt: anInteger
  | index |
  index := 0.
  1 to: runs size do:
    [:each |
    index + (runs at: each) >= anInteger
      ifTrue: [^values at: each].
    index := index + (runs at: each)
```

With this implementation, an access pattern like the one above will now be slightly slower than the equivalent OrderedCollection because of the overhead of checking for the common case. Accessing the RunArray in reverse is now proportional to the number of runs squared.

INTERVAL

Another kind of run-length encoded collection is Interval. An Interval is created with a beginning number, an ending number, and an optional step number (1 is the default). #(1 2 3 4) and Interval from: 1 to: 4 are equivalent objects for most purposes. Number>>to: and to:by: are shorthand for Interval class>>from:to: and from:to:by:.

Intervals are commonly used to represent ranges of numbers, such as a selection in a piece of text. A common idiom is using an Interval with collect:.

```
foo
  ^(1 to: self size) collect: [:each | each -> (self at: each)]
```

Species is sent to an object when a copy is being made for use in one of the enumeration methods collect: and select:. The default implementation in Object just returns the class of the receiver. SequenceableCollection implements collect: and select:, and it expects the result of self species to respond to at:put:. Since Intervals don't respond to at:put:, they have to override species to return the class Array.

SORTEDCOLLECTION

Another dynamically sized collection is the SortedCollection. Unlike Ordered-Collections, which order their elements according to the order in which they were added, SortedCollections rely on a two-argument block to determine, pairwise, the order for elements. This block defaults to [:a :b | a <= b], so simple SortedCollections sort their elements from lowest to highest.

One thing to watch out for when using SortedCollections is sending them add: when you don't have to. add: does a binary search of the collection, moves all of the elements after the added object down one, and inserts the added object. Moving the elements to make room takes time proportional to the size of the collection. If you know you are going to be adding several elements at once, use addAll:, which will stick the new elements at the end and resort the entire collection. Here is a method for comparing time spent using these two methods (notice that I don't hold myself to the same coding standards in workspaces):

```
| sc r t1 t2 |
sc := SortedCollection new.
r := Random new.
t1 := Time millisecondsToRun:
    [1000 timesRepeat: [sc add: r next]].
sc := SortedCollection new.
t2 := Time millisecondsToRun:
    [sc addAll: ((1 to: 1000) collect: [:each | r next])].
'Add: ', t1 printString, ' addAll: ', t2 printString
```

Executing this results in 'Add: 10725 addAll: 1386'.

STRING

Strings in Smalltalk are like Arrays whose elements are restricted to Characters. Strings are byte indexable for compactness. They redefine the indexing methods to convert from 8-bit numbers to characters and vice versa.

```
String>>at: anInteger
```

```
^Character value: (super at: anInteger)
```

```
String>>at: anInteger put: aCharacter
    ^super at: anInteger put: aCharacter asciiValue
```

It is common to use, to concatenate Strings. You can use , to concatenate any two sequenceable collections (OrderedCollection, Array, RunArray, and so on). Less common is the use of the other collection methods with Strings. You can capitalize all the characters in a String with collect.

```
asUppercase
^self collect: [:each | each asUppercase]
```

Interestingly, even the ParcPlace Release 4.1 image implements this method with five lines containing an explicit loop and indexing.

Digitalk's String class is implemented with the simple model described here. ParcPlace has a much more elaborate implementation that takes care of multibyte characters and different character sets on different platforms, even for odd characters. The design requires six classes for strings and three more for symbols.

SYMBOL

Symbols behave in most ways like Strings, except that if you have two symbols containing the same characters, they are guaranteed to be the same object. So while String>>= takes time proportional to the length of the strings, Symbol>>= takes constant time:

```
Symbol>>= anObject
    ^self == anObject
```

To preserve uniqueness, Symbols cannot be changed once they are created. at:put: is overridden to raise an error.

Like Interval, because Symbols don't respond to at:put:, they override species. Symbol>>species returns the class String. Thus, executing "#abc , #def" returns 'abcdef', a String, not a Symbol.

If you are programming in Smalltalk/V, be careful of creating too many symbols. There is a limit of 2^16 Symbols. While this may seem like a lot, after you have created many new methods and used Symbols for indices in several places, it is very possible to run out of Symbols. The scrambling you have to do to climb out of the "limited Symbol pit" is not pretty.

A last oddity of Symbols and Strings is the asymmetry of =. "'abc' = #abc" returns true because the String receives the message and successfully checks to see that the characters in the receiver are the same as those in the argument. "#abc = 'abc'" returns false because the two objects are not identical. I can remember long debates at Tektronix over the propriety of this strange fact. The upshot of the debates was that it's regrettable things work this way, but the alternatives are all less attractive for one reason or another.

SETS

Sets are dynamically sized collections. They respond to add: and remove: but, unlike OrderedCollections, they don't guarantee any particular ordering on the elements when they are used later (e.g., by do:). Sets also don't have any indexed access (no at: or at:put:).

Sets implement includes:, add: and remove: efficiently by hashing. The element to be added is sent hash, and that value is used modulo the size of the storage allocated for the Set as the index to start looking for a place to put the element (or remove it). Note that storage for a Set will contain more indexed variables than the Set has elements, so hashing is likely to encounter an empty slot. The Set contains an instance variable, *tally*, which records how many of the slots are filled. Set>>size just returns tally.

You can eliminate duplicates from any collection (albeit while losing its ordering) by sending it asSet.

IDENTITYSET

Sets use = to determine if they have found an object. IdentitySets use ==. They are useful where the identity of objects is important. Most applications are in meta-object code, where you are manipulating the objects but not asking them to do anything. For instance, if you designed a remote object system where transparent copies of objects were transmitted over a network, you might store the objects in an IdentitySet. If you transmitted two objects that were = but not ==, and later changed one of them, storing them in an IdentitySet would ensure that they were different objects on the remote systems.

BAG

Instead of discarding duplicate elements like Sets, Bags count them. Executing this code

```
| s |
s := Set new.
s addAll: #(a a b b c).s
size
```

returns 3. Changing it to a Bag

```
| b |
b := Bag new.
b addAll: #(a a b b c).
b size
```

returns 5.

Use Bags anywhere you want a quick implementation of includes—that is, when you don't care about the order of elements and you need a compact representation of duplicate elements.

Bags are not used anywhere in the ParcPlace Release 4.1 image or in Smalltalk/V Mac 1.2. The only time I can remember using Bags is in Profile/V. Every time I take a sample, I put the program counter in a Bag. When I display the profile, I map the stored program counters back to source statements, giving the user profiling at the level of individual statements.

CONCLUSION

The Collection classes are among the most powerful parts of the Smalltalk system. Choosing the right collection for a circumstance has a dramatic influence on the behavior and performance of your system. I have tried to lay out what each major collection class does, what it is good for, what to watch out for, and how it is implemented.

I am amazed at the richness of this seemingly simple set of classes. Originally, I thought I would have to stretch to get enough material for just one column. After two columns that have covered the major issues in using collections, there is still more to be written. I'll give it a rest for now, however, and go on to something else—I'm not sure what just yet. If you have any ideas call me at 408.338.4649 or fax me at 408.338.1115.

11

AN OBJECTWORKS\SMALLTALK 4.1 WRAPPER IDIOM

Smalltalk Report, JANUARY, 1993

Here is a great example of a column I wish I'd never written. It presents *a new control structure to deal with the complexity of the Composite/Wrapper pattern used in the user interface code in VisualWorks. I wrote the column, sent it off, then had a quick talk with David Liebs about the subject. "So you need to talk to a particular wrapper, eh? Why don't you keep a pointer to the wrapper you need to talk to and give it a useful name? Then you can just send it messages." Duh...*

The other aspect of the column I regret is that it seems to condone adding new control structures to Smalltalk. The meta facilities of Smalltalk are extremely powerful, but 99.99 percent of the time, you shouldn't use them. Oh, they'd get the job done alright, but at what cost?

When you write something like #wrapperSend:, you have to take off your application-programmer hat and put on your language-designer hat. The responsibilities of the language designer are ten times as great as those of an application developer. Whatever you do, you have to implement it and test it, sure, but you also have to document it like a new language feature, extend the programming environment to handle it smoothly, and worst of all, maintain it through all future releases of the image.

All that might be worth it, but it's sure worth another look at simpler solutions first. Oh, and then another look after that...

ONE OF THE most significant changes to Smalltalk in recent years is the refactoring of display functionality into the VisualComponent hierarchy of Objectworks\Smalltalk Release 4. I am only beginning to realize the full implications of factoring borders, composition, and layout into their own objects.

Some recurring problems arise in using the new architecture. This column addresses the problem of addressing the right object in an environment of changing compositions of objects. The solution was invented by Jay O'Connor, a bright new Smalltalk programmer I've been working with for the last year. My columns have been getting longer and longer, so I've have tried a different approach this time. I will address a specific problem in a specific context, rather than try to tackle something as general as "Collections: The Big Picture." Let me know what you think. My numbers are listed at the end of the article.

ARCHITECTURE

In the beginning there was **View**. (Well, not entirely the beginning, but back there someplace). And **View** was responsible for rendering a model's data on the screen. To make pretty pictures on the screen, though, **View** picked up a few more responsibilities along the way—drawing borders, composing subviews, transforming coordinates, and clipping display operations. All this responsibility and the state to support it made **View** difficult to subclass, expensive to instantiate, and hard to teach to new programmers.

Two things were needed: to split each of the responsibilities into its own object and to compose the objects so they could work together to achieve the same results as before. Objectworks\Smalltalk Release 4 introduced the new architecture. It has three main families of objects: **VisualComponents** for displaying models, **GraphicsContexts** to translate and clip display operations, and **Wrappers** to modify the **GraphicsContext** on the way down to the **VisualComponent**.

VISUALCOMPONENT

VisualComponent is an abstract superclass. It requires its subclasses to implement **displayOn: aGraphicsContext**, which renders the component. All displaying is done relative to 0@0, so the component need not know where it eventually ends up on the screen. Subclasses also have to implement **preferredBounds**, which returns a **Rectangle** describing the size the component thinks it should be. Layout may make its screen appearance smaller.

VISUALPART

VisualPart adds an instance variable, container, to VisualComponent. A VisualPart is linked to its containing component so it can send itself invalidate when it wants to be redrawn. In the original display model, a View that got an update and wanted to display itself would do it right then. If several Views redisplayed this could result in an annoying flicker. With the invalidation model, all VisualParts wanting to display register their interest, and the next time a Controller goes through an idle loop it notices that redisplay needs to happen, and it all occurs at once.

COMPOSITEPART

A CompositePart puts several VisualComponents together. Their placement and displayed size are subject to a layout object that can flexibly position components in either relative or absolute positions relative to the CompositePart. It is easy to specify locations like "the top third of the composite with a margin of 20 pixels at the top."

WRAPPER

Wrappers pass most messages through to their component. Some messages get intercepted or modified on the way. A translating wrapper, for instance, would change where its component displayed. A color wrapper would change the colors used by its component. Wrappers are supposed to be transparently composable. That is, you should be able to insert new wrappers anywhere between the containing object and the component without interfering with the operation of the component or any of the other wrappers.

BOUNDEDWRAPPER

One of the most common wrappers, BoundedWrapper, translates and clips graphics operations. You'll almost never explicitly create a BoundedWrapper. Adding a component to a composite automatically inserts a Bounded-Wrapper whose size and location are set according to the specified layout.

Bordered Wrapper

You might think that bordering and bounding would be handled in separate wrappers, in the spirit of purity and composability. Instead, apparently for implementation reasons, BorderedWrapper is a subclass of BoundedWrapper. BorderedWrappers compute their preferredBounds by increasing the size of their components' preferredBounds by the size of their border. They implement displayOn: by displaying the border, insetting the clipping bounds, and asking their component to display.

Graphics Context

All graphics operations go through a GraphicsContext. It has symbolic protocol to display images, lines, rectangles, strings, and so on. It also carries along a clipping bounds and translation. Wrappers like BoundedWrapper work by modifying the GraphicsContext passed along to their component. It also carries along a foreground color and background color, so components that operate in two colors need have no knowledge of what colors to use, leaving it up to the GraphicsContext to have the right color set (perhaps by enclosing the component in a wrapper that sets the color).

The heavy reliance of this model on wrappers leads to a problem. You would like to treat the chain of wrappers and the component they enclose as a single unit. You would also like to insulate the wrappers and their component from changes in the wrapper chain.

You could write "container container remove: container" to remove a component from its composite. This assumes that the container is some form of wrapper and its container is a CompositePart. When I started using the new framework I wrote code like this often. I also found it breaking often, because I inevitably wanted to insert new wrappers in the chain. Every time I inserted a new wrapper I'd have to change the length of "container container ..." expressions to match the new setup.

A slightly more modular way to fix this problem is to implement a pass through message in **Wrapper**. The component could say "**container remove: self**" and **Wrapper>>remove: aVisualComponent** could pass the message on to its container. The problem with this solution is that it introduces many messages in **Wrapper**.

IMPLEMENTATION

What we needed was an abstract way to address a message somewhere in the wrapper chain. We wanted to treat the chain as a single object for most operations. First we needed to get the top wrapper in the chain. VisualComponents don't have a container, so they assume there are no wrappers.

```
VisualComponent>>topWrapper
  "By default"
  ^self
```

VisualParts ask their container for the **topWrapper**. Note the nil check. Many methods in VisualPart would be simpler if VisualParts maintained the invariant that their container could not be nil. I have never found a case where it wasn't nil, except after a window has been released. The lack of an invariant leaves you with one more thing to remember—always check the container
before sending it a message.

```
VisualPart>>topWrapper
  container isNil ifTrue: [^self].
  ^container topWrapperFor: self
```

The argument to **topWrapperFor:** will always be the component immediately below the receiver. When you get to an object that isn't a wrapper, you return the object below, which is guaranteed to be either a wrapper or the original component itself:

```
VisualComponent>>topWrapperFor: anObject
  ^anObject
```

```
Wrapper>>topWrapperFor: anObject
    container isNil ifTrue: [^self].
    ^container topWrapperFor: self
```

TopWrapper is useful all by itself. I often keep a collection of VisualComponents that I'm interested in managing. When I want to remove one from a CompositePart, I need—you guessed it—the topWrapper. I can say component topWrapper container remove: component topWrapper. Simple. It no longer matters what part of the chain I hold onto. I can get to the top and bottom easily.

Back to our effort to send messages "somewhere in the chain." We want to send a message to the first wrapper that implements it. The search proceeds from the top wrapper down, so we can insert new wrappers to intercept the message later. This creates the potential for other problems later on, like accidentally shadowing a method in a lower Wrapper, but I haven't found it to be a problem in practice.

```
VisualComponent>>wrapperSend: aSymbol
    ^self topWrapper wrapperDelegate: (Message selector: aSymbol)
```

Using this protocol, a component can say things like self wrapperSend: #disable, assuming that some wrapper in the chain implements disable, but not assuming where in the chain it resides.

Now we need to implement wrapperDelegate:. The default implementation is to perform the message

```
VisualComponent>>wrapperDelegate: aMessage
    ^self perform: aMessage selector withArguments: aMessage
        arguments
```

Wrappers need to be a bit smarter. They perform the message only if they can understand it; otherwise they pass it on to their component (remember, search for the appropriate wrapper proceeds top down).

```
Wrapper>>wrapperDelegate: aMessage
    ^(self respondsTo: aMessage selector)
        ifTrue: [super wrapperDelegate: aMessage]
        ifFalse: [component wrapperDelegate: aMessage]
```

Here is an interesting question: Should the VisualComponent send the message regardless, or ignore it if it isn't understood? I can see both sides. Ignoring it is better for modularity because if you don't have a wrapper that responds, the message disappears without a trace. On the other hand, if someone is counting on the return value, the "doesNotUnderstand" case will cause an error. Besides, I like having a notifier pop up during development if I send a message no one understands. It's usually because I have made a mistake.

WrapperSend: has made my life much easier. I now use wrappers as they were intended: independent bits of functionality that can be composed in different ways with abandon. I no longer pause to think if any of my code depends on the configuration of the wrapper chain.

Another useful implication is that, in using the wrapper pass through mechanism described above, I had to implement my messages in three places: VisualComponent for some default behavior, Wrapper for delegation, and wrapper subclass for implementing the method for the real behavior. With wrapperSend:, I only put it in one place: the class that really implements it. All the other wrappers pass it along automatically.

CONCLUSION

Wrappers make amazingly powerful and flexible interface objects. Coloring, highlighting, visibility, selection, and double buffering are some of the activities that used to be built into interface objects that can now be factored into their own wrapper. Once you have a library of wrappers, you can create new interface objects by composition, never having to create new classes. The possibilities are mind boggling and not nearly fully explored.

12

A SHORT INTRODUCTION TO PATTERN LANGUAGE

Smalltalk Report, FEBRUARY, 1993

Kent comes clean. I'd never tried to explain patterns in print before, not at any length. This was a bit of an experiment for me. Looking at it now I'm a bit disappointed, because the presentation violates one of my cardinal rules of teaching—always go from concrete to abstract. Were I writing this again, I would take some disguised pattern I had presented earlier and present it both in idiom format and pattern format. Oh well...

One thing I like about the column is the emphasis on communication. Looking at the earlier columns, I'm surprised at how little I said about the importance of communicating through code. I'm sure I understood how important communication is, but I hadn't written about it since the early HOOPLA! articles.

THIS WILL BE a departure from my code-oriented columns. For the last six months I've been surreptitiously presenting my material using a technique that I've been working with for the past six years or so. This technique was derived from work done in architecture (buildings, not chips) to help people design comfortable spaces for themselves. The time has come to tell you what I've been leading up to, so that I can directly refer to these concepts in the future.

First, though, I have to tell you about the most thoroughly useful little idiom I have seen in a long time. Ward Cunningham and I recently got to code together on a nifty spreadsheet project, and he showed me a simple idiom for dealing with nil values. It saves me a line in many methods and, since most methods are three or four lines long, that's a significant savings. Here is the implementation:

Donald Knuth has attacked the problem with what he calls "Literate Programming." He shares the insight that programmers ought to write programs for other programmers, not just the computer. His solution is to make programs read like books. When you read a literate program you are reading a combination of prose and code. You can filter out the nonprogram elements and run the result through a compiler to get an executable program.

There are a couple of problems with literate programming as Knuth conceives it. First, his literate programming system is implemented as a 1970s-style textual language. To write a literate program you have to know the programming language, the typesetting language, and the extensions required by the literate programming system. More important, the structure of a literate program is fundamentally linear. It is intended to be read from beginning to end. While this may be appropriate for a monolithic program like TeX, it does not address the problem of describing the intent of an object library, which is intended to be used piecemeal—sometimes just by instantiating objects, sometimes by plugging new objects into existing frameworks, and sometimes by refinement.

What we need is a structure for intention-oriented information that is flexible enough to convey a variety of information at different levels, but structured enough to provide a predictable experience for readers. It has to be able to convey process-oriented information but also describe programs piecemeal. It has to describe both how a program is intended to be used and how it works.

The solution I have been pursuing derives from the work of architect Christopher Alexander, who has spent many years seeking a way for architects to describe generic solutions to architectural problems so that individuals can adapt these solutions to their situations. The solution he found, called *pattern language,* solves all of the problems listed above: it is piecemeal, but also has large-scale structure; its essence describes the application of a solution, but also relates how the solution works; and it describes solutions at all scales, from urban planning to the size and color of trim in a house. His approach is presented in a pair of books from Oxford Press: *The Timeless Way of Building* and *A Pattern Language.*

```
Object>>ifNil: aBlock
    ^self
UndefinedObject>>ifNil: aBlock
    ^aBlock value
```

Simple, huh? Here's what happens when you use it, though. You can transform code that looks like:

```
foo isNil ifTrue: [foo := self computeFoo].
    ^foo
```

into:

```
^foo ifNil: [foo := self computeFoo]
```

The savings comes because ifTrue: and ifFalse: return nil if the receiver is false or true, respectively. IfNil: returns the receiver, which can be any object, instead. I have found ifNil: useful in many more situations than the one listed above. Try it! If you find a clever use, send it to me and I'll write it up.

The one complaint about ifNiL: is that it is slower than "isNil ifTrue:" (or its grosser cousin "== nil ifTrue:"). I claim that if you are focused on anything but achieving the most readable code possible in the middle 80% of a development, you're doing the wrong thing. Besides, it wouldn't be that hard to implement ifNil: as an inline message, just like the other conditionals. If it's not that hard, maybe I should write it up some time. Or maybe you should!

Now back to our regularly scheduled column…

The problem to be solved is describing the intent behind a piece of code to someone who needs to use it. There are plenty of methods for describing how code works (even though most programmers aren't disciplined in using them), but describing how code is supposed to be used is a black art. As the emphasis on programming shifts from just running programs to refining and reusing them, this is a problem of increasing importance.

As objects are supposed to be about reuse, describing intent is of critical importance to us.

Patterns

The unit of knowledge in a pattern language is a pattern. A pattern encodes an adequate solution to a problem known to arise in the process of building a system. A person should be able to read a pattern and know:

- What problems need to be solved before this one can be solved
- What problem the pattern solves
- What constrains the solution to the problem
- What to do to the system to satisfy the pattern
- What problems to solve once this one has been solved

Patterns have a consistent structure. Each has the following sections:

- A name evoking the problem and its solution
- A prologue summarizing what other patterns have to be considered before this one is appropriate
- A one-paragraph preamble describing the crux of the problem solved by the pattern
- A diagram illustrating the problem
- A short essay exploring constraints on the solution
- One or two paragraphs describing how to solve the problem
- An illustration of the solution
- An epilogue summarizing patterns that can be considered once this one is satisfied

Several valuable traits are common to all patterns:

- They always call for concrete actions, even if they are at very high levels. For instance, a design-level pattern might call for splitting one object into two to improve flexibility. A coding pattern might help you give names to arguments.

- They include a complete description of the considerations influencing the solution. Almost no documentation describes the forces acting on a decision, but it is precisely this information that allows you to evaluate an object for usefulness in a particular context.

- They are illustrated with a simple diagram. Alexander's patterns are remarkable for the degree to which their essence can be distilled into a simple line drawing. The effective computer patterns I have discovered also boil down to a little picture.

The word "pattern" takes several meanings in this context. First, each solution represents a pattern of elements. The object that uses an `OrderedCollection` has a specific relationship with the objects it references. Second, the constraints acting on the solution form a pattern. The need to conserve space tugs this way, the desire for greater speed that way. Finally, and most curiously, are common patterns of human behavior. The act of choosing an `OrderedCollection` recurs many times and in many places.

PATTERN LANGUAGE

Patterns do not stand in isolation. The epilogue and prologue sections of each pattern link it to several others. The result can be seen as a kind of lattice, with problems that need to be addressed first higher than those that can be considered later. Much of an expert's skill comes from knowing what to worry about up front and what can be safely postponed. This process-oriented information is often as valuable as the patterns themselves.

The patterns together form a language in the sense that the patterns are terminal symbols and the links between them are the productions. You create well-formed sentences by considering a sequence of patterns in turn. The result is a fully formed system. This is the primary difference between a pattern language and a set of design rules (like the Apple Human Interface Guidelines). The pattern language helps you create a system with the desired properties, not just analyze existing systems for the existence of those properties. A pattern language for good design will lead you to create a system with high coherence and low cohesion, not just describe the properties in isolation.

A complete pattern language for object-oriented programming encompasses patterns at all levels. Broad patterns cover issues like distribution of responsibility and control structures. Subsequent patterns help use the right abstractions in a library. Final patterns deal with variable naming, method naming, breaking methods into smaller methods, factoring code into inheritance hierarchies, and performance tuning.

CONCLUSION

No one has yet written a pattern language for objects like the one outlined above. There is general agreement that the problem of communicating intent is critical to cashing in on the promise of object-oriented programming. Researchers worldwide have turned to pattern languages as a promising approach to the problem. Here are a few I know about:

- Ralph Johnson at the University of Illinois is writing a pattern language for HotDraw, a graphical editing framework.

- Richard Helm and John Vlissides of IBM and Erich Gamma of the Union Bank of Switzerland have been writing a catalog of "design patterns," which capture common design elements of C++ programs.

- Bruce Anderson of the University of Essex is leading an effort to compile an "architecture handbook."

- Oscar Nierstrasz at the University of Geneva has been using patterns to try to achieve reuse.

In subsequent columns I will explicitly use the pattern format where appropriate to describe Smalltalk idioms. I recommend the study of Christopher Alexander's work for those interested in attacking the educational side of the reuse problem. I have enjoyed studying the material both because of the obvious parallels between the pitfalls of professional architects and professional programmers, and because I am now far more sensitive to my physical environment and its effect on my life.

Architecture has the advantage (and disadvantage) of thousands of years of history to mine for patterns. Programming is a new enough discipline that we all have to invent new solutions often. Collecting and disseminating these common patterns will hasten the day we can get on to more interesting questions. As you discover patterns in your own work, please send them to me.

13

WHOLE LOTTA SMALLTALK: THE TECHNOLOGY

Object Magazine, MARCH–APRIL, 1993

You can't write a review without breaking some eggs. That was my conclusion after writing this article. I pretty much trashed the Enfin product as it stood, backed by my review research and a nasty experience at a potentially big client.

I was worried what my friends at Enfin would say after this came out. I was pleasantly surprised to find them supportive—"We know we have these problems. Let us show you how we are addressing them."

I learned that readers appreciate it when you speak your mind plainly, but you'd better have some numbers to back up your opinions.

A FUNNY THING HAPPENED on the way to objects. There was this C++ juggernaut that was supposed to trample all in its path. I can remember hearing all the talk at OOPSLA '86 in Portland about how C++ was *the* language for objects. "Too much momentum." "Too many C programmers." "The alternatives are too flaky." Everything else was going to be trampled. Period. In spite of this, a thriving market has grown around Smalltalk, the granddaddy of pure object languages. It may be a fraction of the C++ market, but it is currently the scene of enormous technical and business energy. I make my living with Smalltalk, so my opinions on the matter are suspect, but I'll present the facts of the products in the market and let you draw your own conclusions.

This article focuses on the technical features of the products involved. It presents a short overview of each product, then compares their performance on a simple set of benchmarks designed to test their implementation. It assumes that you know something about the Smalltalk language and are trying to make a technical decision about which Smalltalk, if any, is right for you. The philosophies and personalities of the companies make for an interesting contrast, too. I will compare them in a future article including interviews with the principals.

We are currently in the middle of a revolution in the Smalltalk world, making it a particularly appropriate time to be writing this kind of article. Back in the old days, the only objects that came with any language were simple data structures, enough metaobjects to write the system itself, and support for rudimentary graphics and user interfaces. Everyone who used an object language was in the business, by necessity, of creating fundamentally new kinds of objects all the time. This limited users to those who were capable of such invention and limited the productivity of those users, because writing new kinds of things is so much harder than reusing existing frameworks.

A consensus has grown recently that the time has come to stop focusing exclusively on *creating* objects and start supporting people who only want to use or elaborate on things that already exist. Several factors contributed to this shift:

- The market of wizards creating new frameworks from scratch was getting saturated. The economics of growth dictated a search for new kinds of customers.

- The pace of innovation in user interfaces slowed, with the major windowing systems settling on roughly the same set of components. This allowed the Smalltalk vendors to stop spending so much energy doing the entire user interface without help from the operating system.

- Enough objects had been created that it was possible to imagine someone writing an application and not having to create new kinds of objects.

- The factors that used to single out Smalltalk—a bundled class library and an interactive programming environment—were no longer unique. Smalltalk had to move on or get trampled by the Borland C++'s of the world.

One interesting fact is that although all the vendors have embraced reuse as a strategic direction, two of them (Digitalk with Smalltalk/V OS/2 2.0 and

ParcPlace Systems with Objectworks\Smalltalk) retain a conventional Smalltalk product in addition to their new, more visually oriented product (PARTS Workbench and VisualWorks, respectively). Easel's Enfin/3 has bundled interface layout and communication objects from the beginning. Also, it is interesting to note that none of the newer products use the word "Smalltalk" in its name. Whether this is a reaction to market resistance to Smalltalk or a healthy focus on solving problems instead of creating technology I'll leave to your analysis.

In what follows I will focus on new products, virtually ignoring the traditional versions. I wrestled with this issue, as I have used and loved Smalltalk the way it was for eight years. My conclusion is that the products presented here are the future of Smalltalk, like it or not, so they deserve our undivided attention. A second limitation of this review is that I compare the OS/2 versions of the products, because that is where the most advanced Digitalk and Easel products run, and it is the one operating system common to all vendors.

PRODUCT OVERVIEW

This section presents a brief overview of the products' appearance and functionality.

PARCPLACE SYSTEMS: VISUALWORKS

VisualWorks is the easiest product to characterize. Take Smalltalk. Add a complete, operating-system-independent screen painter. Finish with a light glaze of new control structures. Voila! VisualWorks.

The screen painter helps you lay out the look of your application from a wide range of visual components: buttons, text, sliders, tables, and static visuals like rectangles and lines (see Figure 13-1). The painter also provides a full set of layout options for relative and absolute positioning and sizing, alignment, and grouping. The most unique feature of the painter is its ability to emulate the appearance of any of the window systems on any of the others. You're on a Mac and you want to see what the interface would look like under OpenWindows? One button, and there it is.

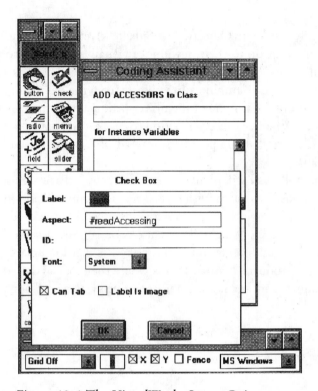

Figure 13-1 The VisualWorks Screen Painter.

When you use VisualWorks, you still have to know how to program in Smalltalk. To specify the behavior of your interface, you use the painter to tell the system that when a button is pushed a certain message is to be sent to the model of the window. Defining what happens then is done in the familiar Smalltalk world of browsers, inspectors, and debuggers.

The biggest departure from traditional Smalltalk is the heavy use made of ValueHolders. Smalltalk has always made a valiant attempt to separate the user interface from the underlying model, leaving the model free to, well, model, without having to be aware that it appeared on the screen. This was accomplished by a dependency mechanism by which the interface could ask to be informed about anything interesting that happened to the model. Any number of interfaces (or none) could be viewing the model at the same time.

In practice, interface information still crept into the model. The model had to broadcast just the right set of updates for the interface to operate. To solve this problem, VisualWorks has adopted the use of ValueHolders (see Figure

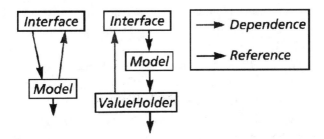

Figure 13-2 Direct dependency and ValueHolders.

13-2). Rather than having the model make direct references to other objects, the model refers to an intermediate object, the ValueHolder, which refers to another object. When the model wants to access the value, it sends the message **value**; when it wants to change the value, it sends **value: anObject**. While this may seem to be a complicated way to change state, it has tremendous advantages in flexibility and modularity. No longer does the model have to broadcast updates; ValueHolder does it automatically whenever its value changes. Also, there is a rich family of ValueHolders, some of which compute values instead of storing them, others of which transform objects provided by other ValueHolders. You can change the operation of the interface without modifying the logic in the model simply by changing what kind of ValueHolders it uses.

VisualWorks is $4,995 for a single license for Unix platforms; $2,995 for Macintosh and Windows. ParcPlace also supplies optional ObjectKits for advanced programming, linking to foreign functions, and accessing popular databases. Applications developed with VisualWorks carry a $350 per-unit runtime license fee. Volume discounts are available. All sales are direct from ParcPlace.

DIGITALK: PARTS WORKBENCH 2.0

PARTS is the product that most enthusiastically embraces the reuse theme. Unlike VisualWorks, which assumes that everyone remains a creator of objects to some extent, PARTS makes a radical split between object creators and object users. When you create parts, you do it in C++, COBOL, or even Smalltalk. A part is defined by the events it generates and messages it receives. Some parts are visual, like a radio button, and some are not, like a dynamic link library (DLL) wrapper. You use a visual wiring-style diagram to match up events and messages (Figure 13-3).

Like VisualWorks, PARTS modifies the "send message to receiver, receiver looks up message, receiver executes method" control structure that has been with Smalltalk since Smalltalk-76. While VisualWorks extends the model of control with ValueHolders, PARTS chooses a completely new structure based on asynchronous events. Each event can trigger any number of messages in any order. Unlike conventional Smalltalk, the event and the message it triggers need not have the same name. Each message can take any number of arguments, created by triggering messages elsewhere in the diagram. The messages themselves are created either in the native language of the part or in PART-Stalk, which is syntactically identical to Smalltalk.

The first big semantic difference between Smalltalk and PARTStalk is that in PARTStalk, you attach scripts to individual instances, not a class. There is no notion of modifying classes in PARTS. You cannot add a new message to all buttons of a certain kind. You can create a new part out of other parts and use it, but each copy is duplicated from the original, and changing the original will not change the copy.

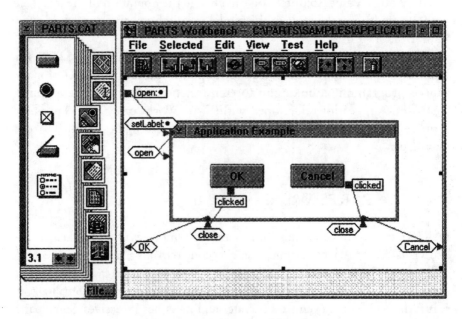

Figure 13-3 PARTS Workbench 2.0.

While this may seem a radical departure from Smalltalk, it is by discarding class and inheritance abstraction that PARTS gets its leverage. If you have ever tried to teach new Smalltalk programmers about all the roles classes play, and tried to keep them from killing themselves designing inheritance hierarchies, you know what I mean. The design of PARTS enforces a strict separation between those who create new kinds of objects and those who specialize existing objects for a particular purpose.

It is tough to compare VisualWorks and PARTS. VisualWorks is Smalltalk, with much of the tedium automated. It will appeal to the market that Smalltalk has always had— technically sophisticated users who want the ultimate power tool. PARTS is aimed at a completely different audience, an audience of programmers who are not adept at abstraction, but know the details of a domain inside out. By enforcing the separation of object creators and objects users, PARTS provides its users with a less flexible but more highly leveraged tool. More highly leveraged, that is, if the parts you want are already available. Otherwise, you fall back on a traditional programming environment—Smalltalk if you are lucky, C++ or COBOL if you are not.

PARTS 2.0 is available now for $1,995 direct from Digitalk, slightly less from mail-order software houses. Digitalk also provides optional database access and COBOL wrapper parts. Smalltalk/V for OS/2 2.0 is $995, Smalltalk/V Windows 2.0 is $495.

EASEL: ENFIN/3

Enfin/3 is definitely the dark horse in this race. It lags behind VisualWorks and PARTS technically but has managed to carve out a solid niche in providing excellent bundled mainframe communications. It is also quite popular in Germany, where IBM has put considerable muscle behind it. The other unique position of Enfin/3 is the company it keeps. Easel bought Enfin in July, 1991. Easel went public selling GUI tools to the OS/2 market. It had 1991 sales of $28 million. Overnight, the purchase put the largest sales and marketing organization behind Enfin.

Figure 13-4 shows Enfin/3 in action. Unlike VisualWorks, which expects its users to be object programmers first and foremost, or PARTS, which visually integrates interface layout and construction, the Enfin model of programming expects users to create interfaces on the contents of relational

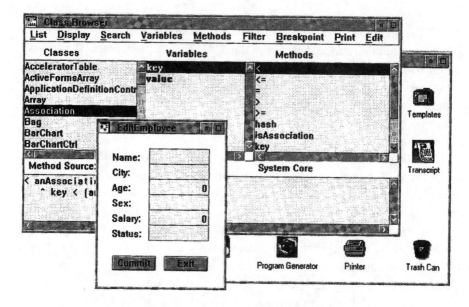

Figure 13-4 Enfin/3 in action.

databases. If processing arises that requires a more sophisticated model than the database can provide, Smalltalk is there to provide more functionality.

Enfin is the youngest of the three products, and it shows in several ways. As you'll see in the benchmark section, it is by far the slowest implementation. The programming environment has none of the grace and integration of VisualWorks nor the innovation of PARTS. The class library is similarly immature. Collection and number classes are only a bit behind the competition, but the user interface abstractions are poorly factored and undocumented.

Enfin/3 with SQL access is $5,995 for OS/2, $3,995 for Windows. EHLLAPI and APPC support are available for $3,995 and $2,500, respectively. There is also a bundled "corporate edition" with all of the above for $10,900. All sales are direct.

IMPLEMENTATION

The implementation of Smalltalk breaks into two parts: statement execution and garbage collection. To compare the quality of the implementations, I use a small set of benchmarks that I have found useful over the years. Please don't make too much of the numbers, however, as they compare only the speed of micro-operations. The quality of Smalltalk code atop these operations and the degree to which the environment encourages experimentation and tuning have more effect on the performance of resulting applications.

The vendors all treat their implementations as the jewel in their technology crowns. While much of the information about how to make Smalltalk run fast is in the public domain, the vendors are touchy about revealing details. The following discussion had to be pieced together from rare public statements and hints in the source code of the systems.

STATEMENT EXECUTION

The best current Smalltalk statement execution technique is called *dynamic translation*. Digitalk and ParcPlace both use it in their latest-generation products. Early Smalltalks compiled source code into a P-code-like bytecode instruction set that was interpreted one byte at a time. To retain the compactness of bytecodes but improve performance, dynamic translation substitutes a runtime compiler for the interpreter. When a method is about to be executed, it is translated from the bytecode form into machine instructions, which are then executed at full speed. The implementation caches recently compiled methods to minimize the translation overhead.

The key to making Smalltalk go fast is to "cheat, but don't get caught," as Dan Ingalls said. The simplicity and generality of Smalltalk's language semantics make for glacial naive implementations. In practice, the full generality of the language is seldom used. The language specifies that every message sent must act as if it was looked up at runtime. For instance, when the message + is sent, the vast majority of the time the receiver and argument will be integers, and not too large. By hard coding the meaning of + in this case, Smalltalk implementations can be sped dramatically.

VisualWorks has always set the standard in Smalltalk performance. In Tables 1 and 2, all results will be normalized to the VisualWorks result. An entry of 6 means that the product in question was six times slower than VisualWorks on the given benchmark. All benchmarks were run on a Zeos 486/33 with 16 megabytes of RAM running OS/2 2.0.

The two most important benchmarks in Table 13-1 are smallIntegerPlus,

Table 13-1 Statement execution benchmark.

Benchmark	What does it measure?	PARTS	Enfin/3
smallIntegerPlus	Simple dispatching overhead.	0.85	13
floatPlus	Allocation and hardware access.	1.8	1
pointCreation	Allocation of small objects.	5.2	9.7
cachedSend	Several sends to same receiver	1	12
uncachedSend	Sends to different classes.	0.89	8
pushContext	Creation of block object.	0.93	11

which suggests how the system will stack up against C for simple operations, and cachedSend, which measures the common case for sending messages. PARTS is at least as good as VisualWorks on both counts. Enfin/3, on the other hand, doesn't show too well. If adding two numbers is slow and you can't send messages quickly, you are likely to have a significant challenge giving your applications decent performance if they do much processing.

GARBAGE COLLECTION

Smalltalk has always been at the forefront of garbage-collection technology. The early pioneers made effective use of automatically deallocated storage to simplify the system. The price of this simplicity was the need for high-performance collection schemes. Still, today the collector is the single most important element for the interactive feel of a Smalltalk system.

The best garbage-collection schemes are based on the generation-scavenging algorithm invented by David Ungar. The insight in this algorithm is that most objects die young, so most of the effort in the collector is spent scanning recently allocated objects. Scavenging collectors have the advantage of causing long pauses very infrequently. PARTS and VisualWorks both use a scavenging collector. Easel has not spoken publicly about their garbage collector.

The benchmarks in Table 13-2 measure object allocation along two axes: whether the objects are large or small and whether they contain references to other objects or binary data (which can be safely ignored by the collec-

Benchmark	What does it measure?	PARTS	Enfin/3
smallObjects	Small, short-lived objects with references.	1.9	9.5
smallByteObjects	Small, short-lived binary objects.	0.67	3.8
largeObjects	Large, short-lived objects with references.	4.8	N/A
largeByteObjects	Large, short-lived binary objects.	2.5	N/A

Table 13-2 Garbage collection benchmark

tor). Enfin/3 was not able to complete the large-object tests because of a limit on the size of objects.

Another collector benchmark is my "killer" list benchmark, which keeps allocating memory forever. It caused all of the systems to abort with an operating system error. The benchmark measures how many objects are allocated before the system dies, and how the performance degrades as more objects are allocated. The code for the killer looks like this:

```
list: anInteger
    | first next |
    first := next := Array new: 5.
    (2 raisedTo: anInteger)
        timesRepeat: [next at: 1 put: (next := Array new: 5)]
```

Figure 13-5 is a graph of the results. I noticed several things from this graph: (1) none of the systems failed gracefully when memory ran out, (2) Enfin ran out of memory much sooner than the other systems, and (3) the performance difference from the smallest benchmark to the largest is a factor of 1,000, but only 250 times as much memory is allocated.

BENCHMARK CONCLUSIONS

On the basis of these benchmarks (admittedly flimsy evidence for any final decision), I conclude that Digitalk has substantially caught up to ParcPlace

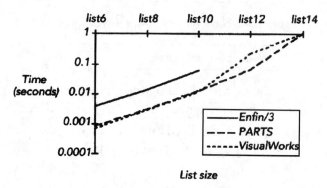

Figure 13-5 Results of the "killer" list benchmark.

when it comes to implementing Smalltalk. Enfin, however, has a long way to go before it can compete technically with its more mature brethren.

CONCLUSION

So, which Smalltalk is best? Here are some obvious answers. If you need to deliver on a variety of Unix platforms in addition to OS/2 and Windows, VisualWorks provides an outstanding solution. If you want to deliver a fully compliant OS/2 application where performance is an issue, PARTS is the right way to go. If you want excellent mainframe access, have modest processing requirements, and want to have a single customer-support number to call if you have problems, Enfin/3 will look attractive.

Beyond these obvious decisions, the waters become murkier. VisualWorks assumes that you have programmers who are able to handle traditional Smalltalk programming. This is not a problem for PARTS, with its visual metaphor and lack of inheritance. However, if the part you need is not in the library, you will have to fall back on Smalltalk/V. There is not yet a strong third-party parts market for PARTS, because it is too new. Enfin/3 is currently not as technically advanced as its competitors. I would only recommend it in cases where the need for a single vendor and mainframe communications are the dominating factors.

14

INSTANCE-SPECIFIC BEHAVIOR: HOW AND WHY

Smalltalk Report, MARCH–APRIL, 1993

After the brief pause in the previous column to discuss philosophy, this column descends again into the depths of techno-minutiae. At least I talked about why you'd want to use instance-specific behavior, and didn't just present it as: "Here's a cool thing you can do with Smalltalk."

The pattern Scriptable Objects still looks pretty good to me. In fact, I like it better as a pattern than many of the patterns that follow.

THIS AND THE next column will discuss technical and philosophical matters. The technical material covers implementing and using instance-specific behavior, the idea that you can attach methods to individual instances rather than to a class. You might use it in animation or in building a Hypercard-like system. It is not a new idea. Lisp-based object systems have had it for years, and languages like Self rely on it exclusively. It is not well known in the Smalltalk community, though, and deserves a place in the mature Smalltalker's bag of tricks.

The philosophical material illuminates the differences between Digitalk's and ParcPlace's view of good Smalltalk style. ParcPlace grew out of a research atmosphere where truth and beauty were admired. Although established in business now, ParcPlace continues to favor elegant solutions. Digitalk has always been driven by the desire to build commercial software and has often been staffed with engineers whose experience comes from other languages. Digitalk's solutions tend to be more pragmatic and the workings easier to follow operationally, even if they don't have the most elegant high-level models.

This month's column will present a pattern for choosing and using instance-specific behavior and its implementation in VisualWorks. In the next issue, I will describe its implementation in Smalltalk/V PM 2.0 and summarize the differences in philosophy revealed by the two implementations.

PATTERN

In my previous column I introduced the idea of a pattern. Before I write a pattern for instance-specific behavior, let me review. A pattern is a program transformation. It takes a program with certain attributes and makes a new program that is somehow better—more concrete, compact, reusable, maintainable, flexible, or efficient. Patterns occur at all levels of programming. Some of them are low-level, like naming arguments and variables; some are tied to a specific language or library, like patterns for using the collection classes; and some are at the level of design, describing ways of dividing behavior between objects. The patterns for instance-specific behavior are at this most far-reaching level.

Notice that I didn't say "abstract" level. Patterns always call for a concrete transformation of a program. Even if the objects are only in your head or on cards, a pattern that applies to embryonic objects will still call for you to do specific things to those objects. I have heard complaints that patterns are too vague, or are connected only to a certain language. The pattern here stands as an example of how it sometimes can apply regardless of language or implementation. Instance-specific behavior is not limited to Smalltalk, and any language that provides it can use the following pattern to guide when its use is appropriate.

Each pattern has the same four parts:

- *Trigger.* How to recognize when the pattern applies. This often takes the form of "You have noticed…"

- *Constraints.* The (often conflicting) constraints on the solution.

- *Solution.* The result of applying the pattern. The insight in the pattern is largely contained in finding the right balance between the constraints.

- *Transformation.* How to transform a program to conform to the pattern.

Here is a pattern I have discovered for instance-specific behavior, observed in Digitalk's PARTS. I don't claim that it is the only reason for using instance specialization. If you find uses for it not covered here, please send them along.

SCRIPTABLE OBJECTS

TRIGGER

- You have objects that need to change their logic at runtime.

- You have added flags—symbols used as messages or blocks in instance variables to account for this variation.

- Your users want to add logic to your objects that you can't anticipate, but they are not prepared to use the full Smalltalk environment.

CONSTRAINTS

- *Code complexity.* The solution must result in less complex code than you currently have.

- *Simple programming model.* If you have users who are not prepared to use all of Smalltalk, the solution must be simple enough for them to understand.

- *Cannot anticipate all needed behavior.* The solution is not simply a matter of adding enough flags and switches. The objects will require entirely new, unanticipated logic after they leave your hands.

- *Expressive power.* The solution should be as powerful as possible and ultimately as expressive as Smalltalk itself.

SOLUTION

Make each instance specializable (see the remainder of the article for implementation details). At runtime, you or your users can change the meaning of any message without affecting other instances. If you want to affect all instances, you can, at your discretion, make it possible to change the class. The solution provides a simple programming model at the expense of expressiveness, but the flexibility of instance specialization makes up for most of the lost power. It should be possible to remove the ad hoc specialization of the original code in favor of a more uniform approach where all changes to logic are done by changing methods.

TRANSFORMATION

Flags: If a method uses a boolean flag to differentiate between cases, replace it with a method that defaults to the case using the default value of the flag. For example, if you have a method like this:

```
display
    isHighlighted
        ifTrue: [self displayHighlighted]
        ifFalse: [self displayUnHighlighted]
```

where isHighlighted defaults to false, you would replace it with the contents of the displayUnHighlighted method. In the methods that set isHighlighted you have to copy the correct method into the instance. You may find that after you have done this throughout the class, you will be able to apply the pattern "Eliminate Dead Variables."

Symbols: If a method uses perform: with a symbol, isolate the perform in its own method (use the pattern "Composing Methods"), and replace it with a method that sends the default symbol as a message. Thus:

```
initialize
    listMessage := #list
getList
    model perform: listMessage
```

would become (in the class):

```
getList
    model list
```

If you wanted to default to the case where listMessage was nil, you could change getList to:

```
getList
    ^#()
```

Any object that set the listMessage would have to instead specialize getList in the instance.

As is the case with flags, after applying the symbol transformation, the instance variable holding the symbol may no longer be needed.

Blocks: The transformation for blocks is similar to the transformation for symbols. The method in the class is the default to which the block is set. The method will have as many arguments as the block did. Thus, a block used for display:

```
initialize
    displayBlock := [:aMedium | aMedium black]
displayOn: aMedium
    displayBlock value: aMedium
```

in the class would become:

```
displayOn: aMedium
    aMedium black
```

Objects that set the block would have to specialize the instance instead. Note that this transformation will work only for blocks that use block temporary or argument variables, or for instance variables of the object being specialized. Blocks used as a full closure, accessing variables in another object creating the block, generally cannot be transformed in this way.

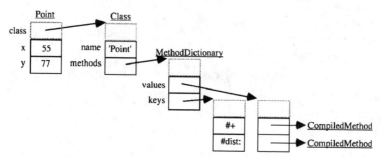

Figure 14-1 Objects supporting method lookup.

PARCPLACE IMPLEMENTATION

RUNTIME STRUCTURES

To understand how to implement instance specialization, you first need to understand how the current model works. As shown in Figure 14-1, every object has a hidden instance variable that holds its class. The class in turn has an instance variable that holds a MethodDictionary, which maps Symbols to CompiledMethods. When an object is sent a message:

1. Its class is fetched.

2. The class MethodDictionary is fetched.

3. The selector of the message is looked up in the dictionary.

4. The CompiledMethod found there is activated.

That's what happens conceptually, but there are many clever tricks to make it go faster in common cases where so much flexibility isn't needed.

CONCEPTUAL MODEL

The way you keep changes to one instance from affecting the others of its class is simple: They don't all have the same class. In Figure 14-1, all Points point to the same class object. To be separately specializable, they all need to point to

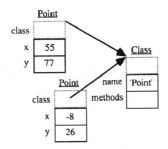

Figure 14-2a A change for instance is a change for all.

different class objects, each of which inherits from the original class Point. That way, methods installed for one instance are installed only in that instance's personal class, not the one shared by all the other instances. Figure 14-2a summarizes this design.

Note that the class of the class of the instances is not Class, it is Behavior. (Isn't it grand to be working in a language that allows you to construct sentences like that and still have them mean something?) Classes are pretty heavyweight objects, so the system provides a simpler superclass, Behavior, which just has methods, subclasses, and superclasses. Unlike Classes, Behaviors are not expected to be named and put in a global dictionary, so they are able to be garbage collected when no one refers to them anymore. They do not introduce instance variables, so specializable instances implemented this way will only have private methods, but not state.

EXAMPLE

CREATING INSTANCE (WORKSPACE VERSION)

When I need to begin implementing a design like the one in Figure 14-2b, I always start in a workspace. After a bit of experimentation, here is the expression I came up with to create a specializable VisualPart:

```
| class instance |
class := Behavior new  "Create a new Behavior"
```

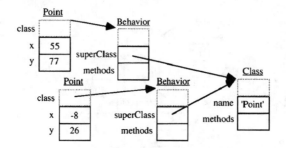

Figure 14-2b Instances can have their own methods.

```
superclass: VisualPart; "Set its superclass"
methodDictionary: MethodDictionary new;
    "Give it a clean MethodDictionary"
setInstanceFormat: VisualPart format. "
    Give instances a reasonable format"
class compile: 'displayOn: aGC' notifying: nil.
    "VisualParts have to implement displayOn:"
instance := class new. "Make the specializable instance"
ScheduledWindow new "Create the window"
    component: instance; "Make the instance its component"
    open. "Open it"
instance inspect "Inspect the instance so we can compile new
methods"
```

Then in the inspector I can execute expressions like:

```
self class compile: 'displayOn: aGraphicsContext
    aGraphicsContext displayString: 'Howdy' at: 100@100'
    notifying: nil
```

and refresh the window. Try inspecting self class in the instance to see that the structure built in the workspace matches the one in Figure 14-2b.

WORKING IT INTO METHODS

Now that we see how to create specializable instances interactively, we need to be able to work the same concepts into permanent behavior. If all instances of a particular class are to be specializable, you can override the class message new:

```
new
    "Create a specializable instance"
    ^Behavior new
        superclass: self;
        format: self format;
        methodDictionary: MethodDictionary new;
        new
```

What if most instances are not specializable? You might only want to create the Behavior when you know the instance needs to be specialized. Here are a group of methods that implement lazy specialization:

```
specialize: aString
    "Compile aString as a method for this instance only"
    self specialize.
    self class compile: aString notifying: nil
```

```
specialize
    self isSpecialized ifTrue: [^self].
    class := Behavior new
        superclass: self class;
        format: self class format;
        methodDictionary: MethodDictionary new.
    self changeClassToThatOf: class basicNew
```

Note the strange method changeClassToThatOf:. It uses this interface, which requires us to waste an object, rather than changeClassTo: so that the primitive implementing it does not need to do complicated checks to make sure that the argument is a valid Behavior:

```
isSpecialized
    ^self class shouldBeRegistered not
```

Only classes that have a name return true for shouldBeRegistered. If we already have specialized an instance using the above algorithm, this test will

165

be correct, while other reasons for creating unnamed classes would render it wrong.

CONCLUSION

You have seen what instance-specific behavior is, why you would choose to use it, and how to implement it in VisualWorks. In the next column I will describe how to implement it in Smalltalk/V PM 2.0, Digitalk's most technically advanced product. The differences in implementation reveal some of the differences in philosophy between the two companies as engineering organizations. These differences will be important to you as you move between systems.

15

INSTANCE-SPECIFIC BEHAVIOR: DIGITALK IMPLEMENTATION AND THE DEEPER MEANING OF IT ALL

Smalltalk Report, MAY, 1993

Well, at least I didn't just present instance-specific behavior as a pointy-hat technique. I tried to extract some cultural lessons from it. Now that the Smalltalk world has contracted to a couple of big players, there isn't enough cultural diversity left to analyze. Ah, the olden days, back when we used to have to walk miles barefoot in the snow to get coal to shovel into our Smalltalk machines... Now I sound like an old fart.

IN THE LAST ISSUE, I wrote about what instance-specific behavior is, why you would choose to use it, and how you implement it in Smalltalk-80 ...er...Objectworks\Smalltalk (which way does the slash go, anyhow?) ...er...VisualWorks (is that a capital *W* or not?). This month's column offers the promised Digitalk Smalltalk/V OS/2 2.0 implementation (thanks to Mike Anderson for the behind-the-scenes info) and a brief discussion of what the implementations reveal about the two engineering organizations.

I say "brief discussion" because as I got to digging around I found many columns' worth of material there for the plucking. I'll cover only issues raised by the implementation of classes and method look-up. Future columns will contrast the styles as they apply to operating system access, user interface frameworks, and other topics.

DIGITALK IMPLEMENTATION

RUNTIME STRUCTURES

The Digitalk implementation of method look-up is slightly different from the ParcPlace model. Actually, until Smalltalk/V OS/2 2.0 (hereafter VOS2) the models were quite similar. The Digitalk implementation did not allow you to create Behaviors and instantiate them easily, so the instance specialization implementation presented in the last issue wouldn't work, but the pictures of the objects would have been identical.

The VOS2 model departs from the "classic" by giving each instance a reference, not to its class, but to an **Array of MethodDictionaries** (see Figure 15-1). In the normal case, the class constructs this array and all instances share it.

The ParcPlace implementation requires an additional indirection to reach the method dictionary, because the virtual machine has to go from the object to the class and from the class to the method dictionary. With the VOS2 model, the virtual machine just has to go from the object to the array. Going up the superclass hierarchy is also faster, because the virtual machine can just march along the array rather than trace references from class to superclass.

Performance is not the primary motivation behind this design, however. More important, given the lack of flexibility in the implementation of **Behavior** and **Class**, this design makes it possible to specify the behavior of objects in many ways. For example, implementing multiple inheritance (ignoring different instance layouts in different classes) is simple. The class is welcome to create the array of method dictionaries any way it wants.

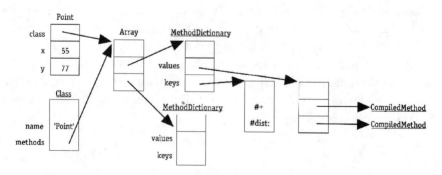

Figure 15-1 VOS2 objects supporting method lookup.

You may be wondering how the message "class" is implemented given the objects above. Each MethodDictionary has an additional instance variable called **class**, which is set to the class where it belongs (each class "owns" one and only one dictionary). The primitive for **class** marches along the array of dictionaries until it finds one whose **class** instance variable is non-nil, and returns that. That way, you can have dictionaries that don't belong to any class, and the scheme still works.

CONCEPTUAL MODEL

What's so special about the class constructing the array? It's just an **Array** whose elements are MethodDictionaries. Any object can build one of those. That's how we'll implement instance specialization. We'll fetch the array that's there and copy it, adding a slot at the beginning containing a fresh Method-Dictionary. Then we can make all the changes we want to the private Method-Dictionary without affecting any other instances.

EXAMPLE

Before we can implement the conceptual model we need access to a couple of hidden primitives to get and set the method dictionaries field of the object.

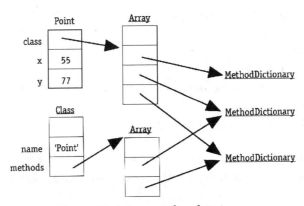

Figure 15-2 A specialized Point.

```
Object>>methodDictionaryField
    "Return the Array of MethodDictionaries for the receiver"
    <primitive: 96>
    self primitiveFailed

Object>>methodDictionaryField: anArray
    "Set the Array of MethodDictionaries for the receiver
    to anArray. anArray must contain MethodDictionaries
    or your system will crash!"
    <primitive: 97>
    self primitiveFailed
```

Now we need to get something on the screen to see the effects of our experiments. Fortunately, that's easy in Smalltalk/V.

```
TopPane new open inspect
```

When we execute the above expression, we get a window and an inspector on that window. In the inspector we can execute the following to get a fresh MethodDictionary to put our specialized methods in

```
| old new |
old := self methodDictionaryField.
new := (Array with: (MethodDictionary newSize: 2)) , old
self methodDictionaryField: new
```

Now we can specialize our window by executing the following in the inspector:

```
| association |
association := Compiler
    compile: 'display Transcript show: "Howdy". super display'
    in: self class
self methodDictionaryField first add: association
```

Now if you execute self display you will see that, indeed, the specialized method is being invoked. (You will have to send the window backColor: for the superclass's display method to work.)

METHODS

I was surprised at how easy it was to implement instance specialization methods that were compatible with the ParcPlace version. I had expected the differences in implementation to leak through into the interface. Hmmm…different implementations, same interface—maybe this object stuff works, after all!

The first method I defined last time was one you would duplicate in any class in which you wanted all instances to be specializable. I don't think this is necessary, since the lazy specialization implemented below works fine. For completeness, though, here it is:

```
new
    ^super new specialize
```

The method I defined in the last issue should have been defined this way, rather than duplicating the specialization code in the class and the instance. I think I did it the way I did because that was how I saw it first implemented by Ward Cunningham when he put scripts into HotDraw.

Next is a method to test whether an instance is ready to be specialized. Since all unspecialized instances of a class share the same array of dictionaries, if the receiver has a different array we will assume it has a private array.

```
Object>>isSpecialized
    ^self methodDictionariesField == self class methodDictionaries
```

Next come the methods for actually specializing the receiver. The first sets up an array with a fresh MethodDictionary.

```
Object>>specialize
    | old new |
    self isSpecialized ifTrue: [^self].
    old := self methodDictionariesField.
    new := (Array with: (MethodDictionary newSize: 2)) , old.
    self methodDictionariesField: new
```

The next one takes a string, compiles it, and installs the result in the private dictionary:

```
Object>>specialize: aString
   | association |
   self specialize.
   association := Compiler compile: aString in: self class.
   self methodDictionariesField first add: association
```

CONTRASTS

What do these two implementations of instance specialization say about their respective systems? For one thing, both of them are simple, clean, and easy to understand. The external protocol is exactly the same. There isn't much to choose from between them. From that standpoint, I would have to say that both systems support a fairly esoteric change to the language semantics with a minimum of fuss.

The ParcPlace implementation is conceptually cleaner to me. The user's model that the behavior of an object is always defined by its class is retained. It's just a little easier to create classes than you thought. The Digitalk implementation requires that you understand the particular mechanism they have lying behind that conceptual model so that you can implement the necessary changes.

When I understood the ParcPlace implementation, I said, "Ah, that makes sense." When I understood the Digitalk implementation, I said, "Cool! That really works?" The ParcPlace model is an extension of the semantics. The Digitalk model is an extension of the implementation.

I am fishing for just the right way to characterize the difference. I don't think I can make it clear yet, but I also don't think it will be the work of a single week, or even a single year, to make it clear. Let's barrel on.

As you get to know both product lines, you will find this same distinction repeated many times. I think that the difference stems from the diverging goals of the technical luminaries at the two companies. The ParcPlace image was driven first by Dan Ingalls and then by Peter Deutsch. Both have strongly developed æsthetic sensibilities to go along with their amazing technical skills. A solution wasn't a solution to them until it was beautiful. Actually, now that both of them have gone on to other things, the ParcPlace models are beginning to show signs of creeping cruft.

Jim Anderson and George Bosworth, on the other hand, are primarily motivated by the belief that software just shouldn't be that hard to write. They produced Smalltalk/V so others could write software more easily. Their success criteria seems to be "if it's better than C, it's good enough." They weren't about to let a little thing like a less-than-perfect conceptual model get in the way of shipping product. Of course, they had a company to run as they were developing their image, unlike ParcPlace in the early (Xerox PARC) years, so they didn't have much choice about the importance of aesthetics.

Don't take this to mean that the ParcPlace image is truth and beauty personified and the Digitalk image is a baling-wire-and-chewing-gum collection of dire hacks. There are areas where each beats the other in both conceptual model and implementation. However, I think it is safe to say that the primary motivations behind the two systems are a contrast between aesthetics and pragmatism.

What this means for the workaday programmer isn't entirely clear. Most of the time, the ParcPlace image provides smooth development. Every once in a while, though, you will encounter a good idea that hasn't been taken quite far enough, and you will have to bend yourself into a pretzel or bypass it entirely to get around it. Put another way, if you are going the ParcPlace way you will have lots of support. If, however, you have the misfortune to want to do something a different way than the original implementor imagined, you may be in trouble. In these cases you will often have to browse around and understand lots of mechanism before you can figure out how to wedge your code in.

The Digitalk world is less coercive, but it's also less supportive. For code that relies heavily on their implementations (i.e., not just instantiating collections) I average more lines of code to get the same functionality. I know there have been cases where the Digitalk implementation has been easier. I don't think a Digitalk project has ever been conceptually simpler, though.

In future columns, I will explore more specifics of the contrast between the systems, and try to quantify why one or the other is better for specific tasks. In the meantime, if you run into situations that are surprisingly hard or easy in either system, please pass them along.

CONCLUSION

Instance specialization has a place in the toolbox of every experienced Smalltalker. You won't use it every day—maybe not even every year—but when you want it, nothing else will do. The implementations for VisualWorks and Smalltalk/V OS/2 2.0 are quite different, but they present the same external interface to the programmer.

The contrasts between the implementations hint at fundamental differences in approach between Digitalk engineering and ParcPlace engineering. I will explore the practical consequences of this difference in future columns.

16

To Accessor or
Not to Accessor?

Smalltalk Report, JUNE, 1993

Why do I keep doing this? I keep bringing up the "should all variables be accessed through methods" debate whenever I see people taking a dogmatic position, that is, one that they don't explain. It wasn't until I rewrote the whole thing as patterns for the book that I realized the key issue here is communication.

I'm a little disappointed reading this now that I didn't try to write Direct Access and Indirect Access as patterns. That would have made the reasoning behind the options much more obvious. I guess I just wasn't ready to use patterns to address such fundamental questions. Now I don't even hesitate- I'm so pattern soaked now I can't help it.

Anyway, if this one bugs you, ignore it, all except the part about making accessors private by default.

A DEBATE HAS BEEN raging on both CompuServe and the Internet lately about the use and abuse of accessing methods for getting and setting the values of instance variables. Since this is the closest thing I've seen to a religious war in a while, I thought I'd weigh in, not with the definitive answer, but with at least a summary of the issues and arguments on both sides. As with most, uh, "discussions" generating lots of heat, the position anyone takes has more to do with attitude and experience than with objective truth.

First, a little background. The classic accessor method comes in two flavors, one for getting the value of an instance variable:

```
Point>>x
    ^x
```

and one for setting an instance variable:

```
Point>>x: aNumber
    x := aNumber
```

Accessing methods are also used to do lazy initialization, or as caches for frequently computed values:

```
View>>controller
    ^controller ifNil: [controller := self getController]
```

ACCESSORS

When I was at Tektronix, Allen Wirfs-Brock (now a Digitalk dude) wrote (or at least discussed writing—it was a while ago) a think piece called "Instance Variables Considered Harmful." His position was that direct reference to instance variables limits inheritance by fixing storage decisions in the superclass that can't be changed in a subclass. His solution was to force all accesses to instance variables to go through a method. If you did an "**inst var refs**" on a variable of such a class, you'd find two users, one to return the value of the variable and one to set the value.

Points make a good example of why inheritance demands consistent use of accessing methods. Suppose you want to make a subclass of Point that obeyed the same protocols, but stored its location in polar coordinates, as r and theta. You can make such a subclass, but you will swiftly discover that you have to override most of the messages in the superclass because they make direct use of the variables x and y. This defeats the purpose of inheritance. In addition, you would have to be prepared to either declare new variables, r and theta, and waste the space for x and y in your subclass, or store r in x and theta in y and keep track of which is which. Neither is an attractive prospect.

If Point had been written with accessing methods, at least the problem with inheritance would not arise. In your subclass, you could override the messages accessing and setting x and y, replacing them with computations converting polar to Cartesian coordinates and vice versa. At the cost of four methods you would have a fully functioning PolarPoint. A more fully factored solution, one that solves the problem of wasted or misnamed storage, would be to have an abstract Point class with no variables, and subclasses CartesianPoint and PolarPoint.

ACCESSORS—NOT!

Many in the Smalltalk community were compelled by this argument (or arrived at the same conclusion independently). Vocal and influential organizations such as Knowledge Systems Corporation made consistent use of accessors a fundamental part of their Smalltalk teaching. Why are there still heathens who refuse to bow to this superior wisdom?

Most easily dismissed is the issue of productivity. All those accessors take too long to write. Most extended Smalltalk environments include support for automatically generating accessing and setting methods. Some are activated when the class is recompiled, asking whether you want accessors for the new methods; others appear when a "message not understood" error occurs by noticing that the receiver has an instance variable of the same name as the offending message. In any case, writing accessors need not be time consuming.

A slightly more serious argument is performance. All those accessors take time to execute. While it is true that accessing a method directly is faster than sending a message, the difference is not as great as you might think. Digitalk and ParcPlace are careful to make sure that looking up a method is fast, particularly in common cases like sending a message to the same class or receiver as you did the last time you were in this method. In addition, the CompiledMethod representing the accessor has special flags set to allow it to be executed quickly, without even the overhead of pushing a frame on the stack. In tight loops where the performance of accessors might still be a problem, you can probably cache the value in a temporary variable, anyway.

The crux of the objection is that accessors violate encapsulation. Accessors make details of your storage strategy visible to the outside world. Messages should present the services an object is willing to provide. Using them to give an abstract view of storage turns those implementation decisions into yet more services. Revealing implementation is exactly what encapsulation is supposed to avoid.

"Just make the accessors private." That's the common solution, but there are two reasons why this isn't a sufficient solution. First, anyone can invoke any method (and will, given enough stress). There is currently no way to make truly private methods that cannot be used outside the class. Digitalk and ParcPlace are both working on this problem. More seriously, programmers are notoriously bad at deciding what should be private and what should be public. How many times have you found "just the right method," only to find it marked **private**? If you use it, you are faced with the possibility that it may go away in the next release. If you don't, you have to violate the encapsulation of the object to do the computation yourself, and you have to be prepared for that computation to break in the next release.

The argument against automatically using accessors rests on the assumption that inheritance is less important than encapsulation. Rick DeNatale of IBM argues that inheritance should be kept "in the family." Anytime you inherit from a class you don't own, your code is subject to unanticipated breakage much more than if you merely refer to an object. If you want to use inheritance, do it only between classes whose change you control. While this may not result in the most elegant solution, it will save you headaches in the long run.

Using this model, you can access variables directly. If you want to make a subclass that needs to access a variable through a message, you use the programming environment to quickly change "x := ..." into "self x: ..." and "x ..." into "self x ...". Encapsulation is retained, and the cost of changing your decision is minimal. If you don't own the superclass or the subclass, you can't do this, as it would involve making changes in code you can't control.

Conclusion

Aesthetics does not provide a compelling argument one way or the other. There's a giddy feeling when you make a subclass the original programmer never anticipated, but only need to make a few changes to make it work. On the other hand, there is satisfaction in thinking you finally have to reveal a variable, only to discover that by recasting the problem you can improve both sender and receiver.

Regardless of how you choose to program, you are faced with the hard choice of deciding which variables should be reflected as messages. Pushing behavior out into objects rather than just getting information from them and making decisions yourself is one of the most difficult, but most rewarding, jobs when programming objects. Making an accessing method public should be done only when you can prove to yourself that there is no way for the object to do the job itself. Making a setting method public requires even more soul-searching, since it gives up even more of an object's sovereignty.

Either way, you accept a discipline not supported by the language. If you choose to use accessors, you and everyone who uses your code must swear an oath never to send messages that invoke methods marked private in the receiver. You also must be wary of using the accessor from outside the object when you really need to add more services to the receiver. If you do not use accessors, you accept the burden of refactoring classes, either making an abstract class or at least adding accessors, should a later inheritance decision make it necessary.

Whichever style you choose, make sure it pervades your team's development. Einstein is reputed to have said, "You can be consistent or inconsistent, but don't be both." The same simplifying assumptions should hold throughout all of your code.

If you use accessors, make them all private at first. Only make them public if you must, and struggle to discover a less centralized solution first. Don't assume that because you access variables through messages you have made all of the abstraction decisions you'll have to make. Using an accessor, internally or externally, should alert you that there may be missing behavior.

If you use variables directly, be prepared to recant your decision when the time comes. If what you thought was state is really a service, make the change everywhere. Don't have external users getting a variable's value through a method and internal users accessing it directly.

So, what's The Answer? In my own code, I change state into service (define an accessing or setting method) only when I am convinced it is necessary. Otherwise, my classes access their variables directly. I think inheritance is overrated. Providing the right set of services has more bearing on the success of a design. There are plenty of successful, experienced folks who would call me a reactionary hick for this (and worse things, for other reasons). Try some code each way and decide for yourself which style you find more comfortable. That's the only right answer.

17

INHERITANCE:
THE REST OF THE STORY

Smalltalk Report, JULY–AUGUST, 1993

As *if one crusade wasn't enough, I had to take on the sacred cow of inheritance as well. This must have been my "caped crusader" phase. I still think inheritance is overrated, but I don't generally get in anyone's face about it anymore. Too many windmills under the bridge, I guess. There I go, sounding old and worn out again.*

I like the way the pattern form makes concrete and clear the technique of separating state-related and service-related code. The how of it is clear, as is the why.

This is one of many attempts I have made to explain the pattern I now call Composed Method. I must have written this pattern six or eight times. Persistence (my wife calls it "stubbornness" for some reason) can make up for lack of raw talent.

The two patterns here are written as transformations and named as a transformation—you have a method and you split it apart or you have a class and you split it apart. I was very big on "patterns as transformations" for a while. All the patterns in the pattern book are written differently— as descriptions of the things created, not the process of creating them.

OF THE THREE TENETS of objects—encapsulation, polymorphism, and inheritance—inheritance generates by far the most controversy. Is it for categorizing analysis objects? Is it for defining common protocols (sets of messages)? Is it for sharing implementation? Is it really the computed goto of the nineties?

The answer is Yes. Inheritance can (and does) do all of the above at different times. The problem comes when you have a single-inheritance system like Smalltalk. You get one opportunity to use inheritance. If you use it in a way that doesn't help you, you have wasted one of the most powerful facilities of the language. On the other hand, if you use it poorly, you can mix up the most ridiculous, unmaintainable program gumbo you've ever seen. How can you walk between the rocks of under-using inheritance and the chasm of using it wrongly?

What's the big deal? Inheritance is the least important of the three facilities that make up objects. You can do valuable, interesting object-oriented programming without using inheritance at all. Programmers still quest after the Holy Grail of inheritance because of the potential it shows when it works well. When you need an object, and there is one out there that is factored well and does almost what you want, there are few experiences in programming better than making a subclass and having a working system after writing two or three methods.

In this and my next several columns, I will focus on various aspects of inheritance. I will present a variety of strategies for taking advantage of inheritance, in the form of patterns. While I don't necessarily use all the patterns in my own programming, casting the strategies in terms of patterns makes it easier to compare and contrast them.

Patterns: Composite Methods

This pattern is the cornerstone of writing objects that can be reused through inheritance. It is also critical for writing objects that you can successfully performance tune. Finally, by forcing you to reveal your intentions through method names, it makes your programs more readable and maintainable.

Context

You have some code that behaves correctly (it does no good to beautify code that doesn't work, unless you have to make it work). You go to subclass it, and realize that to override a method you have to textually copy it into the subclass and change a few lines, forcing you forever after to change both methods.

Another good context for this pattern is when you are looking at a profile that looks flat; that is, no single method stands out as taking more time than others. You need further improvement in performance and believe that the object can deliver it.

PROBLEM

How can you write methods so that they are easy to override, easy to profile, and easy to understand?

CONSTRAINTS

Fewer, larger methods make control flow easy to follow. Lots of little methods make it hard to understand where any work is getting done. Lots of little methods named by what they are intended to do, not how they do it, make understanding the high-level structure of a computation easy. Your programming time is limited. You only want to perform manipulations of the code that will have some payoff down the road. Each message sent costs time, and execution time is limited. You only want to cost yourself execution time if the result will provide some advantage at some point. You don't want to introduce defects in working code. The manipulations must be simple and mechanical to avoid errors as much as possible.

SOLUTION

Make each method do one nameable thing. If a method does several things, separate out one of them, create a method for it, and invoke it in the original method. When you do this, make sure that if the same few lines occur in other methods, those methods are modified to invoke the new one as well.

This solution ignores the cost of message sending. You will get faster programs by using messages to structure your code so that you can more easily tune them than by reducing the number of messages. It also assumes that the eventual reader of the code is comfortable piecing together control as it flows through lots of small methods.

EXAMPLE

A method for parsing a stream to eliminate lines that begin with a pound sign might look like this at first:

```
parse: aStrea
    | writer |
    writer := String new writeStream.
    [aStream atEnd] whileFalse:
        [(aStream peekFor: $#)
            ifTrue: [aStream restOfLine]
            ifFalse: [writer nextPutAll: aStream restOfLine]]
```

Applying "Compose Methods" to parse: to separate line parsing from the overall parsing control structure we get

```
parse: aStream
    | writer |
    writer := String new writeStream.
    [aStream atEnd] whileFalse:
        [self parseLine: aStream onto: writer]
parseLine: inStream onto: outStream
    (aStream peekFor: $#)
        ifTrue: [^aStream restOfLine].
    outStream nextPutAll: aStream restOfLine
```

Notice that by creating parseLine:onto: we are now able to use the return control structure to make the submethod easier to extend. Applying it again to factor out the output Stream creation, we get

```
parse: aStream
    | writer |
    writer := self outputStream.
    [aStream atEnd] whileFalse:
        [self parseLine: aStream onto: writer]
outputStream
    ^String new writeStream
```

Applying it to parseLine:onto: to separate the choice of what is a comment from the behavior when a comment is found we get

```
parseLine: inStream onto: outStream
    (self peekForComment: inStream)
        ifTrue: [inStream restOfLine].
    outStream nextPutAll: inStream restOfLine
```

```
peekForComment: aStream
    ^aStream peekFor: $#
```

Apply it to **peekForComment:** to separate the character you are looking for from the way in which you look for it:

```
peekForComment: aStream
    ^aStream peekFor: self commentCharacter
commentCharacter
    ^$#
```

The final code is much easier to modify in a subclass if you want to change the comment character, write onto something other than a **String**, or extend the parsing to deal with special cases other than comments.

PATTERN: SEPARATE ABSTRACT FROM CONCRETE

This is a pattern I learned from Ken Auer of Knowledge Systems Corporation. He told me about using it to great advantage in a financial services application in which there were many kinds of financial instruments, all implemented similarly.

CONTEXT

You have implemented one object. It has some methods that rely on the values of variables, and others that do not. You can see that you will have to implement many other similar objects in the future.

PROBLEM

How can you create an abstract class that will correctly capture the invariant part of the implementation of a family of objects with only one concrete example?

Constraints

You want to begin using inheritance as early as possible to speed subsequent development, and you want your inheritance choices to be correct so you don't have to spend time refactoring later.

Solution

Create a state-less superclass. Make it the superclass of the class you want to generalize. Put all of the methods in the subclass which don't use variables (directly or through accessors) into the superclass. Leave methods which rely on instance state in the subclass.

This solution strikes a balance between inheriting too early and too late. By making sure you have one working class you know you aren't using inheritance entirely on speculation.

Example

Lets say that we have an **RGBColor** represented as red, green, and blue values between 0 and 1. We can then write methods like

```
hue
    "Complicated code involving the instance variables red, green,
    and blue..."
saturation
    "Complicated code involving the instance variables red, green,
    and blue..."
value
    "Complicated code involving the instance variables red, green,
    and blue..."
complement
    ^self species
        hue: (self hue + 0.5) fractionalPart
        saturation: self saturation
        value: self value
```

Applying "Separate Abstract from Concrete" to **RGBColor** we create **Color** as RGBColor's superclass. We move **complement** to **Color**, because it doesn't rely on any instance variables directly. We leave hue, saturation, and value in RGBColor because they rely do rely on variables.

Now if we want to create **Color** subclasses that store color values in other ways, they can inherit **complement** as long as they implement hue, saturation, and value.

When you apply this pattern you will often find that methods which were implemented initially as requiring variable values can be recast by applying "Compose Methods" so they can be moved into the superclass.

Conclusion

Now that I have written down "Separate Abstract from Concrete," I'm not sure I entirely agree with it. I like to have more than one concrete example before I try to generalize. I use two different patterns, "Factor Several Classes" and "Concrete Superclass" in my own programming. I will present these patterns in the next issue.

Inheritance is strong medicine. Only by understanding the options and trade-offs involved can you avoid the pitfalls and use it to your advantage. If you use different patterns for applying inheritance, please feel free to send them to me.

18

INHERITANCE:
THE REST OF THE STORY (CONT.)

Smalltalk Report, SEPTEMBER, 1993

I *think this was originally titled "Inheritance: The Rest of the Rest of the Story," but it got edited. Oh well.*
  The pattern presented here is another in the "Transformation Series." It recommends letting inheritance evolve from the need to reduce code duplication.

I N THE JUNE ISSUE, where I took on accessor methods, I stated that there was no such thing as a truly private message. I got a message from Niko-las Boyd reminding me that he had written an earlier article describing exactly how to implement really truly private methods. One response I made was that until all the vendors ship systems that provide method privacy, Smalltalk cannot be said to have it. Another is that I'm not sure I'd use it even if I had it. It seems like some of my best "reuse moments" occur when I find a supposedly private method in a server that does exactly what I want. I don't yet have the wisdom to separate public from private with any certainty.

On a different note, I've been thinking about the importance of bad style. In this column, I always try to focus on good style, but in my programming there are at least two phases of project development where maintaining the best possible style is the farthest thing from my mind. When I am trying to get some code up and running I often deliberately ignore good style, figuring that as soon as I have everything running I can simply apply my patterns to the code to get well-struc-tured code that does the same thing. Second, when I am about to ship a system I often violate good style to limit the number of objects I have to change to fix a bug.

What got me thinking about this was a recent visit I made to Intelliware in Toronto. Turns out Intelliware is two very bright but fairly green Smalltalkers,

Greg Betty and Bruno Schmidt (he's not nearly as German as his name). They hired me to spend two days going over the code they had written for a manufacturing application. The wonderful thing was, they had made every mistake in the book. It's no reflection on their intelligence; everyone makes the same mistakes at first.

What made their boo-boos so neat was that I was able to go in and, in two days, teach them a host of the most advanced Smalltalk techniques just by showing them how to correct errors. I'd say, "Oh, look, an isKindOf:. Here's how you can get rid of that and make your program better at the same time." Because I had a concrete context in which to make my observations, they could learn what I was teaching both in the concrete ("Yes, that does clean up the design") and the abstract ("Oh, I see. I can do that any time I would have used isKindOf:").

So, go ahead. Use isKindOf:. Use class == and == nil. Access variables directly. Use perform: a lot. Send a message to get an object that you send a message to. Just don't do any of these things for long. Make a pact with yourself that you won't stand up from your chair (or go to bed, or ship the system, or go to your grave...) without cleaning up first.

Some people are smart enough to write clean code the first time. At least, that's what they tell me. Me, I can't do that. I write it wrong, and then fix it. Hey, it's not like we're writing in C++ and it takes an hour to compile and link our programs. You may as well be making your design decisions based on code that works. Otherwise, you can spend forever speculating about what the *right* way to code something might be.

Pattern: Factor a Superclass

As an alternative to the "Separate Abstract from Concrete" pattern, I'd like to present the way Ward Cunningham taught me to make inheritance decisions. It is very much in keeping with what I wrote above about letting your "mistakes" teach you the "right" thing to do. When you are programming like this, it feels like the program itself is teaching you what to do as you go along.

Context

You have developed two classes which share some of the same methods. You have gotten tired of copying methods from one to the other, or you have noticed yourself updating methods in both in parallel.

Problem

How can you factor classes into inheritance hierarchies that share the most code? (Note that some people will say that this isn't the problem that inheritance should be solving. You wouldn't use this pattern if that was your view of inheritance.)

Constraints

You'd like to start using inheritance as soon as possible. If you're using inheritance you can often program faster because you aren't forever copying code from one class to another (what Sam Adams calls "rape and paste reuse"). Also, if you are using inheritance, you don't run the risk of a multiple update problem, where you have two identical methods, and you change one but not the other. Ideally, for this constraint, you'd like to design your inheritance hierarchy before you ever wrote a line of code.

On the other hand, designed inheritance hierarchies (as opposed to derived inheritance hierarchies) are seldom right. In fact, by making inheritance decisions too soon you can blind yourself to the opportunity to use inheritance in a much better way. This constraint suggests that you should make inheritance decisions only after the entire system is completed.

Solution

If one of the objects has a superset of the other object's variables, make it the subclass. Otherwise, make a common superclass. Move all of the code and variables in common to the superclass and remove them from the subclasses.

EXAMPLE

It is difficult to come up with an example of inheritance that isn't totally obvious. The problem is that before you see it, you can't imagine it, and after you see it, you can't imagine it any other way. So, if this example seems contrived, don't worry, your own problems will be much harder.

Here is an example in VisualWorks I ran across a couple of months ago. I had Figure1, a subclass of VisualPart. It had to be dependent on a several other objects, and it had to delete those dependencies when it was released.

```
Class: Figure1
    Superclass: VisualPart
    Instance variables: dependees

Figure>>initialize
    dependees := OrderedCollection new
```

Rather than use the usual addDependent: way of setting up dependencies, I implemented a new message in Figure1 called dependOn:.

```
Figure1>>dependOn: anObject
    dependees add: anObject.
    anObject addDependent: self
```

When the figure goes away, it needs to detach itself from everyone it depends on.

```
Figure1>>breakDependents
    dependees do: [:each | each removeDependent: self].
    super breakDependents
```

Then I created a Figure2. To get it up and running quickly I just copied the three methods above to Figure2 and set about programming the rest of it.

It was when I went to create Figure3 that I decided to take a break and clean up. I created DependentFigure as a subclass of VisualPart, gave it the variable dependees and the three methods above, made Figure1 and Figure2 subclasses of it, deleted their implementations of initialize, dependOn: and breakDependents, and then implemented Figure3.

OTHER PATTERNS

While you are factoring the code is often a good time to apply "Compose Methods" so you can move more code into the superclass.

CONCLUSION

I have presented a pattern called "Factor a Superclass" as an alternative to "Separate Abstract from Concrete" for creating inheritance hierarchies. Using "Factor a Superclass," you will end up with superclasses that have more state. I'm not sure if this is a good thing or not. On the plus side, you will probably be able to share more implementation. On the minus side, you may find yourself applying the pattern several times to get the final result. You might factor two classes to get a third, then notice that once you look at the world that way you can factor the superclass with a previously unrelated class to get a fourth, and so on.

Beware of juggling inheritance hierarchies too much. You can waste lots of time factoring code first one way, then another, and find that in the end you aren't that much better off than you were when you started. Objects can survive less-than-optimal inheritance much better than they can encapsulation violations or insufficient polymorphism. Most expert designers agree that great inheritance hierarchies are only revealed over time. Make the changes that you can see are obvious wins, but don't worry about getting it instantly, absolutely right. You are better off getting more objects into your system so you have more raw material from which to make decisions.

19

HELPER METHODS AVOID
UNWANTED INHERITANCE

Smalltalk Report, OCTOBER, 1993

This column is really just an application of Composed Method to deal with inheritance. Now I always try to make my code fragments be real code, no As, Bs, and Cs. You can see why from the example here that is written the other way.

The column is interesting in that it contains some of the first explicit links between patterns. Down at the end it says, "Use Composed Method if necessary to set this pattern up." I paid considerably more attention to pattern linking when I wrote the pattern book, and I'll probably pay a lot more attention with my next set of patterns.

Patterns in isolation are all very interesting, but it is when they are linked together that they become powerful. It is only then that you can explain a simple solution to a problem, because you know that the rest of the solution was handled by previous patterns or will be handled by future patterns.

THE TOPIC OF THIS issue's column on Smalltalk idioms, following the general theme of inheritance, is how to manage the use of super. Several issues back I wrote a column entitled "The Dreaded Super," in which I catalogued all the legitimate (and otherwise) uses of super in the existing Smalltalk/V and VisualWorks images. I'm still very proud of that column, but a couple of days ago I discovered I had left out one very important technique in dealing with super.

The pattern that follows, "Helper Methods Avoid Unwanted Inheritance" (not my best name ever), tells how to resolve this problem. The first time I remember anyone talking about the problem was when Richard Peskin of Rutgers brought it up on the net several years ago. A lively "discussion" ensued. The solution is one many Smalltalkers have discovered over the years.

195

Before I jump into the pattern itself, let me say a word about patterns in general. *Hot.* That's the word. Grady Booch and Dick Gabriel have both been trumpeting patterns in other SIGS publications. Ralph Johnson has had a couple of ECOOP/OOPSLA papers published on them. Pete Coad has jumped on the bandwagon in his OOP book (although I think he's missing the point). I have gotten a half dozen calls in the last month or so from people who have heard about my interest and want to tell me what they are doing with patterns.

I think *patterns* will be the next big buzzword in the object world. If you want to get involved, now is a great time to try writing some patterns of your own. Don't get discouraged if your first efforts don't sparkle. It took me six years to get my first pattern that I didn't want to immediately crumple up and throw away. It shouldn't take you nearly as long.

Here are some criteria I use when evaluating a pattern:

- *Does it make me change my program?* The best patterns don't just say, "Hey, here is a useful configuration of objects." The patterns I find most powerful say, "If you find yourself with this problem, create this useful configuration of objects and it will be solved."

- *Does it explain its assumptions?* Each pattern implicitly contains assumptions about what is most important about the decision it describes. If a pattern says, "We want simple programs, we want fast programs, we want programs we can write quickly, but in this case the most important thing is getting the program running quickly," I have a much better basis for evaluating it.

- *Does it contain an illustration?* Good patterns can invariably be reduced to a single picture. Drawing that picture, or writing a code fragment example can sharpen your understanding considerably.

Give it a try. I'd be glad to critique your efforts, or you could try passing them around to other Smalltalk or C++ programmers you know.

PATTERN: HELPER METHODS AVOID UNWANTED INHERITANCE

CONTEXT

When you are using "**super**" at the bottom of a three-deep inheritance tree, you may find yourself wanting to inherit the root class's behavior, but not the immediate superclass's.

PROBLEM

In this case, you almost want to be able to say something stronger than **super**, like "give me that class's method but no one else's." Experience with C++, which has such a facility, says that using such a feature is a maintenance nightmare. How can you take advantage of inheritance, share code, and remain within Smalltalk's simple control structures?

CONSTRAINTS

- *Code sharing.* The resulting program should contain as much code sharing as possible.

- *Use inheritance.* The resulting code should use inheritance. Inheritance may be important for simplifying the implementation of the rest of the class.

- *Simple code.* The result should be no more complex than necessary. This recommends against using "Delegation" or some other pattern that requires extensive code changes.

SOLUTION

Put the behavior you don't want to inherit in its own method. Invoke that method from the method that contains the send to "**super**". Override the

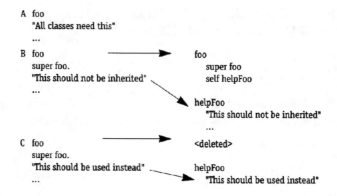

Figure 19-1 Invoking helper methods avoid unwanted inheritance.

new method in the subclass to either do nothing, or replace its behavior with behavior appropriate to the subclass (Figure 19-1).

EXAMPLE

This problem often occurs in initialization code.

    A>>initialize
        "Initialize generic structure"
        ...

    B>>initialize
        super initialize.
        "Allocate machine resources"
        ...

Now we want to write C, a subclass of B that uses other machine resources. If we write:

    C>>initialize
        super initialize.
        "Allocate other machine resources"
        ...

we will allocate B's machine resources and C's, too, which is not what we wanted. If we don't send to super, we don't get the generic initialization from A. If we copy A's initialization into C, we have a multiple update problem with the code in A and C. The right solution is to use Compose Methods to introduce a helper method in B that allocates machine resources:

```
B>>initialize
    super initialize.
    self initializeMachineResources

B>>initializeMachineResources
    "Allocate machine resources"
    ...
```

Then we can override initializeMachineResources in C:

```
C>>initializeMachineResources
    "Allocate other machine resources"
    ...
```

We can delete initialize in C. The logic in B works just fine to invoke its specialized behavior.

This solution satisfies all of the constraints: Inheritance is still used, the maximum amount of code is being shared, and the resulting code is only slightly more complex than the original (same number of methods, one more method name).

OTHER PATTERNS

You may have to invoke "Compose Methods" before you can separate out the single method you want to override but not invoke.

20

IT'S NOT JUST THE CASE

Smalltalk Report, NOVEMBER–DECEMBER 1993

Okay, back to tilting at windmills. Sometimes I think people just don't get Smalltalk. Why in the world would you want a grungy old explicit case statement when you have a superior substitute in the polymorphic message? How could you read and write Smalltalk code for enough years to be able to implement new language features and not understand that you didn't need them?

I guess my tights and cape aren't far enough at the back of the closet...

THIS MONTH'S topic is case statements: practical necessity or pernicious contaminant? My interest in the topic comes from several areas at once. SmalltalkAgents has added a form of case statement to their Smalltalk for the Macintosh. CompuServe has hosted a lively discussion of isKindOf: and its relatives. Finally, net news has had a discussion of case statements. What's the deal?

Cutting right to the punch line, I think case statements are an inappropriate holdover from procedural thinking. While vital in procedural languages, their use in object programs is obviated by the much more powerful mechanism of the polymorphic message send. Anytime you find yourself wishing for or using a case statement, you have an opportunity to take advantage of objects instead. The noncase version will yield a more maintainable, more flexible, more readable, and faster solution.

Of course, I can't just say case statements are bad, I have to demonstrate how to avoid or eliminate them. Here is the first of two patterns that go a long way toward getting rid of the need for case statements.

Pattern: Turn Class Tests Into Messages

Context: To get code running, you occasionally have to insert an explicit test for the class of an object, either through sending it the message class or isKindOf:, or by introducing a testing method like isInteger, which is implemented in Integer to return true and in Object to return false.

Problem: Class tests, explicit or implicit, are a maintenance nightmare. An operation like refactoring an inheritance hierarchy can break seemingly unrelated code. How can you eliminate class testing?

Constraints:
Limited impact. You'd like the solution to affect as little code as possible.
Readability. The solution should reveal more of the programmer's intent than the original code.
Maintainability. The solution should yield code that is less susceptible to breaking because of unrelated changes than the original.

I did a little research into the various images' use of class tests. Table 20-1 provides the raw results. These numbers need a little interpretation. There are legitimate uses for isKindOf:, like writing generic comparison methods. There are also legitimate uses of class. It is used heavily in V Mac 2.0 to return instance-invariant information.

The most interesting comparison in Table 20-1 is between V Win 2.0 and V Mac 2.0. Both images come from a common base and share a lot of code. The Mac image shows the effects of being worked on after Digitalk bought

	V Win 2.0	V Mac 2.0	VisualWorks 1.0	ENVY for VisualWorks
Senders of isKindOf:	44	26	161	214
Senders of isMemberOf:	3	1	26	26
Senders of class	156	810	573	823
is... methods in Object	43	18	11	13

Table 20-1 How various images use class tests.

Instantiations, which brought a new sense of discipline to Digitalk's code. Both the reduction in the reliance on isKindOf: and in the increase in the use of class, not for class testing, but for instance-invariant behavior seem to be the result of the strict programming style developed in Portland.

Solution: Replace the test with a message. Implement the conditionally executed code as the method in the class tested for. Implement the conditionally executed code as the method in the class tested for. Implement an empty method (or one that returns a default answer) in all the other classes the object could be.

Example: Here is an example from the V Win 2.0 image. The method ApplicationWindow>>isTextModified returns true if any of the pane's children has modified text. It looks like this:

```
ApplicationWindow>>isTextModified
    children
        detect: [:each | (each isKindOf: TextPane)
            and : [each modified]]
        ifNone: [^false]
    ^turn
```

This method will break if you add new text editing panes that don't inherit from TextPane. Using the transformation described above, we implement two methods:

```
TextPane>>isTextModified
    ^self modified "This is the conditionally executed code"
```

```
Pane>>isTextModified
    ^false
```

Then the original method simplifies to:

```
ApplicationWindow>>isTextModified
    children
        detect: [:each | each isTextModified]
```

```
        ifNone: [^false]
    ^true
```

This transformation has done two things. First, the code is easier to read. I can read it as saying, "I have modified text if any of my children have modified text." No such simple statement can be made about the original. Second, the intent of my code is much clearer. If I want to create a subclass of Pane that edits text, it is clear from browsing the code in Pane that I will have to override isTextModified. Before, whatever behavior depends on checking for modified text (like prompting before closing a window) would simply not have worked, and you would have a chore figuring out why.

OTHER PATTERNS

You may be able to factor the implementations of the blank methods higher in the hierarchy ("Move Common Methods Up").

What if you have an object that can be in one of three states, and you have to take the state into account in several methods? Seems like a natural use of a case statement, doesn't it? In my next column, I'll present the Multiplexer pattern, which improves your design in such a situation at the same time it eliminates the need for a case statement.

21

CRC: Finding Objects
the Easy Way

Object Magazine, November–December, 1993

This article gives the longer version of the story I told above in introducing the original CRC article. I was glad Marie Lenzi gave me the chance to write it, because I was able to make an explicit public statement that Ward invented CRC, even though my name came first on the original article.

T HIS ISN'T ANOTHER introduction to objects with CRC. It is a philosophical look back at CRC's place in the grand scheme of things. It presents what CRC is under the hood, where it came from, and what it is good for.

Not a methodology

What is an article on CRC doing in an issue on methodologies? CRC isn't a methodology. What? Your consultants told you otherwise? Well, as the narrator at the beginning of any number of Disney movies would say: I was there at the beginning, so let me tell you what really happened.

Perspective

Before I get rolling, let me say that CRC was really Ward Cunningham's idea. As you'll see later in the article, his was the insight that really tied together several strands we had been pursuing together. You'll also see how I got my name first on the paper that introduced it to the public eye. Really, though—Ward did it, I helped. I hope that sets the record straight. Now, back to your regularly scheduled article.

First, what does CRC stand for (besides truth, justice, and the object-oriented way)? The first C stands for *class*, the name of the object. The names you give to objects take on a life of their own, becoming part of the everyday vocabulary of programmers and, eventually, users. Time invested choosing names is time well spent. The R stands for *responsibilities*, the job description of the object. Responsibilities are best described in short, active verb phrases. The second C stands for *collaborators*, the other objects this one relies on to get its job done. As I am widely quoted as saying (although I don't remember saying it, and it's trite if I did): "No object is an island."

Rather than worry about all the possible issues that could be dealt with during design, CRC tells us that by focusing on class, responsibilities, and collaborators early in design we will arrive at systems that make good use of objects. This is not to say that there aren't other issues to be dealt with during design, just that picking names and distributing responsibilities have the largest downstream effects, and therefore should be done first.

CARDS

You will hear people talk not just about CRC, but about CRC cards. CRC is the attitude, the cards are one way to make it concrete. CRC cards use ordinary index cards, one per object, spread out on a large, flat surface.

CRC cards are a particularly convenient way of handling CRC information. New objects can be created quickly, responsibilities created and moved from object to object, and scenarios tested physically, by grabbing several cards and waving them around. None of the many attempts at computerizing the cards has caught on, probably because plain index cards have so many advantages:

- Machine independent
- Language independent
- Easily backed up (photocopier)

- Intuitive interface (pen and ink)
- Physical
- Cheap

As the editor said when I showed her this article, "The minute someone turns on a computer, all human interaction ceases." This may not be a fundamental attribute of computers, but it certainly characterizes almost all computers in wide use today.

WHY IT ISN'T A METHODOLOGY

If forced to put a label on CRC, I call it an object-finding method. That doesn't make it a methodology, numerous scholarly papers to the contrary. To me a methodology should explain how to go from concept through shipping several versions of a program. CRC doesn't do all that, so it isn't a methodology. It can, however, be of help at several spots along the way, as described in the last section.

HISTORY

I thought I'd take this chance to tell the story of how CRC came to be. It lends a human side to what has so far been a dry, technical article, and it serves as a lesson in how innovation takes root. Of course, this is just the story from my perspective. You should talk to the other actors directly if you want a balanced picture.

TEKTRONIX

It all started in the Computer Research Lab at Tektronix in Portland, OR. Ward Cunningham and I had been working together for about two years, he as the master, I as the student, in the mysteries of Smalltalk and object-oriented thinking. We developed a very productive collaborative style sharing a single computer, keyboard, and mouse. We were able to program as fast as we could come up with new ideas. In other words, programming was no longer the bottleneck in our research; thinking was.

Dry spells in the idea well led us to take walks around the Tektronix campus. It was during these walks that we came up with the idea of teaching other people how to program the way we did. The problem, we recognized, was that we had to learn an enormous amount of detail about the Smalltalk library, programming environment, and user interface before we were able to program like that. How could people with less Smalltalk background have a taste of what we called the "browser experience?"

Another thread that ties into the CRC story was our developing philosophy of objects. I ran across the addendum to the 1987 OOPSLA proceedings the other day. In it I am quoted (during Norm Kerth's famous "Where do objects come from?" workshop) as saying that "…finding objects isn't the hard part of design; the hard part is distributing behaviors among objects" (p. 14). I may have said it, but the thinking was something Ward and I had developed together.

CAPITOLA

After I left Tektronix in 1987, Ward and I wanted to continue collaborating. In early December of that year I organized a workshop attended by Dave Thomas, Kurt Schmucker, Ward, and me, ostensibly to begin writing a book on object-oriented design. We sat together in a beach house in Capitola, CA, for three days and talked. The book came to naught, but the workshop was still valuable. Early on in the discussions, Ward got fixated on the idea of what he called responsibility diagrams. He was sure that if we could just figure out how to diagram responsibility we'd have the core of the design problem licked. I didn't have a clue what he was talking about, but I had seen enough big ideas germinate in his brain that I was sure this was going to be a good one.

THE STACK

During 1988 Ward was still at Tektronix, consulting with a group working on a Smalltalk-powered oscilloscope. He had just gotten Hypercard, so he wrote a stack for designing objects. Each object had its own card. The name of the object went in the upper left corner, the responsibilities down the left, and the collaborators on the right. Typing in a new collaborator would create a card for that object, if necessary. Clicking on it would take you to that card.

Doing interviews and then going back to his Macintosh to key in the information got tedious. He had read in the Hypercard documentation that it was a good idea to prototype stacks by writing them on index cards first. A month later he was considering presenting the design of the scope as a case study. Ward says, "It came to me in a flash. I had to figure out how to communicate what I was doing when I was working with those guys at the blackboard. Just to try it, I wrote out HotDraw [a semantic drawing editor framework we wrote] in the middle of one night. The next morning I did designs with three different people. I was pleased with how similar the designs came out."

I remember a long call shortly after that in which Ward told my group at Apple (Joshua Susser and Diana Merry-Shapiro) about CRC. The microphone in my speaker phone was broken, so Ward had to just ramble on for an hour with no feedback. We sat entranced. At the end of that call it was clear to me that the wave that started on that Capitola beach was breaking. This was great stuff.

OOPSLA '89

In 1986, Dan Ingalls, the OOPSLA program chair, had published a little technical paper. I wanted to follow his lead, and CRC seemed the right vehicle. It was a cool idea, not too earth-shattering, and it could be summed up in a few pages.

Ward and I may program smoothly together, but writing is another matter entirely. I spew out pages of stuff, then go back and slash. Ward has to craft each sentence, each word as he goes along. To keep the peace we made the rule that whoever wrote the first draft of a paper got to be first author. Whoever had an idea in the first place would usually write the first draft, but if one of us got fed up with the other's pace, we'd get credit. It is a great way of making sure papers get written.

The OOPSLA deadline was approaching, and Ward still hadn't sent me anything, so I quickly threw together a draft and sent it to him by courier. In it, I changed the name of the method to Name, Responsibilities, and Helpers and I specified 3"×5" cards. When the paper came back, the name of the method had been changed back to CRC and the cards had grown an inch each way to accommodate Ward's messy handwriting.

We had a long talk about the name, but Ward was adamant. His second son, Christopher Ryer Cunningham, had been born around that time (his wife insists the boy was named after the method, not the other way around). The title took even longer. Finally we settled on what I think is still my best title, "A Laboratory for Teaching Object-Oriented Thinking." We knew CRC was good for design, but all we could prove at that time was that it was good for getting learners over the hump in learning to think like objects.

AND THEN...

My second child, Lincoln, was busy not being born during OOPSLA, so I missed Ward's presentation. I changed jobs to a startup, so I was out of touch with how the paper was received in the months after it hit the street. I figured it was another case of an idea whose time hadn't yet come. I was astonished at the next OOPSLA when, during a design workshop, someone asked who in the room had tried CRC and every hand went up, including hands attached to some very big names.

Since then CRC has gone in some surprising directions. Dave Thomas has been instrumental in getting it publicized to the many new object folks. Jim Coplien at AT&T is using it to map out human organizations. Sam Adams and the folks at Knowledge Systems Corp are basing an exciting new programming environment on it. And, of course, Rebecca Wirfs-Brock and colleagues at Tektronix expanded on it enormously in their book on responsibility driven design, *Designing Object-Oriented Software*.

SO WHAT?

Fireside reminiscence aside, if CRC isn't a methodology, what is it good for?

TEACHING

As I said earlier, the first public application of CRC was teaching how to think from the objects' perspective. CRC cards are particularly good at this because they defer so many details of objects. I taught a class at a large computer company for several years in which I got the students doing object design before I ever introduced any vocabulary. None of this standing up and saying (puts on stuffy, self-important voice), "The three most important concepts in object-oriented are encapsulation, polymorphism, and inheritance." The students designed objects for an automatic teller machine first. Then I was able to point to their concrete experiences and give names to them.

BRAINSTORMING

At the beginning of any group development, there is often considerable diversity of opinion about how a system should be put together. Sitting a core development team around a table and going through a day or two of CRC sessions is a great way to make everyone's ideas concrete. One feature of CRC is that it allows everyone to contribute what they are comfortable contributing. Someone who is familiar with objects can wade in and sling new objects and responsibilities, while someone who might not know objects but does know the problem very well can often contribute the scenario that brings the proposed system to its knees.

DESIGN

For small groups of experienced developers working in an advanced object language, CRC may be all the design notation they need. I have seen five person-year projects driven entirely by a couple of weeks of CRC.

USER INVOLVEMENT

Because CRC presents an approachable view of objects, managers and users can often follow the gist of your object designs. I remember one case where I was presenting a programming environment design to a FORTRAN programmer and he caught a fundamental error. All the usual good effects ascribed to user involvement happen with CRC, and the users don't have to learn any obscure "circles-and-arrows" notation.

DESIGN REVIEW

Using CRC to review designs forces developers to focus first on the "big picture." My rule of thumb is that if a system doesn't boil down to three or four objects, it doesn't have a clear architecture. An additional advantage, alluded to above, is that managers can understand CRC presentations. If your managers can actually understand the design, perhaps they will be willing to lighten up on those productivity-sucking, tree-killing piles of paper documentation.

When I present a design using CRC, I start with a clean set of cards. Working from a prepared set always tempts me to introduce too much complexity too soon. If I have to write everything over from scratch, I can't introduce complexity any faster than I can write.

GROUP DYNAMICS

Grady Booch told me about this use of CRC, and I have used it several times since. As a consultant, I come into many highly charged interpersonal situations. My first job is to figure out who is being heard and who should be heard. CRC is a great nonsense detector. A quick design review with CRC tells me who knows the system and who knows objects.

CONCLUSION

You've seen how CRC focuses design on what objects are called and how they divide the work to be done by a system. You've learned how it grew from a desire to quickly give novices the essential experience of objects. You've seen how it can work in practice.

All that's left is to try it. Get a pack of index cards and a nice pen, pick a problem, give yourself plenty of space, and go to it. I suggest starting with one object and letting the system grow from there. Pick up the cards as you talk about them; it will help you think about the system from each object's perspective. Struggle to find the right words—object names should be consistently drawn from a single metaphor; responsibilities should contain active verbs. That's it. Your first objects (or your thousandth) for less than a buck. Enjoy.

22

DEATH TO CASE STATEMENTS

Smalltalk Report, JANUARY, 1994

There are two notable points to make about this paper. First, it is one of the first times Ward and I published any pattern-related material (we presented some stuff at OOPSLA 87 in Orlando, I in Norm Kerth's "Where Do Objects Come From" workshop, Ward on a panel). Second, it argues that the worst problem of reuse is one of communication, not technology or economics.

The paper started out life as a Tektronix technical report. Ward and I had the habit of writing up just about everything we did as a TR. After we had written this, I think we submitted it as a position paper for some conference or workshop. Somehow, JOOP got hold of a copy and contacted us about publishing it.

The paper can be summed up as: "We created two sets of abstractions. The first was communicated as literate source code. The second was communicated as patterns for its reuse. The first set of objects was misused; the second was used correctly. We conclude that the problem of reuse is one of effectively communicating the intent of the code."

HOLD ON A SEC . . . .
Before I finish bashing case statements, I'd like to return to the scene of an earlier crime, my perfidious assault on that bastion of Smalltalk orthodoxy, the ubiquitous accessor method. (Whew! That's a ten-buck sentence if I ever seen one.) I argued that the violation of encapsulation provided by accessor methods more than offset any benefit of inheritance reuse. I talked to several readers at OOPSLA who were offended by that column, although no one wrote me directly. Well folks, none of those beer-soaked conversations convinced me differently in Washington, and a couple of recent events leave me even more sure that insisting all variable access go through a message is a bad idea.

Here's the basic problem: Beginners don't get the message that accessor methods should be private by default. They hear the rule, *access variables only through a message,* and they think, "Great, here's one thing I can do to make sure I'm not messing up." They're using their new object and they say, "Hey, if I just had that variable over there I could solve my problem." Next thing you know, representation decisions have leaked all over, none of the objects have grown the behavior they need, and progress slows to a crawl.

I was at a client recently where they had misused accessor methods all over the place. The biggest problem was in changing collections behind the owning object's back. They wrote code like this:

```
Schedule>>initialize
    tasks := OrderedCollection new

Schedule>>tasks
    ^tasks
```

Then in user interface code they would write:

```
ScheduleView>>addTaskButton
    ...
    model tasks add: newTask
```

The problem with this code is that it assumes that tasks returns an object that responds to add:. If they changed the representation in Schedule to store tasks as a Dictionary instead of an OrderedCollection, the ScheduleView code breaks. The implementation of Schedule has leaked out, and that's exactly the kind of problem objects are supposed to help us avoid.

Later on in this same assignment, the horror that accessing methods are there to avoid happened to me—I changed an instance variable so that it was lazily initialized. I had to change all those methods that directly accessed the variable so they sent a message instead. It took me all of three minutes and I was done.

The point here is not that accessor methods are useless. There are definitely cases where judicious use of accessors can improve code. However, teaching beginners always to use accessors before they are able to understand the need to keep some methods private avoids reuse problems far down the road at the cost of encouraging them to violate encapsulation.

Enough about accessors. If you don't agree, let me know. I'd love to see a reasoned discussion of this issue, since accessors are accepted as an article of faith by so many people, and I see lots of bad code being written while adhering to the letter of the "accessor law."

The real purpose of this article is to complete my thoughts about case statements from last issue. QKS' SmalltalkAgents has introduced a case construct. I'm making the argument that case statements in an object language are superfluous and that they prevent discovering important new objects. Rather than just complaining about case statements, though, I'll show you how to turn a situation that uses case logic into a richer use of objects. (This is typical of patterns: They don't just describe a good or bad situation, they tell you how to get from bad to good.)

Pattern: Objects from States

Problem: Parallel case statements are a maintenance nightmare. Changing one instance of the case without changing the others can lead to subtle bugs. How can you use objects to eliminate case statements?

Constraints: One of the goals of any programming activity is to not introduce any more complexity than necessary. Creating methods and classes that don't have any payoff is a common programming mistake. The solution to the case statement problem should create only new classes and methods that pay for their existence with reduced maintenance, improved readability, and increased flexibility.

The solution must eliminate the case logic that causes maintenance problems. Why are case statements a problem? Essentially, multiple case statements with the same cases introduce a multiple update problem. You can't correctly change one statement without changing all the others, and this relationship is entirely implicit. While you might be able to keep track of where all the cases are today, a year from now you (or worse, someone else) will have to know to look for them all, and know where to look.

Finally, the solution should set the stage for further growth of our objects. Some of the most valuable objects you can find are the ones that are not obvious from the user's view of the world. These are the objects that structure not the world, but our computational model of the world. (Other patterns like this are "Objects from Collections," "Objects from Instance Variables," and "Objects from Methods"). Taking advantage of the appearance of case logic should make programs more explicit and more flexible.

Solution: Make an object for each state. Make a variable in the original object to hold the current state. Move the logic in each case into the corresponding state object. Delegate to the current state instead of executing in the original object. Make the state changing methods assign a different state object to the state variable.

Example: Consider a visual object that can be in one of three states—enabled, disabled, or invisible. The state is represented by storing a Symbol in the variable state. A couple of the methods might be:

Visual>>display
    state = #enabled ifTrue: [...display enabled... .
    state = #disabled ifTrue: [...display disabled... .
    state = #invisible ifTrue: [...do nothing...

Visual>>extent
    state = #enabled | (state = #disabled) ifTrue: [^40@40 .
    state = #invisible ifTrue: [^0@0 .

Visual>>enable
    state := #enabled

Visual>>disable
    state := #disabled

Visual>>disappear
    state := #invisible

Applying "Objects from States," we first make an object for each state:

EnabledVisual, DisabledVisual, InvisibleVisual, subclasses of Object.

We can use the variable state to hold an instance of one of these. Moving the logic into the state objects yields

```
EnabledVisual>>display
    ...display enabled...

EnabledVisual>>extent
    ^40@40

DisabledVisual>>display
    ...display disabled...

DisabledVisual>>extent
    ^40@40

InvisibleVisual>>display
    "Do nothing"

InvisibleVisual>>extent
    ^0@0
```

Then Visual has to change to invoke the state:

```
Visual>>display
    state display

Visual>>extent
    ^state extent
```

Finally, the state-changing methods have to change.

```
Visual>>enable
    state := EnabledVisual new

Visual>>disable
    state := DisabledVisual new
```

```
Visual>>disappear
    state := InvisibleVisual new
```

OTHER PATTERNS

After you've applied "Objects from States," you may have to use the "Delegate or Call Back" pattern to fully move each state's logic into the state object. You may be able to use "Factor a Superclass" to simplify the implementation of the states and prevent multiple update problems.

CONCLUSION

This and the previous column have shown how to eliminate most uses of case-type logic. The remaining examples of case statements don't appear frequently enough to justify a new language construct. The power of Smalltalk lies primarily in its simplicity, out of which richness can grow without undue complexity. Every new feature must pay for itself by solving a problem affecting a large part of the community. On this grounds, case statements just don't cut it.

What's next? In this pattern, I referred to several others that created new objects. I think I'll spend at least a couple more months exploring this theme. See you in the next issue with the second installment of "Daddy, where do objects come from?"

23

WHERE DO OBJECTS COME FROM?

Smalltalk Report, MARCH–APRIL, 1994

The previous column got me started examining why people create classes. About this time, I had collected enough patterns to begin thinking about the patterns book. Of course, at first I was going to cover all of programming/analysis/design/project management/etc. in a single book. This exploration was the beginning of trying to write the analysis/design portion of the book.

One of the things I like about writing a column is that it forces you to think hard about a topic at regular intervals. I'm the kind of person who dives deep into a topic until I'm bored, and then drifts until something else catches my eye. I get to study lots of cool stuff that way, but I don't really penetrate to insight. Writing a column returns me to roughly the same place every month and pushes me to find something new. The result is much more valuable thinking.

PREVIOUSLY, I talked about how objects could be created from the states of objects that acted like finite-state machines (the "Objects from States" pattern). I'll continue on the theme of where objects come from for this and several issues.

I won't be saying much about the conventional source of objects, the user's world. There are lots of books that will tell you how to find those objects. Instead, I'll focus on finding new objects in running programs.

In all programming, many of the most important design insights don't come until after a program has been deployed for awhile. Smalltalk is unique in that it is possible to fold those insights back into the program. Polymorphism, in particular, is invaluable for introducing new objects without disturbing existing ones. Unlike programs written in more conventional languages, Smalltalk programs can get better and better, and easier to extend over time. Such programs tend to spin off reusable pieces, as well, which multiplies their value.

Ward Cunningham is a pioneer of this technique, which he calls episodic design. In an episodic design process, design doesn't happen all at once, as in the barnacle-encrusted waterfall model. Instead, design happens in episodes, whenever you understand an issue well enough to know that your previous design is limited in some way.

To avoid overdesigning, design episodes are typically triggered by the desire to add a new feature. Some features seem to slide right in with little effort. Others must be forced in at the cost of violating good design. When encountering the latter, an episodic designer will first 'make a place' for the feature by fixing the design so it's easy to add.

Design episodes typically consist of finding new objects, new responsibilities, or new collaborations. New objects often come about to add degrees of freedom to your program. For example, you may have thought initially that interest calculation was a simple computation, so it was buried in a method in FinancialInstrument. In adding new functionality, you realize there are many different ways to calculate interest, so you need an InterestCalculator, which a FinancialInstrument collaborates with to compute interest. Then you can add new InterestCalculators without disturbing the rest of the design.

When creating new objects, you might think a flash of insight is required to discover them. Not so. While some objects come out of the blue, most can be found in the program itself.

The next couple of columns will explore where you can find some of these derived objects. This month's pattern helps you find objects you just didn't quite want to create when you found them in the first place. The programming "convenience" it represents is particularly common in former LISP programmers, but I've seen it come from C and assembly language hacks, too.

Pattern: Objects from Collections

Problem: Collections where two or more methods in the same or different objects have to agree on a fixed set of indexes are a maintenance headache (the same observation applies to Associations or Points being used to represent a duple). The programming environment doesn't help you find where all these implicitly meaningful indexes are used. If you have such a collection, how can you make it easy to maintain?

Constraints:

Simplicity. The reason such collections arise in the first place is because creating classes is a fairly heavyweight activity. You have to find the right name ("System of Names") for the class, then you have to find the right name for the messages, then you have use the programming environment to define it. Once it's there, you have to document and maintain it. Where you can't imagine the object being used anywhere else, like returning two values from a method, you aren't likely to bother.

Readability. The problem with simply using collections instead of an object is that even in the small it fails to convey the intent of the code. A good example from the VisualWorks 1.0 image is Browser>spawn-Edits:from:. It creates a three-element array with the text to edit, the start of the selection, and the end of the selection. This array gets passed through two intermediate methods before it is finally torn apart in Browser class>setTextView:fromTextState: and turned into messages for the newly created text editor. Reading the code, the only clue you have to the contents of the array is the names of the temporaries in the latter method.

Maintainability. Closely allied with readability is the issue of how hard the code is to maintain. If I wanted to add a fourth element to the array in the above example, perhaps for a special font for the selection, I would probably go to Browser>spawnEdits:from: and Browserclass>setText-View:fromTextState: and make the change. However, this would break the debugger, which also spawns edits. This hidden multiple update problem is the best reason for making collections into objects.

Solution: Create a new class. Give it the same number of instance variables as the size of the collection. Name the variables according to what goes in them.

Example: To simplify the above example, let's say you wanted to be able

221

to spawn a text editor. TextEditor has a method **textstate:**, which takes as a parameter a three-element array:

```
TextEditor>textState: anArray
    self text: (anArray at: 1).
    self selectFrom: (anArray at: 2) to: (anArray at: 3)
```

Our browser uses this method:

```
MyBrowser>spawnEdits
    | array |
    array:= Array
        with: self text
        with: self selectionStart
        with: self selectionStop.
    TextEditor open textState: array
```

Both methods are now vulnerable to change in the other. By creating an object from the collection, we solve this problem:

```
TextState
    variables: text selectionStart selectionStop

TextState class>text: aString selectFrom: startInteger to:
stopInteger
    ^self new
    setText: aString
    selectionStart: startInteger
    selectionStop: stopInteger

TextState>setText: aString selectionStart: startInteger
selectionStop: stopInteger
    text := aString.
    selectionStart := startInteger.
    selectionStop := stopInteger
```

Then we can use a TextState in the TextEditor:

```
TextEditor>textState: aTextState
    self text: aTextState text.
    self selectFrom: aTextState selectionStart to: aTextState
selectionstop
```

And create it in MyBrowser:

```
MyBrowser>textState
    ^TextState
        text: self text
        selectionStart: self selectionStart
        selectionStop: self selectionStop
```

```
MyBrowser>spawnEdits
TextEditor open textState: self textState
```

The result is code that is slightly more complicated, but much easier to read and maintain. The beauty of "Objects from Collections" is not just in the immediate results. The new objects often become the home of important behavior in their own right. Code that lived uneasily in one of the objects that understood the format of the array can now live comfortably in the new object. Also, the new object becomes a new degree of freedom in the system. If there are a variety of ways the information can be structured or used, you can capture that variety in a family of objects all responding to the new object's protocol.

In the next issue, we will examine two more patterns for creating objects from code: "Objects from Variables" and "Objects from Methods."

24

PATTERNS AND SOFTWARE
DEVELOPMENT

Dr. Dobb's Journal, FEBRUARY 1994

This is my abortive attempt to bring patterns to the masses. Dr. Dobbs (which I used to read as a Silicon Valley brat in the late '70s) called to ask for a pattern article. I thought, "Here is my chance to step outside the narrow confines of the object universe."

Ha. Nobody got it. I'm sure I misjudged my audience, but I think there are more serious problems with the presentation here. Looking at the paper again, though, I'll be hanged if I can figure what. I'll take a shot at it, though.

One of the problems is certainly that I am talking about a different kind of pattern here than most people talk about. The patterns in the Design Patterns book, for example, show you how people use objects over and over. You can take the same approach to using a particular framework, however. People use MVC the same way over and over. You can write the things they do as patterns.

Part of the problem with the paper now that I look at it is that I got away from Ward's question, "What is the one thing you want the reader to take away?" This paper is all over the place. Another problem is that the paper isn't explicit about even those points that it does make. It tells a story (kinda), but it doesn't come out and say, "Communication is the problem."

The one good thing to come out of the article was about two months of intense discussion on a CompuServe forum devoted to software engineering. After the article had been out for a month or so, I got this email, "Er, uh, would you mind terribly coming over and explaining just what the hell you mean?"

I'm constantly amazed by how diffident people are with me, via email or in person. Hey, I'm just a guy in sweats sitting in a cold office with a poorly behaved dog at my feet.

P ATTERNS ARE A WAY of developing and packaging reusable software components. The idea of patterns is gaining attention in certain programming circles—especially those based on object-oriented languages and paradigms. At last fall's OOPSLA '93 conference, the foreground topics focused on mainstream development methodologies (such as the second-generation versions of Booch, Rumbaugh, Schlaer-Mellor, and the like), but smoldering in the background was much discussion around patterns. This subject will likely catch fire in the coming year.

Driving the discussion of patterns is the ongoing need to create truly reusable software—the long-awaited benefit of OO languages and methodologies that has yet to materialize.

In this article, I'll look at patterns as a method of guiding reuse. Although some of this discussion may be abstract, it draws upon my ten years of experience as a programmer and current vendor of object tools (Profile/V and the Object Explorer).

Patterns should not be confused with methodologies. A methodology tells you how to write down the decisions you have made. A pattern tells you which decisions to make, when and how to make them, and why they are the right decisions. Methodologies are free of content: Once you imagine a specific solution to a problem, a methodology gives you the wherewithal for writing it down and arriving at a correct implementation. By contrast, patterns are all content.

Abstractors and Elaborators

I divide the world of software development into two parts: the abstractor, creating reusable pieces; and the elaborator, massaging those pieces to fit the needs of a user. Microsoft has lately been promulgating a roughly similar vision, in which software development is divided into two categories: component builders (for example, programmers who write a DLLs or class libraries in C or C++), and solution builders (those who use high-level tools such as Paris, Visual Basic, PowerBuilder, or an application framework in conjunction with low-level DLL components to construct application-level solutions for end users). The abstractor/elaborator categorization is more general, so I'll stick with it.

The economics of reusable software are dominated by the cost of communicating between abstractor and elaborator. For example, if an abstractor takes 1000 hours to create a piece of reusable software, and 100 elaborators each take 100 hours to understand how to use it, then the elaborators have collectively spent ten times as many hours as the abstractor. Obviously, these numbers are hypothetical, but six months to create a reusable component and two-and-a-half weeks to learn how to use to use it effectively are well within the realm of possibility.

Making the abstractor more efficient (by providing, say, a faster computer or whizzy debugger) won't reduce the total effort spent on writing software; if you view the abstractor and the elaborators as belonging to the same economic domain (say, a large corporation or organization), the equation's total is little changed. The only way to significantly affect the sum is to either reduce the number of elaborators (a bad thing, because it implies that software is not being reused, and thus more work is done from scratch), or reduce the time they spend figuring out the software.

This is nothing new. The old story of maintenance taking up 70 percent of the resources is really another way of saying the same thing. The new wrinkle is that, when you introduce software reuse into the equation, it isn't just one hapless programmer trying to figure out an obscure piece of code—it's hundreds.

Constructing a software component so that it is reusable is a step forward, but nowadays it's not enough. The abstractor needs to do more. Why should the abstractor care? In one model of reuse, there is a development team within a company building software components for other teams to use; in this model, making the elaborators more efficient reduces the development resources required. The company can then use the freed-up resources to shorten time-to-market, increase features, reduce development cost or improve quality.

In another model of software reuse (the market model), reusable components are available for developers on the open market (for example, the Visual Basic add-on market). Here, if you are a VBX vendor (abstractor) and your customers (elaborators) are able to produce finished applications sooner, you will have a substantial edge over your competition.

If the time it takes elaborators to figure out reusable software is an important issue and solving the problem has significant payback, how can we reduce the time necessary to understand how to reuse software? What is it that, in the hands of elaborators, would make them more successful, sooner? Another way of asking the question is, what do abstractors know that they aren't communicating?

What's missing is a way for abstractors to communicate their intent. The abstractor, in building a piece of reusable software, is solving a whole set of future problems. Indeed, most reusable software results from the experience of being an elaborator several times, then having a flash of insight that solves a number of elaborator problems once and for all. The abstractor needs to communicate which problems a reusable component is intended to solve, how to think about the problem, how this thought process is embodied in the software, in what order to pursue subissues of the problem, and so on. Communicating with elaborators is more important than, say, using a better programming environment.

If you need to communicate what you were thinking about when you wrote your reusable software, what form would such communication take? Of course there are the usual mechanisms—a tutorial, reference manual, comments in the code, the coding conventions used by the source (if it is available to the elaborator), and, of course, word of mouth—bits of advice passed from guru to novice.

Researchers and developers have been exploring another approach, which falls under the rubric of patterns. I'll discuss the abstract definition later, first, I'll provide a concrete example of how patterns can be used to communicate the programmer's intent.

A Multicurrency Library

Let's take as an example a class library for handling multicurrency transactions. There are two principal classes: a *Money* entity, which has a value and a currency, and a *CurrencyExchange,* which can convert a *Money* in one currency to a *Money* in another. How can you use these objects? What is the intent behind the design? Here are three patterns that describe it. While by no means complete, a set of 15 or 20 such patterns would provide any elaborator a good start on reusing the library.

The Money Object Pattern

> *Problem:* How to represent a monetary value in a system which needs to deal with many different currencies.

Constraints: One important concern in a system dealing with financial calculations is efficiency—making sure the calculations run in a timely manner and use as little memory as possible. The simplest representation of monetary values, and one which maps well onto the hardware, is representing them as fixed or floating-point numbers.

While you'd like your system to be as efficient as possible, you'd also like it to be flexible. For instance, you'd like to be able to decide as late as possible in which precision computations should occur. The rapidity of change of most financial systems dictates that flexibility is more important than efficiency for most applications—you can always buy faster hardware. When you need real number crunching, you can translate from and to a representation more flexible than simple numbers.

Another consideration, related to flexibility, is that a system handling multiple currencies should be as simple to use as possible. Only code concerned with creating or printing currency values should be aware that many currencies are possible. The rest of the code should look as much as possible like you are just using numbers.

Solution: When you need to represent a monetary value, create an instance of Money whose value is the value you need to represent and whose currency is the standard, three-character abbreviation (USD for United States dollars, for instance).

The Money Arithmetic Pattern

Problem: How can you do arithmetic with Money?

Constraints: Money arithmetic should be as simple as possible. Taking this constraint to the extreme would lead you to allow Money and numbers to freely interoperate, perhaps with a default currency to allow conversion of numbers to Money.

A far more important principle than mere programming convenience is making sure financial algorithms are correct. Restricting the combinations of values that can operate together arithmetically can catch many programming errors which might otherwise produce answers that seem reasonable, but are incorrect.

Solution: Send a Money the message + or – with another Money as the parameter, or * or / with a number as the parameter. A Money will be the result of any of these messages. Adding a Money and a number, or multiplying two Moneys will result in an error.

THE MONEY PRINT PATTERN

Problem: How can you print a Money?

Constraints: The simplest possible design has a single global exchange rate. Asking a Money to print itself would cause it to convert to the common currency and print.

This simplest solution ignores the complexity of most financial systems, which must deal with multiple exchange rates—some historical, some current (perhaps kept up-to-date with currency exchanges), some projected. By specifying an exchange rate (in the form of a CurrencyExchange) your printing code will be slightly more complicated, but much more flexible as a result.

Solution: Print Money by sending CurrencyExchange the message "print" with Money as an argument. Money will be printed in the CurrencyExchange's preferred currency. There is a second message, printCurrency, which takes two arguments. The first is the Money to be printed, and the second is the currency (again, a three-character string containing a standard abbreviation) in which to print it.

PATTERNS

As you can see, a pattern has three parts:

- *Problem.* The first part of every pattern is the problem it solves. This is stated as a question in a sentence or two. The problem sets the stage for the pattern, letting readers quickly decide whether the patterns applies to their situation.

PATTERN RESOURCES

—

The idea of patterns capturing design expertise originated with the architect Christopher Alexander. His books The Timeless Way of Building and A Pattern Language (both from Oxford Press) are required reading for anyone who wants to get serious about patterns. A forthcoming Addison-Wesley book, Design Patterns: Micro-architectures for Object-Oriented Design, by Erich Gamma et al., catalogs some of the most common object patterns.

The Hillside Group is a nonprofit corporation founded to promote communication to and through computers by all potential users, focusing initially on patterns as a strategy. The founding members are myself, Ken Auer, Grady Booch, Jim Coplien, Ralph Johnson, Hal Hildebrand, and Ward Cunningham. Our sponsors are Rational and the Object Management Group. In August 1994 we will sponsor the first annual Pattern Languages of Programs conference. For more information, contact plop94@ee.pdx.edu. The Hillside Group also has a mailing list, which you can contact at patterns-request@cs.uiuc.edu.

—K.B.

- *Context.* Patterns explicitly describe the context in which they are valid. The context is the set of conflicting constraints acting on any solution to the problem. You saw in Money an example of efficiency vs. flexibility. Other patterns might balance development time and run time, or space and speed.

The constraints aren't just described, however. The pattern also specifies how the constraints are resolved. Money states that flexibility and correctness are more important than raw efficiency. Other patterns might find a balance between two or more constraints, instead of saying that one dominates. The aforementioned patterns really just sketch the context section. A fully developed pattern might have two or three pages of analysis to back up its solution.

- *Solution.* Given the analysis of the constraints in the context section, the solution tells you what to do with your system to resolve the constraints. Supporting the solution is an illustration of it at work—either a diagram or code fragments.

Patterns Form Language

Although patterns are interesting in isolation, it is when they work together, forming a coherent language, that their power becomes apparent. A few times in my life I've been fortunate enough to work with someone who just seems to ask the right questions first. Rather than chasing issues that seem interesting but are ultimately secondary, some people can zero in on the one issue at any given moment that will allow the most progress. A language of patterns can function in much the same way.

By choosing the order in which the patterns are considered, the pattern writer has the chance to guide the reader in dealing with issues in the right order. In the patterns above I have chosen to ignore efficiency for the moment, confident that should the issue arise later, it can be dealt with locally (I can imagine a later pattern which tells how to temporarily suspend the flexibility of Money to gain efficiency). In general, a good pattern language will lead you to address issues with wide scope early, and those with limited impact later.

How can you write your own patterns? The bad news is that applying patterns to programming is a new enough technique that there isn't anything like a body of experience to draw on. However, the Hillside Group has made progress with patterns. (See the accompanying text box entitled, "Pattern Resources.") The first step in writing a pattern is a process of discovery. You notice yourself making the same decision over and over. You might find yourself saying, "Oh, this is just a such and so," or, "Oh, we don't have to worry about that now." These are the moments that you can capture as patterns.

Once you have noticed a recurring decision, you have to invent the pattern that encodes it. First, you must catalog the constraints that make the solution right. You will often find in exploring the constraints that you don't quite have the solution right—either it isn't the right solution, or you've described it too specifically or too generally. Finally, you have to find a problem statement that will help a reader choose when the pattern is appropriate.

A Pattern Checklist

After you have a pattern, you need to evaluate and refine it. Here is my checklist when I'm looking at a new pattern:

- *Does it read well?* Does it have a sense of tension and release? Two thirds of the way through the context section of a good pattern you should be saying, "I never thought of this problem in quite this way. Now that I see all the constraints that have to be satisfied, I can't understand how there is any solution." Then, when you read the solution, you should blink your eyes, drop your shoulders, and give a sigh. Strongly literary patterns will make a bigger impact on the reader, and are likely to be based on deeper insight and clearer thinking than patterns that don't read like a story.

- *Does it tell me what to do?* In the early stage of finding a pattern, I often find that I have really only described a solution without having stated the problem. The typical symptom of these solution-oriented patterns is that they don't tell you what to do and when to create the solution. Solution patterns leave the hard work to the reader—figuring out when a solution is appropriate and how to create it. As a pattern writer, you have this information tucked away in your head somewhere. Introspecting enough to pin it down and express it is what will make your patterns (and the code they support) valuable.

- *Does it stand without being easily broken into other patterns?* I have heard "client-server" suggested as a pattern. While I can imagine a description of it that would read well, it fails the atomicity test. There is really a language of patterns which create client-server architectures. Somewhere in there are the decisions that divide responsibility for computation and storage between a shared server and multiple clients. Just saying "client- server," though, is too vague; it captures too many decisions to be a pattern.

- **Does it fit with other patterns to solve a larger problem?** On the one hand, a pattern needs to stand on its own, without being further decomposable. However, for a pattern to be complete it must work in harmony with others to solve a larger problem. If I can't imagine how a pattern could be part of a larger language, either it isn't a good pattern, or other patterns are out there waiting to be discovered.

Using patterns to enhance reuse is just one of the ways patterns are being applied to programming.

25

DISTRIBUTED SMALLTALK

Object Magazine, FEBRUARY, 1994

Yet another brutal review. I never write a tough review without ques-tioning myself: "Is it just me? Am I just not smart enough to get this prod-uct? Who am I to tell someone else what to do?"

I am just now getting comfortable with writing what I know and trusting my readers to take what I say and add their perspective and experience to it.

SHOULD YOU BE using Distributed Smalltalk? That is the question I'll address here. This isn't a full-blown product review, nor a technical piece. I'll introduce the history and technical background of Distributed Smalltalk as they apply to the question of who should be using it.

First, what is Distributed Smalltalk? It is a Common Object Request Broker Architecture (CORBA)-compliant extension to ParcPlace System's Visual-Works developed and marketed by Hewlett-Packard. "HP? The hardware company? Those C++ guys?"

My first reaction when I saw that HP had done a Smalltalk product was, "What does HP know about Smalltalk?" The answer to this question is twofold. One answer is "a lot." HP has been involved peripherally in Smalltalk since it first escaped Xerox. They were one of the first four companies to write a virtual machine. They have also had pockets of interest in Smalltalk ever since. Their 700 series of workstations has held the title for fastest Smalltalk for several years.

The second answer is "who cares?" What HP has done with Distributed Smalltalk is apply their considerable expertise in distributed applications to add value to Smalltalk. They didn't try to write the whole product them-selves. They took a good single-user system and added transparent distribu-tion. That's why I don't care what HP knows about Smalltalk—what's "Smalltalk" about the product they didn't write, and what's new about the product is something they understand very well.

How It Works

DST (as insiders call it) adds three layers of functionality to VisualWorks as it comes from ParcPlace. First, there is the object request broker (ORB) itself. It fields requests from ORBs on other machines, passes messages to remote objects, and converts objects to and from the byte stream protocol used to communicate with other ORBs. The second layer is a standard set of system services built on the ORB for creating and deleting objects, blah, blah, blah. This is the layer currently being standardized by the Object Management Group (OMG), based in part on input from HP. Finally, DST also contains a distributed desktop built on the standard services.

When DST sends a message to a remote object, the message first encounters a stub object on the local machine called a proxy. The proxy responds to all messages by signalling an error. The error is handled by contacting the local ORB with the receiver, name, and arguments of the message. The ORB uses the proxy to locate and contact the ORB for the remote object. When the remote object finishes processing the message, the remote ORB contacts the local ORB with the result of the computation. The proxy returns the result to the local sender. The sender of the message has no knowledge about the location of the receiver.

The design of any system using distributed objects has to take distribution into account, however. The problem is that some messages are received in microseconds while others can take seconds. So, while the implementation of distribution is transparent, for your design to work well it still has to take distribution into account. For example, in the Smalltalk world it is common for one object to notify any interested objects that some part of it has changed and rely on fast messages to make querying the changed object fast. In a distributed system the changing object should pass along enough information in its broadcast that most dependent objects need not send further messages to update their state.

Because CORBA is a typed protocol, any compliant implementation has to be able to compile the Interface Definition Language (IDL) (this is starting to look like acronym soup!). DST's IDL compiler is nicely integrated with the rest of the environment. Classes that act as IDL definitions have IDL as their "native language." When you want to change an IDL definition, you use the standard Smalltalk browser to edit and change it.

WHO SHOULD USE DST?

One of the tough things about writing this article is that the product is moving so fast. From the time I saw it in June of 1993, the breadth and depth of the functionality have expanded dramatically. Anything I say today is likely to be obsolete six months after it hits the page.

My conservative side suggests waiting for DST to settle down. It is a product in its infancy, and it shows its lack of age in all the predictable ways. The training classes are just beginning. New tools to solve common problems are continually being invented. The consultant community doesn't have experience to offer yet. The code itself can use refinement (this being HP's first big commercial Smalltalk program).

On the other hand, my conservative side never makes me much money, nor does it have a lot of fun. I'm in this because it is the leading edge—let it bleed. If you're from a conservative, risk-averse organization, I'd recommend you wait before jumping into DST. Take another look in a year or so. If you're willing to take some risks for big rewards, however, here are the kinds of projects I think could benefit from DST today.

One kind of project for which I recommend DST already has a Smalltalk program up and running. Sometimes it has been uncomfortably squished into a single image or has grown ad hoc communications (often socket or shared-file based). Because the communications in DST are at such a high level, adopting it will often result in a reduction of the overall complexity of the program. For these projects, DST is a clear win.

If you are going to distribute a Smalltalk application, I recommend you rely only on the basic system services, not the distributed desktop. Although the desktop code is maturing rapidly, you will have to grapple with many details to use it. In the hands of an expert it can be extremely powerful, but beginners will be struggling with details of implementation at a time when they should be thinking about how to distribute their application.

Another kind of project that can benefit from DST is a technology group that wants to experiment with distributed objects and isn't sure what platform to use. Once you're over the learning curve for Smalltalk, DST will allow you to quickly experiment with changes to objects and their interfaces in a way that isn't possible with environments that stick a long compilation step into the development cycle.

One issue to be aware of if you are using DST is that it doesn't contain any abstractions for fault tolerance. The CORBA model assumes that remote machines stay up. If one fails, you'll get a timeout error, but there is no provision for hot backup. It's not that it's not possible, you'll just have to do the work yourself. Another similar issue is persistence. HP has tried several object databases with DST, but it takes some work to add persistence to your application.

CONCLUSION

HP's Distributed Smalltalk isn't for everyone. If you have to distribute your application anyway, you'll have a much easier task if you let a vendor take care of the communications. If you're interested in exploring CORBA-style distributed objects, it makes a superior quick-turnaround environment. Even if you don't fit either of these profiles today, the product is maturing fast enough that you should keep an eye on it for when it can help you.

26

WHERE DO OBJECTS COME FROM?
FROM VARIABLES AND METHODS

Smalltalk Report, MAY, 1994

More thinking about design/modeling. This one covers my pet peeve-people who use fixed-sized collections with meaningful indexes (e.g. "1 is red, 2 is blue, 3 is green"). In my patterns book, I covered this in some detail when I talk about your program talking to you. Darn it, if red, green, and blue go together, then make an object for them, figure out what it should be called, and figure out what it should do. If you don't create the easy objects, how will you ever be able to see to create the hard ones?

L ET'S SEE IF I can get through this third column on how objects are born without blushing. So far we've seen two patterns: "Objects from States" and "Objects from Collections." This time we'll look at two more sources of objects: "Objects from Variables" and "Objects from Methods." All four patterns have one thing in common—they create objects that would be difficult or impossible to invent before you have a running program.

These patterns are part of the reason I am suspicious of any methodology that smacks of the sequence, "design, *then* program." The objects that shape the way I think about my programs almost always come out of the program, not out of my preconceptions. Thinking "the design phase is over, now I just have to push on and finish the implementation" is a sure way to miss these valuable objects and end up with a poorly structured, inflexible application to boot.

Pattern: Objects from Variables

Problem: How can you simplify objects that have grown too many variables?

Constraints: It is common to add a variable to an object during development, then add related variables later. After a while, this process of accretion can lead to objects that have many variables. Such objects are difficult to debug, difficult to explain, and difficult to reuse.

Still, the object more than likely works as desired. You'd like to avoid changing code and risking breaking the system for no reason. You will pay a space penalty for breaking the object up, because each object requires an 8- or 12-byte overhead.

Solution: Take variables that only make sense together and put them in their own object. Move code that only deals with those variables into methods in the new object.

Example: The classic example of this pattern is dimensioned numbers. Because Smalltalk doesn't have a built-in framework for dimensioned numbers, programmers often simulate computing with dimensions by storing a value and a dimension together:

```
Class: Page
    variables: lines widthNumber widthUnits heightNumber
heightUnits
```

Code has to take the different possibilities for units into account:

```
area
    | widthInches heightInches |
    widthInches := widthNumber *
        (widthUnits = #mm ifTrue: [25.4] ifFalse: [1]).
    heightInches := heightNumber *
        (heightNumber == #mm ifTrue: [25.4] ifFalse: [1]).
    ^widthInches * heightInches
```

The number and units for width don't make sense without one another. Take away one variable and the other no longer is useful. The same is true for height. Both are candidates for objects from variables. First we have to create a Length object to hold both the measure and units:

```
Class: Length
    variables: magnitude units
```

Now the Page can be simplified

```
Class: Page
    variables: lines width height
```

and the area method can be simplified, too

```
area
    ^(width * height) inches
```

I'll leave the implementation of Length arithmetic as an exercise for the reader and maybe as the subject of a future column.

Once you have Length, you will find many places to use it. The resulting code will be much cleaner, easier to read, and more flexible. If you have to add cubits as a measure, you won't have to visit a hundred methods, you'll just have to fix Length. Following up on object from states, I suppose this is another way to avoid the need for case statements. Rather than build the cases into many different methods, you build it into one object and hide the *caseness* of it.

How can you know when and how to simplify an object that seems to have too many variables? You should obviously avoid the extremes: no object with fewer than two variables will work because you'd never have enough information in one place to write a readable method. All the variables in the world in one object would result in an entirely unreadable, unreusable mess. How can you walk the delicate line between breaking objects up too much and too little?

One telling sign that this pattern is appropriate is when you have two variables in an object with the same prefix and different suffixes. Thus, if you see headCircumference and headWeight as variables, they likely could be factored into their own object, reducing the original object's variable count by one.

Now for the second pattern *du jour*, "Objects from Methods." This isn't a pattern I have. (This is a usage that has spread quickly in the pattern community. You'll present a pattern and someone will say, "I have that pattern," meaning they use it, even if they haven't ever articulated it before.) Several people I respect have reported excellent results with it, so I'll do my best to make the case for it. Perhaps there is something else in my programming style that causes me to find these objects another way, or maybe I just never find them. I haven't really thought much about it. Anyway, here is the pattern.

Pattern: Objects from Methods

Problem: Sometimes you write a method that is too long to read well. Reduction with the usual techniques (e.g., *compose* methods), doesn't seem to make it read any better. How can you simplify methods that resist easy reduction?

Constraints: Creating a new object is one of the weightiest conceptual decisions you can make when programming with objects. You should never make the decision to create one lightly. If the object in question has no obvious counterpart in the problem domain, you should be even more careful. The increased load on downstream programmers is one reason to create as few kinds of objects as possible. The tendency of objects to leak into the user's consciousness is another.

Objects are great for structuring information, particularly information that has a behavioral or computational component. They are good for representing not just the user's view of a program, but the programmer's view as well. When you have tried simpler methods of writing a computation and failed to produce a result that effectively communicates your intent as a programmer, you are justified in creating new objects to simplify your computation.

Methods that are candidates for this treatment have several features in common. First, they are long. Two, three, and four line methods composed out of other provocatively named methods generally communicate well.

Second, they are not easily shortened by splitting them into smaller methods. This may be because the parts of the method don't make sense when separated, or it may be because you have to pass so many parameters to the submethods that you have trouble naming them all meaningfully. The submethods may also need to return two or more values. Finally, such methods often have many temporary variables (resulting in the many parameters to the submethods).

Solution: Create an object encompassing some of the temporary variables from the complex methods that manipulate those variables into the new object. In the original method, create one of the new objects and invoke it.

Example: As I said in the preamble, I don't have a good example of this pattern. I have used object languages that didn't have points, however, and I can imagine discovering them using this pattern. If you have a method that displays a sequence of pictures:

```
display
| x y |
  x := y := 0.
  10 timesRepeat:
    [picture displayAtX: x y: y.
    x := x + 2.
    y := y + 2]
```

Using objects from methods, we notice that x and y are used together. We create a point object with x and y variables. We can then simplify the above method to the following:

```
display
  | p |
  p := Point x: 0 y: 0.
  10 timesRepeat:
    [picture displayAt: p.
    p := p + 2]
```

I don't find this example compelling, but if you had an algorithm that used a half dozen points, you could easily get lost in the thisX, thisY, thatX, thatY's. The transformation would make much more difference.

Ward Cunningham told me a story of using this pattern on a piece of financial software. There was one method that was long and ugly, but it was important because it computed the value of a bond at a given moment. As soon as they turned the method into its own object, the computation came into focus. These advanced objects became the centerpiece of their caching strategy.

In my next column, I will end my series on the origin of objects by examining two common patterns for finding objects: "Objects from the User's World" and "Objects from the Interface."

27

BIRDS, BEES, AND BROWSERS—
OBVIOUS SOURCES OF OBJECTS

Smalltalk Report, JUNE, 1994

I was kind of running out of gas for the column by this time. "Objects from the Interface" is a five-paragraph description of a topic that really deserves a book, namely how to factor user interface code. However, I really wanted to present "Objects from the User's World," and I had to pair it with something to make it long enough.

I always worry when I'm writing if what I'm doing will be long enough. Long after it was clear that the patterns book was way, way too big, I was worried if I could produce enough pages. I think this comes from early writing experiences where I had minimum word counts. I got an "F" on a paper in fourth grade for submitting a 50-word paper, 43 words of which were "very." That should have told me something about me and about the schooling system I was experiencing.

THIS IS THE FOURTH and final installment in my series on where objects come from. I deliberately started with the unusual and difficult ways of finding objects. There are lots of books that will tell you how easy it is to find objects. Just underline the nouns! The fatuous phrase that keeps popping up is, "…there for the picking." Or maybe it's "plucking." In any case, none of the objects you'll find with "Objects from States," "Objects from Variables," "Objects from Collections," or "Objects from Methods" is there for the picking. They are, rather, deep, powerful objects that will change the way you see and structure your systems.

That's not to say that program-derived objects are the only important objects. There are a couple of kinds of objects that are necessary for a well-structured application. They just aren't sufficient to take full advantage of all the benefits objects can offer. Here are two patterns that capture the way I think about obvious objects: "Objects from the User's World" and "Objects from the Interface."

Pattern: Objects from the User's World

Problem: What are the best objects to start a design with?

Constraints: The way the user sees the world should have a profound impact on the way the system presents information. Sometimes a computer program can be a user's bridge to a deeper understanding of a domain. However, having a software engineer second guess the user is a chancy proposition at best.

Some people say, "I can structure the internals of my system any way I want to. What I present to the user is just a function of the user interface." In my experience, this is simply not so. The structure of the internals of the system will find its way into the thoughts and vocabulary of the user in the most insidious way. Even if it is communicated only in what you tell the user is easy and what is difficult to implement, the user will build a mental model of what is inside the system.

Unfortunately, the way the user thinks about the world isn't necessarily the best way to model the world computationally. In spite of the difficulties, though, it is more important to present the best possible interface to the user than to make the system simpler to implement. Therefore...

Solution: Begin the system with objects from the user's world. Plan to decouple these objects from the way you format them on the screen, leaving only the computational model.

Comment: This is a pattern Ward Cunningham and I named years ago when we first began exploring patterns. Looking at it again was interesting. I was reminded why having the user's objects at the center is so important. So many effects flow subtly from the object model to the user. I always know a project is in trouble if I come in and the Parsers and Process Schedulers are in the middle of the table.

Pattern: Objects from the Interface

Problem: How can you best represent a modern interface with objects?

Constraints: A natural tendency is to want to make big user interface objects—an entire table, a row of buttons, etc. This may be a legacy from procedural programming, wherein separating functionality into pieces is difficult. The problem with this approach is that the result is inflexible. If you want to add another button to the row or change the way the table behaves, you may have to touch many parts of the code.

A better approach is to make many smaller-grained user interface objects. The more you can compose your user interface out of small objects, the more flexibility you have, and flexibility is at a premium in user interface design and implementation. The user interface is the part of the system that will remain unstable longest, long after the underlying model has shaken out.

Solution: Find objects in the user interface. As much as possible, make each identifiable thing in the interface into an object and build larger entities by composing them together. The lowest-level user-interface objects become like the tokens in a programming language.

Comments: I sort of like the way "Objects from the User's World" turned out, but I think "Objects from the Interface" isn't very good. Actually, the design of objects to support user interface is the result of a whole system of patterns. I think I succumbed to "big patternitis," the disease in which you want to look comprehensive and you end up saying something so vague as to be unusable. I'll leave that pattern there, though, as an example of how not to do it.

This concludes a four-part series on where objects come from. Looking back, I can see I have wandered pretty far afield from the hard, practical information I wanted to present in this column. I'm not sure what I'll do next, but I think I may even give patterns a rest for a while. Maybe something about what goes on under the hood in VisualWorks and V. Maybe some virtual machine secrets. What do you think? Let me know at 70761.1216@compuserve.com.

28

USING PATTERNS: DESIGN

Smalltalk Report, JULY–AUGUST, 1994

Just when I write something that is too short, I write some that is too long. I was really in the groove of writing columns by this time, and I'd wait until the last minute. Sometimes, as in the previous column, this left me a little short. Sometimes as in this column, I ended up starting something I couldn't finish.

This column points to one of my weaknesses as a writer—I don't turn to pictures nearly soon enough. The material covered here would make much more sense with a few well-chosen pictures. If you get bogged down, try drawing the pictures yourself. That's what I do, even if I don't often publish them.

I KIND OF RAN out of steam towards the end of that last series on creating new objects. I think the message that many of the most important objects are not the ones you find by underlining nouns in problem statements is still valid. The objects that emerge (if you're watching for them) late in the game, during what is typically thought of as maintenance, can profoundly affect how you as a programmer view the system. By the time I got to the fourth part, though, I was tired of the topic. Those last couple of patterns still deserve some reexamination in the future.

This month I'm making a new start, and once again the topic is too large for a single column. The problem is how patterns can be used. I have presented probably a dozen patterns over the past year, but I haven't said anything about how they are used. Using patterns is a topic of current interest to me, because I've started teaching a three-day course on how to write and use patterns, and my students are asking me how to apply all these great patterns they are writing.

I divide the use of patterns into three categories: explaining designs, designing, and documenting for reuse. This series will address all three uses of patterns and introduce several new patterns in the process.

EXPLAINING

Even if you don't use patterns explicitly in design, they are a great way to explain the architecture of a system. Look for a paper Ralph Johnson and I wrote in the coming ECOOP'94 proceedings for an example which uses patterns to describe the HotDraw drawing editor framework (the paper is also available via ftp from st.cs.uiuc.edu).

DESIGNING

Nothing says you have to wait to use patterns until the design is finished. Considering patterns by name during design can result in clearer, more consistent, and more productive designs. If you're working in a team, patterns can become the basis of much more efficient communications between team members. I find that even when I design alone, patterns keep me from taking shortcuts that cost me time down the road.

REUSE

The patterns used for explaining and designing are very general purpose software engineering patterns. They are intended for an audience of professional programmers who are used to making judgments based on experience and taste. There is another programming audience, however, one that is potentially much larger than just hackers. This audience are those who program by necessity, not by choice. They are the biologists, chemists, and business people of the world who can't find a program that does what they want, but they don't want to learn any more about programming than they must to get their job done. Patterns are a great way of communicating how to reuse a framework (as opposed to merely telling them how it works).

I'll deal with all three uses of patterns in the months ahead. I'll start with design—how you can use patterns to help you design better, faster, and with greater confidence.

DESIGNING WITH PATTERNS

The stereotyped Smalltalk programmers design as they program. There's never a "paper" design; instead the design of the program is reflected in the code and changed as a result of manipulations in the browser. Ignore for a moment that this picture doesn't reflect any of the diversity that currently exists in the Smalltalk world, which includes many programmers following explicit, nonprogramming-environment-based methods. What can patterns offer the lone wolf, the "design-as-you-go" programmer?

One great thing about patterns is they provide you with easy-to-digest descriptions of design techniques. Even if you have been using Smalltalk for years, there are likely tricks that other designers know that you don't. Reading and writing patterns gives you a way to communicate your design knowledge with others and have them fill you in on techniques you don't know.

One of the things I like about patterns is that they force me to be consistent in my designs. After I formulate a pattern I can often go back to my existing programs and see how they would have been better had I consistently used the pattern. An example is using "each" for the parameter to a block used for iteration. I used to get creative with the parameter names, trying to call them something meaningful. By just using "each" I can program faster, because I don't stop to choose a name; I can read the code better, because I know what to expect; and I am more likely to put complex expressions in the block into their own method, because "each" doesn't work well if you are programming a block with 20 lines in it.

Finally, no one ever really just codes for themselves, for the moment. Someone will read your code, even if it is just you six months later. The consistency and explicitness of patterns, if their use is documented, become important sign posts on the road to understanding what you were getting at when you wrote the code in the first place.

Now let's move into an example of using patterns for design. I'll introduce a specification that we need to design to, then alternately tell you about new patterns and show how they advance the design. In real design, you'll be working mostly with patterns you already have in front of you. The purpose of the discussion isn't to show you a real design session, but rather to convince you that patterns could be valuable during design, and coincidentally introduce some new patterns.

The Problem: TV with Remote Control

Here's the example I'll use for the rest of the articles on design with patterns. The problem is to design the software to run a television, including a remote control. For now we'll support two simple stories (some people call them "use cases"): when someone presses a channel button the channel (one of ten) changes, and when the television notices a commercial starting it flashes a light on the mute button of the remote control.

We are given several pieces of software to begin with:

- A keyboard library that returns the last key pressed (0–9 for the 10 channels, -1 for no new key press, and 10 for mute)

- An infrared communication library that sends and receives bytes,

- A tuner library that changes channels

- An object that watches a video stream and broadcasts messages whenever it notices the start of a commercial

I'm assuming that both the television and the remote control have processors capable of executing objects, and that they are linked with a communication channel based on infrared.

Big Objects—Objects from the User's World

We'll implement the "change a channel in response to a keypress" story first. The first problem to be solved is finding the large-scale objects in the system. The last issue contained a pattern, "Objects from the User's World," which addressed this problem. The problem statement of that pattern was, "What are the best objects to start a design with?" Sounds like the right pattern to me.

The solution of "Objects from the User's World" is to begin the system with objects that the user thinks about. Two objects spring to my mind that fit this criteria. RemoteControl has the responsibility for translating user input into commands (that is, given some user input, the RemoteControl will decide what messages to send to the rest of the system). Television has responsibility for changing channels. I'm imagining protocol in Smalltalk like channel: anInteger.

RemoteControl * translate user input into commands
Television * change channels

If I want to execute the story, first the RemoteControl has to take the input of a channel button being pressed, then translate it into a message to the Television to change the channel.

KEYBOARD—"OBJECTIFIED LIBRARY" AND "EVENT"

This scenario is plausible as far as it goes, but it isn't nearly detailed enough to begin programming. The next problem we solve is getting the keystrokes into the RemoteControl to begin the computation. The first part of this problem is reading the keystrokes in the first place. Recall that we have a library that lets us read the keystrokes. We need to surface those functions in object terms. Here's the pattern we will use:

Pattern: Objectified Library

How can you integrate a function library with a system built from objects?

All modern object languages provide facilities for calling functions written using older languages. The design problem is how to integrate the functions conceptually with the rest of the system. The simplest solution is to call the functions wherever you need to in your code. This has the advantage of simplicity, because you don't have to introduce any new objects.

Just calling the functions from wherever introduces problems of its own. First, external libraries change at a rate that isn't synchronized with changes to your objects. New releases of a library may come at a time when you don't want to change much of your system. By scattering the calls to the library all over your system, you make yourself vulnerable to having to touch many parts of your system.

Second, because the world is moving more and more towards objects, any function library is likely to be replaced by objects. Scattering calls to the library means that you will have to revisit much of your design should that happen.

Finally, scattered calls to the function library don't communicate well. In particular, you cannot easily answer the common question, "How is the library being used?" Answering this question is important both for making the kind of design updates required above, and to use the library with other objects.

Therefore: Create an object to represent the library. Give it external protocol using Smalltalk naming conventions and accepting and returning standard objects.

Using **"Objectified Library,"** we create a Keyboard object whose responsibility in the design is to read keystrokes, and which accomplishes it by calling the keyboard library.

```
Keyboard * read keystrokes
```

Running the story again, we have the RemoteControl asking the Keyboard for the next keystroke, then translating that into a message to the Television to change the channel.

Notice that the solution to **"Objectified Library"** tells us to "accept and return standard objects." What object should the Keyboard return? Here is a pattern that you are probably familiar with that answers this question:

Pattern: Event

How do you represent interesting events from the outside world?

The simplest solution to representing outside events is to cause a message to be sent to the object which handles the event, passing as parameters what happened. Unfortunately, the parameters are seldom a simple, atomic object. Also, the system is often interested in other, related information from other sensors such as the clock (i.e., a timestamp). Passing all of the information as separate parameters leads to long, unwieldy message names and introduces the risk that some parameters will get out of sync with others.

Simplicity of naming is not the only important issue working against simply sending a message. Many times the parameters to be included with an event are time valued and must be collected immediately to be correct. The collection of the parameters doesn't involve complex processing, so it can easily be done in a lightweight but higher-priority process than the process in which the reaction to the event is determined. Splitting the collection of the parameters from their processing introduces the need to create a protocol between the tasks. Simple protocols provide flexibility, and a single object as the protocol is simplest of all.

Bundling the parameters together into an object introduces its own costs. First, there is the additional complexity in the system of having an additional class. Second, there will be a runtime cost associated with creating the object. However, these costs are easily dealt with later, while the difficulties associated with not having the parameters together will adversely affect the whole design.

> ***Therefore:*** Create an **Event** object. Give it protocol to return information describing what happened outside the system to create the event and report what else interesting was happening at the time.

Our **Event** object will carry along what key was pressed to create the **Event**. The Event object will be a good place to hide the interpretation of the keystroke (i.e., the difference between 0–9 and 10). We'll be able to add testing protocol like isChannel, which will insulate the rest of the system from the details of the keyboard.

We have to change the responsibility of **Keyboard** a little to reflect that the **Keyboard** is responsible for creating the events:

Keyboard * Create events from keystrokes

Running the story, we now have the **RemoteControl** asking the **Keyboard** for an **Event**, then using the **Event** to send a "change channel" message to the **Television**.

CONCLUSION

This article has used one pattern from the previous issue, "Objects from the User's World," and two new ones, "Objectified Library" and "Event," to create the first four objects in our system: RemoteControl, Television, Keyboard, and Event.

That's all I have space for in this issue. Next time we'll decide how the objects are going to be distributed between the two processors, including a nifty pattern I learned while consulting on a telecom project called Half Objects. We'll also get into more of the details of how "Events" get turned into commands.

If you have good examples of applications of any of the patterns I present, or if you have alternative patterns that you think are better, please let me know. Patterns are just getting started and there are no right answers, only a bunch of committed people searching.

29

PATTERNS GENERATE ARCHITECTURES

WITH RALPH JOHNSON
ECOOP '94—Object-Oriented Programming, AUGUST, 1994

T*his was a very important article for me. I had been writing solo for some time. I needed to collaborate more, especially since I had been independent for almost a year and I was getting lonely for technical collaboration.*

Bruce Anderson organized this fantastic workshop for IBM at its educational site in Thornwood, New York. Ralph Johnson was another one of the teachers. Late one night, I grabbed him and said, "I bet we can describe HotDraw using patterns." He didn't know quite what I meant, but he has learned to humor me (probably because he's big enough to just bop me if I get out hand). There in a spartan little room in IBM's training facility in upstate New York, we tried to recreate HotDraw using only patterns—this pattern tells us to create this object, then this pattern splits it in two, then...

The result was one of those crackling moments when you know you have something. Early the next morning, I described HotDraw to Desmond D'Souza, first using CRC cards the way I always had, then using the patterns. He confirmed that the pattern description communicated the "why" of the design much more clearly.

Ralph and I were confident enough of our findings that we wrote up the paper with a sweeping conclusion—any object architecture can be derived by applying a set of patterns.

Richard Helm (another of the Design Pattern authors) and I applied this technique in Sydney last year. While a guy stood and chalk-talked us through his system, we didn't say a word; we just looked at each other. At the end, we knew we both had the same pattern-ized description of the system. I'm not so confident that the telepathy part of the technique scales, however, so I haven't written it up for a scholarly journal.

Another important aspect of this paper was that it returned, however briefly,

257

to the world of academia. I came out of school and into a research lab think-
ing of myself as a scholar, made some contributions, then dropped out for five
years. Publishing in ECOOP, even though I'm sure I couldn't have done
without Ralph's help, reminded me of where I started. I'm not sure if I'll pub-
lish scholarly papers again, but it's nice to know I can if I have to.

Abstract

We need ways to describe designs that communicate the reasons for our design decisions, not just the results. Design patterns have been proposed as
ways of communicating design information. This paper shows that patterns
can be used to derive an architecture from its problem statement. The resulting description makes it easier to understand the purpose of the various
architectural features.

Introduction

Design is hard. One way to avoid the act of design is to reuse existing designs. But reusing designs requires reaming them, or at least some parts of
them, and communicating complex designs is hard, too. One reason for this
is that existing design notations focus on communicating the "what" of designs, but almost completely ignore the "why." However, the "why" of a design is crucial for customizing it to a particular problem. We need ways of
describing designs that communicate the reasons for our design decisions,
not just the results.

One approach to improving design, currently receiving interest primarily
outside the object community, is the idea of "architecture" [Garlan93]. An architecture is the way the parts work together to make the whole. The way architectures are notated, applied, and discovered are all topics of active research.

A closely related idea inside the object community is that of "framework"
[Deutsch89] [Johnson88]. A framework is the reusable design of a system or
a part of a system expressed as a set of abstract classes and the way instances
of (subclasses of) those classes collaborate. Frameworks are a particular way
of representing architectures, so there are architectures that can't be expressed

as frameworks. Nevertheless, the two ideas overlap. Both are attempts to reuse design, and examples of one are sometimes used as examples of the other.

Another approach to design in the object community is "patterns." There were OOPSLA workshops in 1991 and 1992 on "an architecture handbook" [Anderson93] and ones in 1992 and 1993 on "patterns"[Coad93], with an overlap between the two groups, which shows a link between architectures and patterns. Much of the work on patterns focuses on patterns of relationships between objects as the building-blocks of larger architectures [Coad92] [Gamma93].

Our original interest in patterns [Kerth88] was sparked by the work of an architect Christopher Alexander, whose patterns encode knowledge of the design and construction of communities and buildings [Alexander77] [Alexander79]. His use of the word "pattern" takes on more meaning than the usual dictionary definition. Alexander's patterns are both a description of a recurring pattern of architectural elements and a rule for how and when ta create that pattern. They are the recurring decisions made by experts, written so that those less skilled can use them. They describe more of the "why" of design than a simple description of a set of relationships between objects.

We call patterns like Alexander's that describe when a pattern should be applied "generative patterns." Generative patterns share the many advantages of non generative patterns; they provide a language for designers that makes it easier to plan, talk about, and document designs. They have the added advantage of being easier for non-experts to use and providing a rationale for a design after the fact. This paper focuses on the last advantage.

This paper shows that patterns can be used to derive architectures, much as a mathematical theorem can be proved from a set of axioms. When patterns are used in this way, they illuminate and motivate architectures. Deriving an architecture from patterns records the design decisions that were made, and why they were made that way. This makes it easier to modify the architecture if circumstances change.

PATTERNS

Two kinds of patterns are needed to derive HotDraw: object-oriented design patterns and graphics patterns. This is probably typical of most architectures; some patterns will be generic and some will be specific to the application domain.

Each pattern follows this format:

- *Preconditions* The patterns that must be satisfied before this one is valid. The sequence in which patterns are considered is one of the most important skills possessed by experts.

- *Problem* A summary of the problem addressed by the pattern. The problem statement is used by the reader to decide if the pattern is applicable.

- *Constraints* The constraints describe the conflicting (sometimes mutually exclusive) forces acting on any solution to the problem. Typical examples are tradeoffs between execution time and execution space, or development time and program complexity. Clearly stating priorities between constraints makes patterns easy to debate.

- *Solution* A two or three sentence summary of the solution to the problem. The solution is often accompanied by a diagram illustrating the activity required to transform a system from one that doesn't satisfy the pattern to one that does.

The graphics patterns are Model-View-Controller, Collect Damage, and Update at User Speed. All of the other patterns except Editor are in the Design Pattern Catalog [Gamma94].

The versions of the patterns in this paper differ from the versions in the Catalog in two ways. The most obvious difference is that the versions in this paper are much shorter, but that is out of necessity, not preference. A fully expressed pattern contains at least two or three pages of discussion of constraints and an illustration or example showing how it works. Another difference is that the versions in this paper are more generative that the versions in the Catalog. In other words, we emphasize the conditions under which the pattern applies, the transformation each causes in the design as it comes into existence. The patterns in the Catalog do not entirely ignore when they are applicable, since the intent is similar to the problem in our patterns. However, they often have a list of possible causes, and in general focus more on the solution and its variants than on when to use the solution. Although we have only rewritten a few of the patterns in the Catalog to be more generative, we have no reason to believe that all of them couldn't be.

An example of a generative pattern for object-oriented software is "Objects for States," which says that you can transform an object which changes behavior depending on state into two objects, the first of which has the invariant parts of the original object, and a family of objects which it can refer to, one for each state in the original object.

HotDraw

The architecture that is derived is that of HotDraw, a framework for structured graphics editors. A previous paper presented a set of patterns for using HotDraw [Johnson92]. In contrast, this paper describes the patterns that create HotDraw. Patterns can be used at many levels, and what is derived at one level can be considered a basic pattern at another level.

HotDraw provides a reusable architecture for direct-manipulation, graphics-editor-like applications that is implemented in Smalltalk-80. (Versions have been implemented for other environments, since the only pattern that depends on the environment is the one that chooses a user-interface framework, and since there is a lot of commonality among user-interface frameworks, all the versions are similar.) It supports:

- Many kinds of figures in the drawing

- A programmable palette of tools

- Different handles for different figures

- Smooth animation

This paper describes HotDraw from the top down, much like the proof of a theorem. It gives reasons for the design decisions in HotDraw, which, as Parnas says, are not always the original reasons for these design decisions [Parnas86]. Thus, the derivation of HotDraw is a rationalization of HotDraw, and is only partly related to the history of its design.

The purpose of this derivation, however, is not to show people how HotDraw was developed, but to let them understand it. Although people usually start to use a framework by modifying examples and recombining components in different ways, experts need to have a deeper understanding of the framework. We believe that the derivation reflects the understanding that an expert has.

DERIVING HOT DRAW

Describing an architecture with patterns is like the process of cell division and specialization that drives growth in biological organisms. The design starts as a fuzzy cloud representing the system to be realized. As patterns are applied to the cloud, parts of it come into focus. When no more patterns are applicable, the design is finished.

Each step of the following discussion will briefly describe what problem needs to be solved, the pattern that is used to solve it, and the effect the pattern has on the design.

USER INTERFACE

The first problem to solve is getting the drawing on the screen so it can be displayed and manipulated. The following pattern tells us that we need to divide the responsibilities between three objects.

MODEL-VIEW-CONTROLLER [KRASNER88]

Preconditions. A system is going to have a graphical user-interface.

Problem. Graphical user-interfaces can be hard to build. Users demand programs that are easy to use, easy to learn, and powerful, and a good user interface is necessary to achieve these goals. How should the responsibilities of implementing a user interface be divided between objects?

Constraints. Modem graphical user interfaces have a small number of recurring visual elements. Because user-interfaces need to be consistent, we depend on a few interaction techniques, such as menus, buttons, scrollbars, and lists. The effort that someone puts into reaming how to use one program, or one part of one program, should apply to other programs and other parts of the same program.

In implementing a user interface, we must strike a balance between a design that uses many objects but is difficult to learn and one that uses few objects and sacrifices flexibility. One important axis of flexibility is the information that is displayed. A second axis of flexibility, independent of display, is interpreting user gestures and mapping them into state changes. A third degree of freedom is the ability to put multiple user interfaces on the same information. Therefore:

Solution. Divide your system into three objects: a Model, View and Controller. The Model is responsible for maintaining state and surfacing the behavior necessary to support the user interface. The View is responsible for displaying an up-to-date version of the Model. The Controller is responsible for mapping user gestures to changes of state in the model.

Applying Model-View-Controller to our system we derive three objects: Drawing, to hold the drawing, Drawing View, to display it, and Drawing Controller to parse user gestures into changes to the drawing.

MANY ELEMENTS IN A DRAWING

Next we notice that Drawings need to contain many figures. This leads us to the Composite pattern.

COMPOSITE

Preconditions. A composite object is an object with many components; a folder consists of a set of documents, a book consists of a set of chapters, a company consists of a set of departments.

Problem. A naive modeling of composite objects leads to many similar classes specialized primarily by the types of their components.

Constraints. Consider a text editing system with "chapter," "section," "subsection," "paragraph," "word," "item," etc. We could have a large number of classes, each of which was really just a collection of its components. Some have titles, some always start a new page, but in general they are quite similar. On the one hand, the composite object is "obviously" different from its components. On the other hand, it is easier to reuse and understand a design that minimizes the number of classes by making its classes be polymorphic and composable in any combination. We don't want to make every "text-element" have a list of components; some will be atomic. But we would like a scheme that lets us avoid having to duplicate code and to design a lot of classes.

Therefore:

Solution. Make an abstract class that represents both the composite and its components. Then make the classes of the composite and the components be its concrete subclasses. The subclasses have to implement all the operations defined in the superclass. Some operations are implemented in every use of the Composite pattern, such as "iterate over components," which will do nothing for leaf classes, but will have a more complicated implementation for true composite classes. But most operations are application specific.

Applying Composite to Drawing creates two new classes: Figure, for the generic thing in a drawing, and PrimitiveFigure for figures that contain no sub-parts. Drawing takes the role of the branching part of the composite.

Notice that using Composite here implies that we can nest Drawings within Drawings.

INTERPRETING INPUT

Which tool is selected in the palette changes how input is parsed. Applying Objects for States to DrawingController solves this problem.

OBJECTS FOR STATES

Preconditions. An object whose behavior depends on its state.

Problem. It is common for an object whose behavior depends on its state to explicitly check the value of its variables using if or case statements. Although this technique can work well when there are only few states, it produces programs that are hard to understand and extend. It also introduces a multiple update problem in maintenance, where all cases must be updated in parallel to preserve correct behavior.

Constraints. On the one hand, encoding dependence on state by if statements makes a design compact; there are fewer objects to understand and fewer procedures to track down. On the other hand, it can be hard to tell which states are important, and hard to tell when a state transition occurs, since an object's states arc determined by the set of values some of its variables can take on, and a state transition is an assignment statement. Moreover, adding a new state might require changing all of the object's methods. If an object has only two or three states, and it is unlikely to need a new state, then it is probably better to encode state dependency directly in methods. Otherwise, states should be represented as objects.

Therefore:

Solution. Implement an object whose behavior depends on its state and that has more than a couple of states, or when the set of possible states is likely to change in the future, by representing the states by objects and having the object act as a "multiplexor," delegating messages to its current state.

A design that uses "encode state in object" can be transformed into one that uses "represent states as objects" by the following 5 steps:

1. Enumerate the possible states of the object.

2. Make a class for each state.

3. Give object an instance variable that contains its current state.

4. If a method of the object depends on its state, move it to the state-classes, and replace it with a method that simply delegates the operation to the current state. Add the object as an argument to the message that it delegates so that the state-classes can access its instance variables.

5. Move a method to the state-classes by copying it to every class, changing every instance variable access to use the original object (which has been passed as an argument to the message), and deleting all the parts of the method that are for other states.

The result of this transformation is that there will be a new class for each state of the original object, and much of the code in the class of the original object will have been moved to the classes of the states. You can add a new state by adding a new class, but the code for the object is now spread among several classes.

You can often use Factor a Superclass (not described here) to reduce the size of the code after applying Objects for States.

Each state object will be a Tool. The DrawingController will have a new attribute to hold the current tool.

CREATE THE OBJECT TO HELP DRAWINGCONTROLLER

Where are Tools created? DrawingController's responsibility is only to manage which Tool is current and delegate input parsing to the currentTool. However, different kinds of drawings will need different sets of Tools.

EDITOR

Preconditions. You have a collection of dissimilar objects, probably after applying Composite.

Problem. Often an object in a collection will have a specialized operation that you want to invoke, but most objects in the collection will not support that operation. Should we have an abstract superclass that supports all operations and let specialized operations produce errors for most subclasses? Should we provide a way for clients to determine whether an object has a particular operation?

For example, consider a collection of vehicles. They will all support "turn left" and "turn right" operations, but only a few (e.g. submarines, helicopters) will have "go up" and "go down" operations. Should we have the superclass Vehicle support al operations and let "go up" and "go down" produce errors for most subclasses? Should we provide a way for clients to determine whether a vehicle is a submarine and hence whether it supports "go up"?

Constraints. Systems are hard to understand if they have many classes, each with a specialized interface. A good design should minimize the number of different interfaces that you have to learn. On the other hand, the problem we are working on often requires that different objects support different operations, so we are forced to have different interfaces. We can either try to design a very general interface and force-fit many classes to it, try to hide some of the interfaces (reducing the apparent complexity, if not the actual complexity), or just live with a complicated system.

If each class has one client that uses its specialized interface, then the Editor pattern can be used to give all of them the same interface.

Solution. Hide the specialized interfaces by making an object (an editor) that represents the client of the object, and making each object responsible for producing its editor. Instead of using a specialized interface directly, you ask the object for its editor and then invoke the editor. The editor will be the only object that knows the private interface of the specialized object. The name "Editor" comes from the use of this pattern in a hypermedia system, where following a link to an object will always invoke an editor for that object.

It is important that there is a standard interface to the editor. Often the editor is a user interface object, and it will have a standard user interface object interface.

Example: Given a set of vehicles, where some can go up and down, but others can only go right or left, give each vehicle a "controls" operation that returns a set of controls, such as steering wheels, knobs, and dials. The user then has operations like "turn right" and "push" that operate on these controls, which will in turn control the direction of the vehicle. The only controls for a vehicle like a car will be for fuming left and right and for controlling velocity, but a submarine will also have controls for going up and down.

We have an object (DrawingController) that manipulates an object (Drawing) through objects with standard protocol (Tools). This is half the Editor pattern. We can finish the pattern by giving Drawing the responsibility for resuming a standard set of Tools.

Update the display when a Figure changes appearance

How can we be sure that changes to the drawing are reflected on the screen?

Observer

Preconditions. Two objects must be synchronized. Changes in one object must be reflected in the other.

Problem. If changing one object requires changing another then there is a constraint between them. But we don't want every client to have to know about this constraint. Moreover, we aren't even sure how many objects need to be changed when the first object is changed. Different instances of the same class might have different numbers of dependents, or the dependents might change over time.

Constraints. To make objects as reusable as possible, we do not want to hard-code constraints into them. Objects should be responsible only for their own state, not for the state of other objects. On the other hand, if there is a constraint between the states of two objects then that constraint must be recorded somewhere. In some way changes to the first object must be translated into changes to the second.

Therefore:

Solution. Have an object involved in a constraint keep a list of dependents. Each time it changes, it notifies all its dependents. When an object is notified that something it depends on has changed, it takes appropriate action. In general, an object can have many dependents, and a change to the object will require only some of its dependents to change. But each dependent will be able to determine whether the change to the object was significant and can ignore those that are not.

Applying Observer to Figure, we add each Figure's enclosing Drawing as a dependent, and the DrawingView as a dependent of the top-most Drawing.

Notice that we could have made the relationship between a Figure and its Drawing one-to-one (calling the Drawing the Figure's parent, for instance). Having done this, though, if we ever wanted to keep the Figure and some other object synchronized, we would have to duplicate code to update both the parent and another object.

Only redisplay changed part of the drawing

If several parts of the drawing change simultaneously (from the user's perspective), then we would like those parts of the drawing to update as a unit.

Collect Damage

Preconditions. A program has an internal representation of an picture. It periodical! changes part of the picture, and then must update the display to correspond to the internal representation.

Problem. To be efficient, a program should display as little of the picture as possible' How do you display just the part of the picture that changed?

Constraints. Each time you change part of the picture, you could display the part that; changed. This would be the simplest solution. However, there is a large constant overhead for redisplaying, as potentially the entire representation of the picture must be traversed. For efficiency, you would like to only redisplay once, even if you sever. parts of the picture changed.

Another issue is that the user expects a single action (for example, changing the color c a certain kind of Figure) to result in a single redisplay. Updating a little at a tame give the impression that the system is slow.

Therefore:

Solution. Have the graphics system keep track of the part of the image that has changed. Associate a damaged region with the image. Every time a part of the image changes, add its area to the damaged region. Adding, deleting, or changing the color of a part of the image will add its area to the damaged region. Moving a part of the image will add both its old and new areas to the damaged region. This can usually be done automatically by the graphics-system, assuming that the graphical elements that make up the image are considered part of the graphics system, and not the application program.

Note that we haven't said how redisplay is initiated, just that it will take place only in the damaged region.

Applying Collect Damage to DrawingView adds an attribute damagedRegion, and applying it to Figure causes it to broadcast a message before and after all appearance changes.

In a language like Smalltalk with anonymous functions, you can embed the "damaging" idiom in a method "damageAround: aBlock."

INITIATE THE REDISPLAY

Now that we are collecting damaged regions, we need some way to make sure they get redisplayed.

UPDATE AT USER SPEED

Preconditions. You are writing a program that is animation a visual display in real-dine, probably in response to user input. You are Collecting Damage.

Problem. When should you update the display?

Constraints. If you update the display too often, your application will spend all its time performing low-level graphics operations, and it may not be able to keep up with the animation. If you don't update the display often enough, the animation will be jerky.

A possible solution to this problem is to spawn an independent thread of control to update the display. By varying the rate at which it cycles, you can tradeoff the amount of system resources required to keep the display consistent and the smoothness of updates. However, this solution requires introducing and maintaining a monitor on the top-most Drawing, to avoid redisplaying it while it is in an inconsistent state.

Solution. Update the drawing at the same speed that the user makes gestures. This implies that you redisplay the drawing once for each user event, which implies that there should be a loop in the program that reads an event, handles the event, and then updates the drawing (by repairing damage). If events come in faster than your program can handle them then you should not redisplay between them.

Add responsibility to DrawingController to tell the DrawingView to redisplay the damaged region after routing each event to the current Tool.

This pattern is different than the convention of many editors, which drag outlines around (which as a Pattern might be called Intermediate Changes to Outlines). It gives a more immediate feel to the application.

CREATE HANDLES

The next problem to solve is where to create handles. Different Figures will require different handles, but the enclosing Drawing should be insulated from these differences.

271

The Editor pattern solves this problem. Applying Editor to Figure creates a Handle object. Each figure must be responsible for resuming a set of Handles that modify it.

Since it must be displayable in the Drawing, Handle can be simply implemented by making it a subclass of figure.

Manage handles

Once we have Handles, we need to manage them. They need to be managed together, since selecting a different Figure causes all of the previous Handles to be discarded. They exist in a limbo between the Drawing and the DrawingView. We cannot manage them in the Drawing, since Drawings nest and we would not know at which level to store them. On the other hand, the DrawingView already is busy collecting damage and displaying the Drawing. We need somewhere new to put the Handles.

Wrapper

Preconditions. We have a set of classes that can be composed in different ways to make an application. We probably use Composite and Observer so that we can make many kinds of systems out of a fairly static set of parts.

Problem. We want to add a responsibility to an object, but we don't want to have make a lot more classes or make it more complicated.

Constraints. Adding the responsibility in a subclass would ensure that the old class was not made more complicated. However, we might want to reuse that responsibility for another object. Multiple inheritance would let us statically assign it to another object, but multiple inheritance can lead to an explosion of classes, and many languages do not support it. Moreover, multiple inheritance does not support dynamically reassigning a responsibility to another object.

Solution. One way to add a responsibility to an object is with a wrapper. A T-wrapper "wraps" an instance of T and supports the T protocol by forwarding operations to the T, handling directly only those operations that relate to the responsibility it is designed to fulfill.

Applying Wrapper to Drawing creates a new object, SelectionDrawing. SelectionDrawing has protocol to hide and show sets of handles. All other messages it passes through to its Drawing.

SelectionDrawing can be implemented simply by making it a subclass of Drawing that has two Figures. The first is a Drawing that will contain all of the Handles. The second is the Drawing to be wrapped.

CONCLUSION

The HotDraw architecture is not magic, but is the logical result of a set of design patterns. In the past, we have explained the architecture as "Drawing, Figure, Tool, and Handle." The pattern-based derivation puts each of these classes in perspective. It explains exactly why each was created and what problem it solves. Presented this way, HotDraw becomes much easier to re-implement, or to modify should circumstances so warrant. This is a completely different approach to describing the design of a framework than more formal approaches like Contracts [Helm90] The more formal results only explain what the design is, but a pattern-based derivation explains why.

We didn't choose these patterns by chance. We had been talking about patterns for a long time, but usually tried to defend an action we were taking in terms of some pattern we knew. This was the first time we had tried to explain an existing design in terms of the sequence of design decisions that led to it. It was not hard to come up with the general sequence, though it took work to make the pattern descriptions clear even though they are short, and we did not completely succeed.

When we attempted to derive HotDraw from the patterns described in the Design Pattern Catalog, we immediately realized that the Catalog had none of the graphics patterns that HotDraw would need. It turned out that it did not have the Editor pattern, either, so the derivation of HotDraw showed us that we needed to describe a new object-oriented design pattern. This is similar to the proof process in mathematics, where the presentation of a proof hides most of its history, and where advances in mathematics are often caused by break-downs in proofs. Catalogs of design patterns will mature as people try to explain designs in terms of patterns, and find patterns that are missing from the catalogs.

A pattern-based derivation of an architecture is like the presentation of a mathematical theorem. Beginning with a problem to solve, you use well-known, independent steps to incrementally refine the problem to a solution. The result is that you not only understand the final system, you understand the reasoning that led to it. This should make it easier for programmers to use and extend systems documented with pattern-based derivations.

REFERENCES

[Alexander77] Christopher Alexander, Sara Ishikawa and Murray Silverstein, with Max Jacobson, Ingrid Fiksdahl-King and Shlomo Angel. *A Pattern Language.* Oxford University Press, New York, 1977.

[Alexander79] Christopher Alexander. *The Timeless Way of Building.* Oxford University Press, New York, 1979.

[Anderson93] Bruce Anderson. Workshop Report—Towards an Architecture Handbook. OOPSLA'92: Addendum to the Proceedings, printed as *OOPSLA Messenger,* 4(2): 109–114, April 1993.

[Coad92] Peter Coad, "Object-Oriented Patterns," *Communications of the ACM,* 35(9):153-159, 1992.

[Coad93] Peter Coad and Mark Mayfield. Workshop Report—Patterns. OOPSLA'92: Addendum to the Proceedings, printed as *OOPSLA Messenger,* 4(2): 93-95, April 1993

[Deutsch89] L. Peter Deutsch. "Design Reuse and Frameworks in the Smalltalk-80 Programming System," pp. 55–71, *Software Reusability, Vol 11,* ed. Ted J. Biggerstaff and Alan J. Perlis, ACM Press, 1989.

[Gamma93] Erich Gamma, Richard Helm, Ralph Johnson, and John Vlissides, "Design patterns: Abstraction and reuse of object-oriented design." In *European Conference on Object-oriented Programming,* Kaiserlauten, German, July 1993. Published as Lecture notes in Computer Science #707, pp. 406 431, Springer-Verlag.

[Gamma94] Erich Gamma, Richard Helm, Ralph Johnson, and John Vlissides. *Design Patterns: Elements of Object-Oriented Software Architecture.* Addison-Wesley, 1994.

[Garlan93] David Garlan and Mary Shaw, "An Introduction to Software Architecture," in *Advances in Software Engineering and Knowledge Engineering* Volume I, World Scientific Publishing Company, 1993.

[Helm90] Richard Helm and Ian M. Holland and Dipayan Gangopadhyay, "Contracts: Specifying Behavioral Compositions in Object-Oriented Systems," OOPSLA '90 Proceedings, SIGPLAN Notices, 25(10), pp.169-180, Vancouver BC, October 1990.

[Johnson88] Ralph E. Johnson and Brian Foote, "Designing Reusable Classes," *Journal of Object-Oriented Programming,* 1(2):22-25, 1988.

[Johnson92] Ralph E. Johnson, "Documenting Frameworks with Patterns," OOPSLA '92 Proceedings, SIGPLAN Notices, 27(10): 63-76, Vancouver BC, October 1992.

[Kerth88] Norman Kerth, John Hogg, Lynn Stein, and Harry Porter, "Summary of Discussions from OOPSLA's-87's Methodology and OOP Workshop," OOPSLA'87: Addendum to the Proceedings, printed as *SIGPLAN Notices,* 23(5): 9–16, 1988.

[Krasner88] Glenn E. Krasner and Stephen T. Pope, "A Cookbook for Using the Model-View Controller User Interface Paradigm in Smalltalk-80," *Journal of Object-Oriented Programming.* 1(3): 26–49, 1988.

[Parnas86] David L. Parnas and P.C. Clement, "A Rational Design Process: How and Why to Fake It," *IEEE Transactions on Software Engineering,* SE-12:2 February 1986.

$$\boxed{30}$$

Simple Smalltalk Testing

Smalltalk Report, October, 1994

This was the column that generated the most interest and email for me, all of it positive. Other than that, there's not much to say, except "Get to work writing tests—yeah, you, the Smalltalk hacker."

Y OU CAN'T ARGUE with inspiration (or deadlines). I started to write the final column in the sequence about using patterns for design, but what came out was this. It describes some work I have been doing with a framework that takes the tedium out of writing tests. I'll get back to the pattern stuff in the next issue.

Smalltalk has suffered because it lacks a testing culture. This column describes a simple testing strategy and a framework to support it. The testing strategy and framework are not intended to be complete solutions, but, rather, are intended to be starting points from which industrial strength tools and procedures can be constructed.

The article is divided into four sections:

- *Philosophy.* Describes the philosophy of writing and running tests embodied by the framework. Read this section for general background.

- *Framework.* A literate program version of the testing framework. Read this for in-depth knowledge of how the framework operates.

- *Example.* An example of using the testing framework to test part of the methods in Set.

- *Cookbook.* A simple cookbook for writing your own tests.

PHILOSOPHY

The most radical philosophy espoused here is a rejection of user-interface-based tests. In my experience, tests based on user interface scripts are too brittle to be useful. Testers spend more time keeping the tests up to date and tracking down false failures and false successes than they do writing new tests.

My solution is to write the tests (and check the results) in Smalltalk. Although this approach has the disadvantage that your testers need to be able to write simple Smalltalk programs, the resulting tests are much more stable.

FAILURES AND ERRORS

The framework distinguishes between failures and errors. A failure is an anticipated problem. When you write tests, you check for expected results. If you get a different answer, that is a failure. An error is more catastrophic; it indicates an error condition that you didn't check for.

UNIT TESTING

I recommend that developers write their own unit tests, one per class. The framework supports the writing of suites of tests, which can be attached to a class. I recommend that all classes respond to the message testsuite, returning a suite containing the unit tests. I recommend that developers spend 25–50% of their time developing tests.

INTEGRATION TESTING

I recommend that an independent tester write integration tests. Where should the integration tests go? The recent movement of user-interface frameworks to better facilitate programmatic access provides one answer—drive the user interface, but do it with the tests. In VisualWorks (the dialect used in the implementation below), you can open in ApplicationModel and begin stuffing values into its ValueHolders, causing all sorts of havoc, with very little trouble.

Running Tests

One final bit of philosophy. It is tempting to set up a bunch of test data, then run a bunch of tests, then clean up. In my experience, this procedure always causes more problems that it is worth. Tests end up interacting with one another, and a failure in one test can prevent subsequent tests from running. The testing framework makes it easy to set up a common set of test data, but the data will be created and thrown away for each test. The potential performance problems with this approach shouldn't be a big deal because suites of tests can run unobserved.

Framework

The smallest unit of testing is the **TestCase**. When a **TestCase** runs, it sets up its test data, runs a test method, then discards the test data. Because many cases may want to share the same test data, **TestCase** chooses which method to run with the instance variable **selector**, and which will be performed to run the test method.

```
Class: TestCase
    super class: Object
    instance variables: selector
    class variable: FailedCheckSignal
```

TestCases are always created with a selector. The class method **selector:** ensures this.

```
TestCase class>>selector: aSymbol
    ^self new setSelector: aSymbol
TestCase>>setSelector: aSymbol
    selector := aSymbol
```

The simplest way to run a **TestCase** is just to send it the message run. run invokes the setup code, performs the selector, then runs the tear-down code.

Notice that the tear-down code is run regardless of whether there is an error in performing the test.

```
TestCase>>run
    self setUp.
    [self performTest]
        valueNowOrOnUnwindDo: [self tearDown]!
```

Subclasses of TestCase are expected to create and destroy test fixtures in setUp and tearDown, respectively. TestCase itself provides stubs for these methods that do nothing:

```
TestCase>>setUp
    "Run whatever code you need to get ready for the test to run."
TestCase>>tearDown
    "Release whatever resources you used for the test."
```

PerformTest just performs the selector:

```
TestCase>>performTest
    self perform: selector
```

A single TestCase is hardly ever interesting once you have gotten it running. In production, you will want to run suites of TestCases. Aggregating Test-Cases is the job of the TestSuite:

```
Class: TestSuite
    super class: Object
    instance variables: name testCases
```

When a TestSuite is created, it is initialized to prepare it to hold TestCases. TestSuites are also named, so you can identify them even if you have, for example, read them in from secondary storage:

```
TestSuite class>>named: aString
    ^self new setname: aString
TestSuite>>setName: aString
    name := astring.
```

```
testCases := OrderedCollection new
```

TestSuites have an accessing method for their name in anticipation of user interfaces that will have to display them:

```
TestSuite>>name
    ^name
```

TestSuites have protocol for adding one or more TestCases:

```
TestSuite>>addTestCase: aTestCase
    testCases add: aTestCase
TestSuite>>addTestCases: aCollection
    aCollection do: [:each | self addTestCase: each]
```

When you run a TestSuite, you'd like all of its TestCases to run. It's not quite that simple, though. Running a suite is different from running a single test case. For example, if you have a suite that represents the acceptance test for your application, after it runs, you'd like to know how long the suite ran and which of the cases had problems. This is information you would like to be able to store away for future reference.

TestResult solves this problem. Running a TestCase just executes the test method and returns the TestCase. Running a TestSuite, however, returns a TestResult that records the information described above—the start and stop times of the run, the name of the suite, and any failures or errors:

```
Class: TestResult
    super class: Object
    instance variables: startTime stopTime testName
        failures errors
```

When you run a TestSuite, it creates a TestResult, which is time stamped before and after the TestCases are run:

```
TestSuite>>run
    | result |
    result := self defaultTestResult
    result start.
    self run: result.
```

```
    result stop.
    ^result
```

The default TestResult is constructed by the TestSuite:

```
TestSuite>>defaultTestResult
    ^self defaultTestResultClass test: self
TestSuite>>defaultTestResultClass
    ^TestResult
```

A TestResult is always created on a TestSuite:

```
TestResult class>>test: aTest
    ^self new setTest: aTest
TestResult>>setTest: aTest
    testName := aTest name.
    failures := OrderedCollection new.
    errors := OrderedCollection new
```

TestResults are timestamped by sending them the messages start and stop:

```
TestResult>>start
    startTime := Date dateAndTimeNow
TestResult>>stop
    stopTime := Date dateAndTimeNow
```

When a TestSuite runs for a given TestResult, it simply runs each of its Test-Cases with that TestResult:

```
TestSuite>>run: aTestResult
    testCases do: [:each | each run: aTestResult]
```

Because the selector run: is the same in both TestSuite and TestCase, it is trivial to construct TestSuites which contain other TestSuites, instead of or in addition to containing TestCases. When a TestCase runs for a given Test-Result, it should either silently run correctly, add an error to the TestResult, or add a failure to the TestResult. Catching errors is simple—use the system-supplied errorSignal. Catching failures must be supported by the Test-Case itself. First, we need a Signal:

```
TestCase class>>initialize
    FailedCheckSignal := self errorSignal newSignal
        notifierString: 'Check failed - ';
        nameclass: self message: #checksignal
```

Now we need a way of accessing it:

```
TestCase>>failedCheckSignal
    ^FailedCheckSignal
```

Now, when the TestCase runs with a TestResult, it must catch errors and failures and inform the TestResult, and it must run the tearDown code regardless of whether the test executed correctly. This results in the ugliest method in the framework, because there are two nested error handlers and valueNowOrOnUnwindDo: in one method:

```
TestCase>>run: aTestResult
    self setUp.
    [self errorSignal
        handle: [:ex | aTestResult error: ex errorString in: self]
        do: [self failedCheckSignal
            handle: [.ex | aTestResult failure: ex errorString in: self]
            do: [selfPerformTest]]]
            valueNowOrOnUnwindDo:
                [self teardown]
```

When a TestResult is told that an error or failure happened, it records that fact in one of its two collections. For simplicity, the record is just a two element array, but it probably should be a first-class object with a time stamp and more details of the blowup:

```
TestResult>>error: aString in: aTestCase
    errors add: (Array with: aTestCase with: aString)
TestResult>>failure: aString in: aTestCase
```

```
failures add: (Array with: aTestCase with: aString)
```

The error case gets invoked if there is ever an uncaught error (for example, message not understood) in the testing method. How do the failures get invoked? TestCase provides two methods that simplify checking for failure. The first, should: ablock, signals a failure if the evaluation of aBlock returns false. The second, shouldnt: ablock, does just the opposite.

```
should: aBlock
    aBlock value ifFalse: [self failedCheckSignal raise]
shouldnt: aBlock
    aBlock value ifTrue: [self failedCheckSignal raise]
```

Testing methods will likely run some code, then check the results inside should: and shouldnt: blocks.

EXAMPLE

Okay, that's how it works, but how do you use it? Here's a short example that tests a few of the messages supported by Sets. First we subclass Test-Case, because we'll always want a couple of interesting Sets around to play with:

```
Class: SetTestCase
    super class: TestCase
    instance variables: empty full
```

Now we need to initialize these variables, so we subclass setUp.

```
SetTestCase>>setUp
    empty :- Set new.
    full := Set with: #abc with: 5
```

Now we need a testing method. Let's test to see if adding an element to a Set really works:

```
SetTestCase>>testAdd
    empty add: 5.
    self should: [empty includes: 5]
```

Now we can run a test case by evaluating:

```
(SetTestCase selector. #testAdd) run.
```

Here's a case that uses shouldnt:. It reads "after removing 5 from full, full should include #abc and it shouldn't include 5."

```
SetTestCase>>testRemove
    full remove: 5.
    self should: [full includes: #abc].
    self shouldnt: [full includes: 5]
```

Here's one that makes sure an error is signaled if you try to do keyed access:

```
SetTestCase>>testIllegal
    self should: [self errorSignal
        handle:[:ex | true] do: [empty at: 5. false]]
```

Now we can put together a TestSuite.

```
| suite |
suite := TestSuite named: 'Set Tests'.
suite addTestCase: (SetTestCase selector: #testAdd).
suite addTestCase: (SetTestCase selector: #testRemove).
suite addTestCase: (SetTestcase selector: #testIllegal).
^suite
```

Figure 30-1 shows an Object Explorer picture of the suite and of the TestResult we get back when we run it.

The test methods shown above only cover a fraction of the functionality in **Set**. Writing tests for all the public methods in **Set** is a daunting task. However, as Hal Hildebrand told me after using an earlier version of this framework, "If the underlying objects don't work, nothing else matters. You have to write the tests to make sure everything is working."

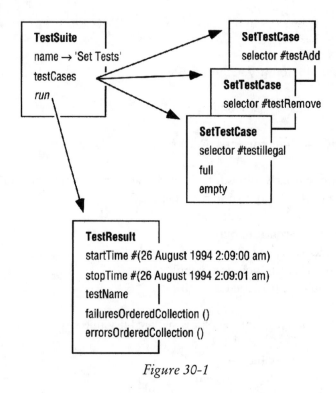

Figure 30-1

COOKBOOK

Here are simple steps you can follow to write your own tests:

1. **Scope the tests.** Decide whether you want to test one object or several cooperating objects. Subclass **TestCase**, prefixing the name of your test scope.

2. **Create test fixture.** Find a few configurations of your objects that will exercise the code you want to test. Add an instance variable to your **Test-Case** subclass for each configuration. Override **setUp** to create the configurations.

3. **Write the test methods.** Write a method for each distinct test you want to perform. Use **should:** and **shouldnt:** wherever you can check for correct or incorrect results. As you write each method, test it by creating an instance of your **TestCase** subclass and sending it **run**.

4. Create the suite. Write a method in one of the classes you are testing that collects all of the TestCases into a TestSuite and returns it.

CONCLUSION

This column has presented the philosophy and implementation of a simple testing strategy for Smalltalk. The strategy has the advantages that it is simple and lightweight and that it produces tests that are stable. It is not complete or perfect, but it's a whole lot better than no programmatic tests at all.

31

ARCHITECTURAL PROTOTYPE: TELEVISION REMOTE CONTROL

―――――

Smalltalk Report, NOVEMBER–DECEMBER, 1994

O*ooooh, my first process pattern. All of the patterns I had written to date talked about programming things. This column introduced the first pattern that talks explicitly about people activities.*

Jim Coplien was one of the first people to start writing lots of good patterns. Even though he is a good programmer, he chose to write his patterns out of his experience analyzing software development organizations. I was skeptical at first—what do these patterns of how people behave have to do with programming? It was around the time of this article that I began to realize that his perspective was as important as mine. It doesn't matter how good a job you do if you're doing the wrong job.

To make up for all the icky squishy stuff, I made sure I included plenty of code in the column. As aggressive as I think I am, looking at these columns reminds me that I go in the water half a toe at a time.

NOW, WHERE WAS I? Oh, yes. Last issue I talked about my philosophy of testing and presented a framework that supported writing unit and integration tests. But before that, I was talking about how to use patterns. I have spent a couple of issues designing the software to run a television and remote control, using patterns to guide every design decision. Here are the CRC descriptions of the objects we found, and the patterns that created them:

By the time I have this many objects designed, especially with clients who aren't really familiar with objects all the way through implementation, I find that most people's understanding of the design is so vague as to be actively dangerous. Everyone is thinking of a different implementation (or trying hard not to think of any implementation at all). It is about at this point that I like to write a quick sketch of the architecture in Smalltalk to bring everyone's focus back to something concrete.

Sometimes I call this a "spike," because we are driving a spike through the entire design. We are not searching for completeness. Instead, we want to illustrate the kinds of responsibilities accepted by all the major objects in the system. Because people variously associate "spike" with volleyball, railroads, or dogs, I have begun using "architectural prototype" to describe this implementation.

What does all this architectural prototype stuff have to do with patterns? I have two answers. First, "Architectural Prototype" is a pattern, but at a completely different level than most of the patterns I have discussed in this column. See below for the pattern itself. The second answer is a bit more complicated. I never design objects without wanting to see them implemented. Especially with designs guided by patterns, I find that the translation of the design into code is both straightforward and enlightening.

Pattern: Architectural Prototype
When do you put design ideas into code?

In the beginning, programmers just sat down and wrote their code. Any preparatory work was either entirely mental, or scratched on the back of sheets of line printer paper. Experience soon showed that while this approach worked for smart people working on small projects, larger team efforts required coordination before coding to avoid the enormous costs of revising already running code to match data structures, resolve names, and ensure reliable computations. Software engineering has a nearly unbroken record of pushing more and more work "up front," before coding begins.

The urge to resolve all possible issues before coding rests on good economics. The later in development a problem is discovered, the more it costs. A dogmatic adherence to "design first, then code" ignores two very important issues.

First, the goal of "up-front" development is to set up clear, effective, concise communications among the members of the team. A good design creates a shared vocabulary and mindset among the people who will have to implement, manage, and use the resulting system. Design notations both help and hinder this process. Because they are abstract, they encourage discussing essentials without descending into unimportant implementation details. That abstraction cuts both ways, though. The meaning of design documents are subject to human interpretation. It may be months before it is apparent that a team's understanding has diverged.

Second, code is no longer the boat anchor it used to be. Modular development supported by a modern, object-oriented language and programming environment results in code that is less expensive to write and easier to modify, even late in development, than were the products of earlier generations of programming languages. The cost curve supporting "design first, then code," has changed.

Together, these two points demonstrate that early coding is both necessary, to overcome the vagueness of design notations, and practical, because doing so will not invoke inordinate costs.

What code should you write early? The same constraints apply to early code that apply to early design. You'd like to make decisions with far-reaching effects. Big decisions are the ones that will be most important to communicate early. You'd like to avoid making decisions with small effects. Their presence in the code will obscure the important points you are exploring.

Implement a system when you have enough objects that their interaction is no longer obvious to everyone. Use simple algorithms and data structures. Implement only a single variation where there will be many in the final system.

You may also need an Interface Prototype to aid in communication with users.

THE TELEVISION PROTOTYPE

The goal in an architectural prototype is to demonstrate and communicate the architecture as simply as possible. I was talking to Ward Cunningham the other day and he said, "My job is to write five method classes." That is exactly what I am talking about.

The user interface to an architectural prototype should be extremely simple. If you can run it from a Workspace, so much the better. The goal of the prototype is not to demonstrate a whizzy interface, but communicate from programmer to programmer. User interface code is some of the hardest to get and keep clean. Any interface you don't need will detract from the primary purpose of the prototype.

REMOTE CONTROL

For the television prototype, we will start on the remote control side. Recall that we have:

Object	Responsibilities
Keyboard	create Events from keystrokes
RemoteControl	read keyboard Events
EventStream	read and write Events
InfraredStream	read and write bytes

Figure 31-1 summarizes the Smalltalk objects I came up with and their relationships.

We will start processing by sending character: aCharacter to the Keyboard to simulate the Keyboard noticing that a button has been pressed.

```
Keyboard>>character: aCharacter
    control event: (Event on: aCharacter)
```

Creating an Event sets its character and timeStamp.

```
Event class>>on: aCharacter
    ^self new setCharacter: aCharacter
```

```
Event>>setCharacter: aCharacter
```

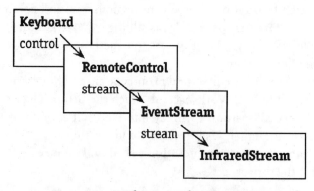

Figure 31-1 Objects in the Remote Control.

```
character := aCharacter.
timeStamp := Time now
```

The **RemoteControl** doesn't try to process the Event, it just passes it along to its other half inside the television:

```
RemoteControl>>event:
    stream nextPut: anEvent
```

The **EventStream** lives to transform Events to and from bytes. I picked the simplest format I could think of, **storeString**. All objects can produce a **store-String**, which when compiled results in an equivalent object:

```
EventStream>>nextPut: anEvent
    anEvent storeOn: stream.
    ^anEvent
```

I'll defer the implementation of **InfraredStream** for a moment, since it is the trickiest piece of code and the least interesting architecturally.

TELEVISION

On the television side, we have the following objects:

Object	Responsibilities
TelevisionControl	map Events to commands
Television	change channels
EventStream	read and write Events
InfraredStream	read and write bytes

In the television, the **EventStream** and **InfraredStream** will be reading rather than writing as they were in the remote control.

Figure 31-2 is a picture of the objects in the Television.

We will start processing by sending the **TelevisionControl** the message "poll." This interface (and **Keyboard>>character:** used above) let us defer decisions about how control really works. Decisions like polling versus interrupts are important, but don't affect a well-factored architecture that much:

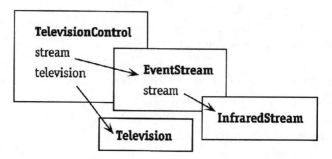

Figure 31-2 Objects in the Remote Control.

TelevisionControl>>poll
    stream atEnd
        ifFalse: [self event: stream next]

Getting the next **Event** from the **EventStream** is accomplished by compiling the characters in the InfraredStream.

EventStream>>next
    ^Compiler evaluate: stream upToEnd

Again, we will defer discussing InfraredStream until later. The **atEnd** test for **EventStream** delegates to the InfraredStream:

EventStream>>atEnd

	Table 31-1	
Object	Pattern
Event	Event
Keyboard—Create events from keystrokes	Objectified Library
RemoteControl—read keyboard events	Objects from the User's World, Half Object
EventStream—Read and write Events	Formatting Stream
InfraredStream—Read and write bytes	Objectified Library
TelevisionControl—Map user input to commands	HalfObject
Television—Change channels	Objects from the User's World

^stream atEnd

TelevisionControls respond to an Event by sending the channel: anInteger message to the Television:

    TelevisionControl>>event: anEvent
        television channel: anEvent digit

Events find their digit by getting the digitValue of their character:

    Event>>digit
        ^character digitValue

Finally, Televisions just print the channel to the transcript to show that they have received the message:

    Television>>channel: anInteger
        Transcript cr; show: 'Channel: ', anInteger printString

Figure 31-3 shows the effect of executing the prototype. The Keyboard has been sent character: 2. The TelevisionControl has been sent "poll." The new channel has been printed on the transcript.

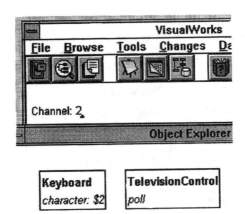

Figure 31-3 Executing the prototype.

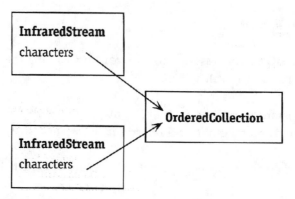

Figure 31-4 Streams sharing a Collection.

INFRAREDSTREAM

I promised to talk about how **InfraredStream** was implemented. We are trying to simulate two address spaces talking over an infrared beam. The implementation of the infrared protocol isn't interesting to the architecture, so we can simulate simply without worrying about how correct it is (although later we might want to take into account communication errors).

The trick is to have both **InfraredStreams** share a common OrderedCollection. The collection will contain the characters that have been written to one beam that haven't yet been read by the other. Figure 31-4 shows how the two streams look when they are connected.

Writing to an **InfraredStream** puts the character on the end of the collection:

```
InfraredStream>>nextPut: aCharacter
    characters addLast: aCharacter.
    ^aCharacter
```

Reading takes the first character off of the collection:

```
InfraredStream>>next
    ^characters removeFirst
```

The atEnd test tests whether the collection is empty:

```
InfraredStream>>atEnd
    ^characters isEmpty
```

Finally, upToEnd returns an OrderedCollection by default. We need it to return a String, because the result will be compiled by the EventStream. We can do this by overriding contentsSpecies.

```
InfraredStream>>contentsSpecies
    ^String
```

CONCLUSION

The architectural prototypes I've done for paying clients have been bigger than the television prototype presented here. Yours likely will be larger, too. The key point to remember is that you should write an architectural prototype to bring design discussions back down to earth. Whenever the abstractness of design is causing people to talk past each other, or fear of making concrete, "could-be-proven-wrong" decisions is slowing progress, a little bit of code goes a long way towards advancing the project.

In the next issue I will begin to discuss how patterns can be used to document reuse.

32

DEMAND LOADING FOR VISUALWORKS

Smalltalk Report, JANUARY, 1995

This was about where I started losing interest in writing the column. I had written this nice bit of code for a client, and I ran into a publishing deadline, so I turned it into a literate program and sent it off.

You'll notice that there are eight more columns after this one. Once again, my reluctance to change shows through. My lesson: once you decide not to do something, do not pass go, do not collect $200 (yep, that's the going rate). Quit and get on with something else.

In my case, I was distracted by trying to keep my business going (which in itself was too big a job for one person) and trying to get my patterns book done.

Not that this is a terrible column, or that it gives bad advice. The technique is useful, and belongs in every wizard's black bag. When I don't feel like writing the column, though, I shouldn't write the column.

BEFORE I JUMP into this month's column, I'd like to tell you a little about what I learned at Digitalk's DevCon this year.

RANT

One thing I learned is that Digitalk is finally coming around to the idea that third-party support is important to their success. The slow growth of the third-party parts market has hurt them, I think, and they want to fix that. Their Partners Program, the third-party catalog to be shipped with their product, and their public and private statements at DevCon give me hope that they are coming around. Their past neglect was made painfully apparent by the number of repeat third-party vendors showing in booths (three, I think).

The wackos are still around. Despite all of their best efforts to put Smalltalk in a blue suit with wingtip shoes, DevCon is still the place to meet interesting folks. I found more odd, interesting, intriguing, stimulating perspectives at DevCon than OOPSLA, the ParcPlace User's Conference (which was a great party for other reasons), and all the commercial object conferences combined. I don't know what it is about V, but it still attracts a fun crowd.

The last thing I learned is more disturbing. I talked to Greg and Bruno from Intelliware in Toronto while I was there. You recall that I mentioned how much they learned when I visited them a couple of years ago. Apparently some readers (not you, of course) read what I had written very differently than I had intended. Greg and Bruno are still taking grief from that one brief comment, as if I had said they were stupid or bad programmers.

Let me be very clear about this. I have a world of respect for them. They had the guts to start their own business on what was then a pretty risky technology, they had the smarts to make it work, shipping an impressive manufacturing application to the automotive industry, and I believe they have the technical talent to go a long way from there. Last but not least, they knew they needed help, so they asked for it and got it. They really "got" patterns. I expect great things of them in the future.

The lesson for me is that I have to be very careful about what I write. People out there are taking what I write seriously, so I have to take what I write seriously, but without taking myself seriously (the dirty diapers help). The lesson for you is to read, yes, but make your own conclusions. I'm sitting here in my living room/office with a deadline, not coming off a mountain with stone tablets.

I feel better having gotten that off my chest.

PROBLEM

No patterns this time. Instead, I'll show you some code I wrote for a client who was having performance problems. It is interesting for several reasons:

- It shows how you can use inheritance to separate the design from the implementation.

- It shows an appropriate use of a dangerous low-level feature.

- It shows how important it can be to understand your underlying Smalltalk implementation.

I described this code to Jon Hylands at the Object People. He proceeded to show me an implementation of the same idea for V. Great minds run in the same gutters, eh Jon?

The client and I discovered that we were thrashing Windows virtual memory. The only solution was to reduce the memory requirements somehow. The Stripper begins to address the footprint problem by removing unused classes before deployment (in addition to removing certain classes to satisfy the standard runtime license agreement). Unfortunately, it is not always possible to statically determine which classes will be used at runtime. Aggressive stripping—removing classes that may be used but you think won't be used—further reduces footprint, but at the cost of correctness. You'll get a smaller image, but will it run?

This column describes a complimentary approach to reducing memory footprint—demand loading. Rather than discarding objects that may not be used, demand loading waits until a value is wanted, then loads it from disk. The implementation makes this process transparent to the runtime code. To invoke demand loading, you need only add a step to the standard Stripper that sets up the variables to be so loaded.

OVERVIEW

When I have a VisualWorks problem that I can't solve, I talk it over with David Liebs. I generally only understand half of what he says, but the half I get is usually enough to get me unstuck. I had tried a couple of different approaches to demand loading without success, and there was a lot riding on an answer for me and the client, so I asked David. He immediately told me the trick that got me going (thanks, David!).

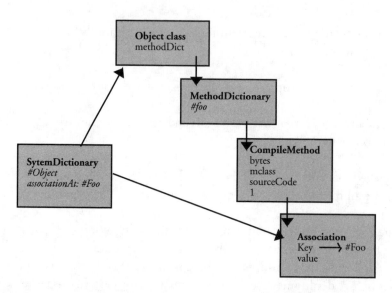

Figure 32-1 A compiled method referring to a global variable.

Global, Pool, and Class variables are stored as **Associations**, where the key is the name of the variable and the value is the value. If you have a method that uses the value of a global variable, the compiled version of that method refers to the same **Association** as the **Dictionary** that owns it. For example, if we compile

```
Object>>foo
    ^Foo
```

where **Foo** is a global variable, we get Figure 32-1.

In VisualWorks, unbeknownst to you, when you access one of these variables, the dynamic translator sends "value" to the **Association** to get the value. This gives us the leverage we need to implement demand loading.

The strategy is to replace the standard Associations for demand-loaded variables with a **LoadingAssociation** that overrides "value." If the value is already in the image, the **LoadingAssociation** just returns it. However, if the value has not yet been loaded, the **LoadingAssociation** uses a stored file name to retrieve the value before returning it.

Actually implementing this requires a bit more detail, as classes are handled specially by the Binary Object Streaming Service (BOSS). **LoadingAs-**

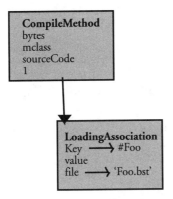

Figure 32-2 A demand loading global.

sociation provides the framework that ClassLoadingAssociation exploits
to load classes.

LOADINGASSOCIATION

LoadingAssociation is a subclass of Association. It will demand load arbitrary objects, so it could be used for lazily initializing large static data structures. For purposes of demand loading classes, however, it mostly acts as an
abstract superclass. Since its implementation is simpler than ClassLoading
Association, it is still a good place to begin studying the implementation of
demand loading.

> Class: LoadingAssociation
> superclass: Association
> instance variables: file

The instance variable "file" holds a string, which is the name of the file from
which the value will be loaded.

When a LoadingAssociation is asked for its value, it first checks to see
whether it has a value. If not, it reads the value from the file.

```
LoadingAssociation>>value
    value isNil ifTrue: [self readValue].
    ^super value
```

Reading a value requires that the LoadingAssociation open a BOSS reader on a ReadStream on the file, read the value, then make sure the file gets closed.

```
LoadingAssociation>>readValue
    | stream |
    stream := BinaryObjectStorage onOldNoScan:
        self filename readStream.
    [value := self readValueFrom: stream]
        valueNowOrOnUnwindDo: [stream close]
```

Reading the value is placed in a separate method because reading classes will be different than reading arbitrary objects. The implementation here simply reads the next object from the BOSS stream:

```
LoadingAssociation>>readValueFrom: aStream
    ^aStream next
```

The LoadingAssociation comes up with a concrete file name by concatenating the file instance variable with a default directory. The implementation here uses the same directory in which the image file was found. You could use a class variable for the directory to gain more flexibility, or even add an instance variable to each LoadingAssociation so different objects could be found in different directories:

```
LoadingAssociation>>filename
    ^self directory construct: file
LoadingAssociation>>directory
    ^Filename defaultDirectory
```

Creating a LoadingAssociation is simple. The class message replace: anAssociation file: aString creates a LoadingAssociation, writes the value of anAssociation to disk, and removes the reference to the value from the

LoadingAssociation. If there are no other references to the object, it will be deallocated by the garbage collector:

```
LoadingAssociation class>>replace: anAssociation file: aString
    ^self new replace: anAssociation file: aString
```

There is also a convenient method to unload a global variable that takes a Symbol as a parameter instead of an Association:

```
LoadingAssociation class>>replaceGlobal: aSymbol file: aString
    ^self replace: (Smalltalk associationAt: aSymbol) file: aString
```

The implementation of replace:file: is a bit tricky. CompiledMethods contain references to the Associations that were found at compile time. Thus, if we want to demand load a global variable, it is not enough to simply remove the Association from the SystemDictionary and replace it with a LoadingAssociation. We have to change all references to the old Association into references to the LoadingAssociation that will replace it. Kids, don't try this at home!

```
LoadingAssociation>>replace: anAssociation file: aString
    file := aString.
    key := anAssociation key.
    value := anAssociation value.
    self unloadValue.
    anAssociation become: self
```

Unloading the object just writes it to disk and removes the reference. It is in its own method because you may want to dynamically unload objects at some point in the future (this capability is not currently used). As currently written, LoadingAssociation is directed at reading, not writing, values. You could change this by adding a flag that was set when a LoadingAssociation was written to (by overriding value:):

```
LoadingAssociation>>unloadValue
    self writeValue.
    value := nil
```

Writing a value is analogous to reading one. The inner unwind block is there in preparation for fail-soft value writing (although unloadValue still overwrites the value instance variable, duh):

```
LoadingAssociation>>writeValue
  | stream oldValue |
  stream := BinaryObjectStorage onNew: self filename writeStream
  oldValue := value.
  [[self writeValueOn: stream]
    valueOnUnwindDo: [value := oldValue]]
      valueNowOrOnUnwindDo: [stream close]
```

Again, the details of writing the value on a stream are broken out to facilitate ClassLoadingAssociation:

```
LoadingAssociation>>writeValueOn: aStream
  aStream nextPut: value
```

ClassLoadingAssociation

ClassLoadingAssociation takes framework provided by LoadingAssociation and adapts it to the details of reading and writing classes. All of the difficulties come because global variables are routinely accessed by BOSS and the ClassBuilder, which will be used to read and write the values of ClassLoadingAssociation. Thus, we have to worry about having a ClassLoadingAssociation invoked when it is already in the middle of being read or written. The first line of defense is adding an instance variable, isLoading, which will be true while the ClassLoadingAssociation is loading its class:

```
Class: ClassLoadingAssociation
  superclass: LoadingAssociation
  instance variables: isLoading
ClassLoadingAssociation class>>new
  ^super new initialize
ClassLoadingAssociation>>initialize
  isLoading := false
```

Writing classes uses the BOSS protocol nextClassesPut: aCollection, which writes a Collection of classes. Classes are in a special format so that variable references can be correctly resolved when reading classes in and the classes can be installed in the SystemDictionary automatically. The current implementation writes a single class at a time. You could probably get performance improvements by reading clusters of related classes, but the external protocol for writing the classes, and the analysis that would go into creating clusters, would make this solution more complex:

```
ClassLoadingAssociation>>writeValueOn: aStream
    aStream nextPutClasses: (Array with: value)
```

There are two pieces of system code that we have to worry about for re-entrancy. The first is the ClassBuilder. When it runs, it looks to find the current class to see if it should modify the existing class or create a new one from scratch. If there is no class (which is what we are simulating), the ClassBuilder does the right thing for us. But to convince the ClassBuilder that there is no class, the ClassLoadingAssociation has to remove itself entirely from the SystemDictionary. If it just returns nil (or some other bogus value), the ClassBuilder will complain that you are replacing a nonclass value with a class:

```
ClassLoadingAssociation>>readValueFrom: aStream
    isLoading := true.
    Smalltalk removeKey: key.
    ^[aStream nextClasses first]
      valueNowOrOnUnwindDo:
        [isloading := false.
        Smalltalk
          removeKey: key:
          add: self]
```

This method embodies yet more trickiness. Recall that all of the Compiled-Methods in the system that refer to a variable have references to the (in this case ClassLoading) Association. After we have loaded the class, there is a new Association in the system referred to by the SystemDictionary. We have to remove the new Association entirely and put the ClassLoadingAssociation back in the SystemDictionary so all those references are consistent.

The second piece of system code that we have to worry about is Dictionary. In reading in a class and resolving its references, and in executing the "removeKey:"s in readValueFrom: above, the SystemDictionary (a subclass of Dictionary) sends messages to its Associations. Thus, while a ClassLoading-Association is loading, it must avoid restarting the loading process:

```
value
    isLoading ifTrue: [^Object new].
    ^super value
```

Second (and this is the trickiest part of this implementation), when BOSS is writing a class that accesses Pool dictionaries, it uses keyAtValue: to find the name of the Dictionary. Unfortunately, Dictionary>>keyAtValue: sends value to each Association. If we have unloaded some ClassLoadingAssociations already, this causes them to be loaded again, negating the effects we are looking for. A little judicious slicing removes the need to send value in executing keyAtValue:. First, we have Associations test whether their value is identical to a given Object:

```
Association>>valueIs: anObject
    ^value == anObject
```

Second, we invoke this method instead of sending value in keyAtValue:. Rather than replace the implementation in Dictionary, I decided to override the implementation in SystemDictionary, to reduce the possibility of any conflicts:

```
systemDictionary>>keyAtValue: value ifAbsent: exceptionBlock
    self associationsDo:
        [:each | (each valueIs: value) ifTrue: [^each key]].
    ^exceptionBlock value
```

Using Demand Loading

All that remains is to create ClassLoadingAssociations as part of stripping. Stripper provides the method postStrip, which you can modify to unload classes you won't always need right away. Here is an example that unloads the business graphics classes:

```
Stripper>>postStrip
    | classes |
    classes := Smalltalk select:
        [:each |
        each isBehavior
            and: [(each name indexOfSubCollection: 'BG_'startingAt: 1) >
o]].
        ClassLoadingAssociations unloadClasses: classes
```

UnloadClasses writes to a contiguous set of file names. You should only invoke it once per strip to avoid generating the same file names more than once:

```
ClassLoadingAssociation class>>unloadClasses: aCollection
    | classes |
    classes := SystemUtils sortForLoading: aCollection.
    classes
        with: (1 to: classes size)
        do:
            [:eachClass :eachIndex |
            self
                replaceglobal: eachClass name
                file: eachIndex printString , 'c.bst']
```

You will have to experiment with this facility to find the right time/space tradeoff for your application.

CONCLUSION

There are several interesting points to make about the code above:

You have to understand the virtual machine. As much as we'd like this not to be true, when you are writing system code (I'd certainly call **LoadingAssociation** system code, not application code), the more you know about the implementation the better.

The design is subtly platform specific. Jon Hylands's demand loader for V takes a very different approach to solving the same problem. Because Digitalk's implementation of become: is so much slower than ParcPlace's, he uses doesNotUnderstand: to forward all messages to the class.

You can use inheritance to separate design from implementation. In general, I am against using inheritance to express any important concept. In this case, though, it came in very handy. You can read the LoadingAssociation code and understand the design. All of the nasty details about how loading classes interferes with the system are hidden in the subclass. A similar use of inheritance is to create a simple, general superclass and an optimized subclass.

As always, I'm interested in your comments. My column on the testing framework actually garnered me half a dozen email messages. If you're using it for anything interesting, let me know.

33

GARBAGE COLLECTION REVEALED

Smalltalk Report, FEBRUARY, 1995

This column is the site of my greatest disaster as a column writer—I promised something I didn't deliver. This was another one of those "write the first half now and the rest later" columns. Unlike the column about applying patterns to design, however, I didn't know the second half of the material when I started. I still feel bad about this, but I still don't know the material for the second half, so I still can't write it.

I really like this column as a piece of pedagogy. It is an excellent example of lie management. I describe garbage collection simply one way, then simply another, then combine the two for a truer picture of garbage collection. And hey, I even included a bunch of pictures.

THIS MONTH I'll talk about garbage collection. To paraphrase Mark Twain, everybody talks about the garbage collector, but nobody does anything about it. All of the commercial Smalltalks provide some ability to tune the garbage collector, but without knowing what's going on and why, you are unlikely to be able to know when these features are applicable or how to use them. This article discusses the common vocabulary of modern garbage collection. Later, we'll explore what you can do to tune the garbage collector in the various Smalltalks.

THE IDEA

In the early days of programming languages, programmers had to decide at compile time how much memory they needed. Languages like FORTRAN and COBOL had a simple runtime model as a result, but they aren't very flexible. Along came LISP, which let you allocate storage at runtime. LISP was very flexible, but what got allocated needed to get deallocated. The first LISP implementations would run until they filled memory, then die. It was clear that when the system filled memory, much of the storage was no longer in use. It had been used for a while, but then it could be safely reused, because it would never be used by the program again. Rather than make the programmer responsible for deallocation, early Lispers decided to have the system deallocate memory for them.

At first, automatic storage deallocation was considered an artificial intelligence problem. After all, how could you possibly know that a piece of memory would never be accessed again? Only a trained programmer could tell with any certainty, and even they weren't very accurate.

It wasn't long before someone noticed that in a type-safe language (that is, one where you can't arbitrarily create pointers to memory) the problem is conceptually quite simple. Once the last pointer to an object is lost, there is no way to get another pointer to it. Therefore, you can't possibly harm the execution of the program by reusing that memory.

In Figure 33-1, since there are no references to object B, the program is free to reuse the memory it occupies, safe in the knowledge that no part of the program can possibly refer to it again. Object C cannot be reclaimed, because it is referred to by object A. Object A cannot be reclaimed because it is referred to from outside the object memory.

The code that finds objects that are no longer referenced is called the "garbage collector." Your Smalltalk contains a garbage collector. While most

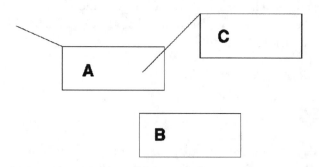

Figure 33-1 Object B's memory can be safely reused.

of its workings are beyond your control, it will occasionally become a most important part of your life. When you are trying to squeeze performance out of a running system, or reduce its memory footprint, you will have to understand what's going on "under the hood."

One common mistaken impression is that the garbage collector runs "occasionally," almost of its own volition. The garbage collector always runs in response to a request for memory it cannot fulfill. The memory allocator looks for the requested memory, but can't find it. It invokes the garbage collector, which reclaims some memory. The memory allocator runs again, returning some of the newly freed memory.

The presence of a garbage collector is an integral part of the Smalltalk programming experience. When you have to explicitly deallocate memory, you program in a very different style. The hard cases are where several parts of the system share an object, and all of them must agree before it can be deallocated. This introduces a pattern of communication to the system that likely wouldn't exist if not for the deallocation problem. A garbage collector, because it needs to have a global view of the system, frees you from having to take a global view. The connections between the parts of a program can be much looser, because they never have to communicate about deallocation. You never have to write otherwise irrational code just to make sure memory gets deallocated correctly.

Your Smalltalk implementation (the virtual machine) provides you with two main resources—message sending and object allocation (and hence garbage collection). The right attitude 95% of the time is to assume that both are free. The right time to stop this charade is when you have gotten the design as clean as you possibly can at the moment and it is obvious that limited machine resources are going to pose a problem for your user. Then you need to have a model in your head of what is going on.

BAKER TWO SPACE

Here's a simple garbage collection algorithm: allocate twice as much space for objects as you think you'll need. Divide the memory in two equal sections, called Old and New. When you allocate an object, allocate it in Old space. (See Figure 33-2.)

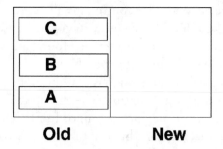

Figure 33-2 Allocating objects in old space.

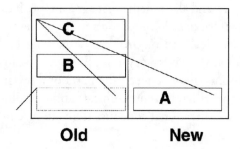

Figure 33-3 Copying a known object to new space.

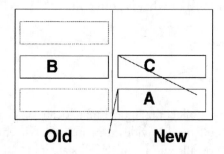

Figure 33-4 Copying a refered-to object to new space.

When you want to allocate an object but Old space is out of room, you have to invoke the garbage collector. The collector runs by starting with a known live object in Old space (in this case A) and copying it to New space. (See Figure 33-3.)

Any object that gets copied to New space has all of its objects copied to New space, too (in this case C). (See Figure 33-4.)

When no more objects remain to be copied, any objects remaining in Old space are not referenced anywhere. In this example, B can be safely ignored. Swap the identities of Old and New space. New objects will be allocated in the same space as the surviving objects. (See Figure 33-5.)

This algorithm is called Baker Two Space after its inventor, Henry Baker. It advantages are that:

- It is simple.

- It automatically compacts surviving objects together, leaving the remaining free space in one big chunk.

Its disadvantages are that:

- It takes twice as much memory as the object actually occupies.

- The copying operation takes time proportional to the number of surviving objects.

Mark and Sweep

The mark and sweep algorithm addresses the disadvantages of the Baker Two Space algorithm (it actually appeared many years before Baker Two Space). All objects are allocated in a single space. (See Figure 33-6.)

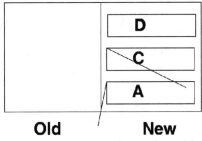

Old / **New**

Figure 33-5 Objects are allocated in old space.

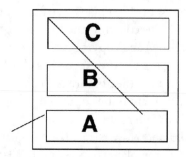

Figure 33-6 Mark and sweep objects in a single space.

As before, when the allocator runs out of space, it invokes the garbage collector. This time, instead of moving surviving objects, they are merely marked as being alive. Objects referred to by marked objects are also marked, recursively, until all the objects that can be marked have been. (See Figure 33- 7.)

After all the surviving objects have been marked, the sweep phase goes through memory from one end to the other. Any object that isn't marked is put on a list of memory available for allocation. While sweeping, the marks are erased to prepare for the next invocation of the garbage collector. (See Figure 33-8.)

The mark and sweep algorithm has the following advantages:

- It doesn't require extra memory.

- It doesn't need to move objects.

However, it has some serious shortcomings:

- The marking phase takes time proportional to the number of surviving objects.

- Worse, the sweeping phase takes time proportional to the size of memory.

- The resulting available memory is fragmented, possibly requiring a separate compaction step to pack the surviving objects together.

GENERATION SCAVENGING

While a graduate student at Berkeley, David Ungar combined the two space and mark and sweep algorithms to create a collector that usually exhibits none of the weaknesses of either, and has some important new properties. He called it generation scavenging.

The observation that makes generation scavenging work is that as a rule objects die young or live forever. That is, many objects are used temporarily during computations. For example, here a Rectangle creates a Point to calculate its extent.

```
Rectangle>>extent
    ^self corner - self origin
```

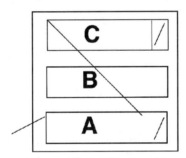

Figure 33-7 After marking.

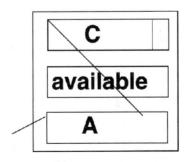

Figure 33-8 After sweeping.

Similarly, a Point creates a new Point to hold the maximum of its coordinates and the parameters coordinates.

```
Point>>max: aPoint
    ^(self x max: aPoint x) @ (self y max: aPoint y)
```

A client might use extent to compute the merged size of several Rectangles.

```
Client>>extent
    ^self rectangles
        inject: 0@0
        into: [:sum :each | sum max: each extent]
```

The Points created by invoking extent only live long enough to get passed as parameters to Point>>max:. The Points created by Point>>max: live over two invocations of the block, one where they are created, the next when they are replaced. If Client has a 100 Rectangles, Client>>extent creates 200 Points, which are all garbage even before the answer is returned.

Generation scavenging uses the demographics of objects to advantage. The relatively expensive two space collector is lavished on newly created objects. The copying operation of the two space collector is called a "scavenge."

The generation scavenger keeps track of the age objects by incrementing a

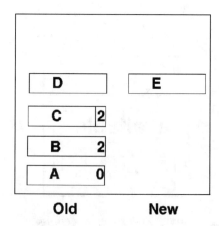

Figure 33-9 D and E are old; A, B, and C are recent.

count every time an object is copied by the two space collector. When the count exceeds a threshold, the object is copied not into New space, but into Tenure space. Tenure space is managed by a mark and sweep collector.

This has the effect of concentrating the collector's efforts on newly created objects, the ones that are likeliest to be collectable. After an object has demonstrated a little longevity, the collector effectively ignores it. Only when tenure space fills or you take a snapshot will the mark and sweep collector examine tenure space.

By concentrating its efforts where garbage is most likely to be found, generation scavenging garbage collectors end up taking only a small fraction of the total time of the system. In general, the collector only takes a few percent, compared with 20–30% for earlier algorithms.

The other valuable property of generation scavenging is that it is insensitive to the number of objects in the system. Recall that the two space algorithm takes time proportional to the number of surviving objects. Since most of the objects in the system are in tenure space, generation scavenging takes time proportional to the number of recently created surviving objects. Limiting the size of New and Old space keeps that number small.

A TENURING MONITOR

All of this is fine in theory, but what about practice? The collector is like a pair of shoes. You don't really notice it unless it is causing you pain. Then you have a serious problem.

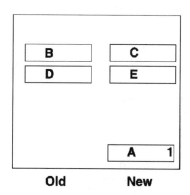

Figure 33-10 B and C have been tenured.

I'm running out of space this month, so I'll have to cover garbage collection tuning in future columns. I'll leave you with a little utility that will to help you begin to understand the interaction of your program with the collector.

The most serious breakdown of a generation scavenger is when it acts like a mark and sweep collector. If objects live just long enough to be tenured, then die, all the efforts spent on scavenging are wasted.

In old versions of Smalltalk/V the execution of the mark and sweep collector was accompanied by a cursor shaped like a vacuum cleaner. This lead to the use of "hoover" as a verb, "I was creating lots of objects, and boy, was I getting hoovered."

The new version of Smalltalk/V, Visual Smalltalk, provides hooks for watching the collector. In particular, the global object **Processor** posts the event flip when a scavenge takes place. You can send the message bytesTenured to find out how many bytes worth of objects were moved to tenure space.

I built the tenuring monitor with **Parts**. I know of no good way to typeset a **Parts** application, so I'll just try to sketch it out well enough for you to reproduce it if you want to.

The design of the user interface is a window with a static text in it. The text displays the number of bytes tenured with every scavenge.

First, we create a window and put a static text into it. Then we need to have the static text notified when a scavenge happens. Give the static text the following script (Digitalk calls them *flips*) and link it to the open event of the window:

```
setDependencies
    Processor
        when: #flip
        send: #UpdateBytes
        to: self
```

When the window closes, the static text should stop getting notified, so define the following script and link it to the **aboutToClose** event of the window:

```
breakDependencies
    Processor
```

```
removeActionsWithReceiver: self
forEvent: #flip
```

Finally, when the static text gets UpdateBytes, it needs to display the number of bytes tenured by the latest scavenge. It gets this number by sending Processor the message bytesTenured. I will describe all the available messages in a later article. Here is the script, which formats the number of bytes tenured for display.

```
updateBytes
    self setValue: Processor bytesTenured printString , ' bytes'
```

Launch the resulting window. Then go operate your favorite interface. You can watch as objects get promoted. If you are doing an operation that you don't think should create any long-lived objects, but lots of bytes are shown as being tenured, you may have a candidate for some tuning. I found drag and drop to be a good example.

This has been a quick introduction to your garbage collector. I will cover what it means in practical terms for the various Smalltalks in future issues. As always, if you have comments or questions, please let me know. I love to hear from you.

34

What? What Happened to Garbage Collection?

Smalltalk Report, March–April, 1995

I *was really stuck trying to write the second half of the garbage collection column. By this time, I felt like I had the column thing wired- sit down, bang out, email. Ka-ching. Not this time. Nothing I tried worked. The column started out late. It kept getting later.*

My solution, as you can see, was to rework material from my by-now-jelling patterns book. I didn't feel particularly good about it, because I knew it wouldn't change anyone's life dramatically, and I always wanted to have an impact. However, it got the column done.

I'LL TELL YOU what happened to garbage collection. I sat down three times to write the next column about garbage collection, and nothing came out. Between that, my wife's ten-game winning streak at Cribbage, and 46 inches of rain so far this year (and it's still January), I'm pretty frustrated.

I've been reading Edward DeBono's book *Thinking Course* (highly recommended). One of the techniques he suggests, and also one I've seen in art, is when you're stuck, do the opposite. In art, if you're having trouble drawing a thing, try to draw something that is completely the opposite. Of course, it's impossible to draw "not a flower," so you end up with something which gets at "flowerness" backwards. I'm writing a column about "not garbage collection." I'm not sure where I'll end up, but at least the column will be done.

CLASS

Bob Williams pointed out a problem with the column I wrote a year and a half ago or so on instance specific behavior. The Smalltalk/V version works fine, but when you specialize an instance in VisualWorks, all of a sudden a bunch of code stops working. The problem? Class tests.

For example, Point comparison (comparison is where this happens most often) is implemented like this:

```
Point>>= aPoint
    ^self class = aPoint class and: [self x = aPoint x & (self y = aPoint
    y)]
```

It's implemented this way so you can put Points and Rectangles and Arrays and Strings and a bunch of other objects that don't respond to x and y in the same Set and not have things blow up. All well and good, until you start specializing instances.

The problem is that "class" returns whatever is in the class field of the object. Instance specialization in VisualWorks operates by creating an anonymous Class (really a Behavior), and setting the class of the instance to it. That way, you can make changes to the Behavior without affecting all the other objects of the same class.

The Point comparison code above, though, will fail, even if two Points are equal. If the receiver has been specialized and the argument has not, the class of the receiver will be reported as this funny Behavior while the class of the argument is just good old Point. Are they equal? No way. Therefore the two Points aren't equal, even if they both print as "2@3".

I turned to David Liebs, my own personal guide to VisualWorks arcana, for ideas. Here's what we came up with.

When you ask an object for its class, it should return a real Class, the thing you defined in the browser. If you want to use instance specific behavior in VisualWorks, you need to make the following changes. Note that if you try the following, the order in which the methods are defined is important. Trashing images is exciting, but it doesn't rank high on the productivity scale.

First, the class primitive, the one that just returns the contents of the receiver's class field, has to be renamed:

```
Object>>primClass
```

```
<primitive: 111>
self primitiveFailed
```

Next, we have to be able to go up the superclass chain looking for a real class. Instances of Class and MetaClass are real.

```
Class>>realClass
    ^self

MetaClass>>realClass
    ^self
```

Behavior, however, needs to ask its superclass for a real class. Note that this code ignores the kinky case of a Behavior without a superclass, which doesn't arise in normal use, nor in the instance specialization code. I'd have to think carefully about what I wanted the code to do in that case.

```
Behavior>>realClass
    ^self superclass realClass
```

Finally, Object>>class needs to be modified so it finds a real class:

```
Object>>class
    ^self primClass realClass
```

Now it works. You can specialize Points and still have "=" work correctly.

FORMATTING

On to the chosen secondary topic for the day—code formatting. What? You think this is a dull, dry, boring topic best relegated to corporate style guides? Not so. As soon suggest that typography is useless, that content is all that matters. The medium is the message—formatting your code is an opportunity to communicate subtle but important information to your readers. It is the first thing people will look at when they see your work. In groups, it is the one topic most likely to cause friction. Everybody has to do it the same or everyone is frustrated, but no one wants to do it like anyone else.

I decided to apply the power of patterns to the problem of source code formatting. Ward Cunningham and I used to have long discussions at Tektronix about just the right way to format a method. Roxie Rochat also produced an excellent style guide, which I didn't entirely agree with, but that took a comprehensive look at the issue of formatting. In the years since, I have often wondered if there were rational rules of formatting, or if it really was just a matter of personal style.

The appearance of the new Cooper and Peters product edIt, with its cool programmable formatting, also drove me to try to canonize my own formatting style.

When I started writing these patterns, I thought I'd end up with fifteen or twenty. As it turns out, I only found five, and **Type Suggesting Parameter Name** isn't really about formatting. The code they turn out isn't exactly like I would have formatted it before I enumerated the patterns, but I like it. It is simple and consistent, and it meets the main goals of code formatting.

What are the goals of formatting? As far as I can tell, the main forces influencing any code formatting style are

- *Minimize height.* Formatting should produce the fewest possible number of lines, consistent with the rest of the constraints. This is important in Smalltalk, because fewer lines translates into more browsers, or less scrolling in the existing browsers.

- *Minimize width.* Formatting should produce code that doesn't have to be either scrolled horizontally or line wrapped. Line wrapping makes reading more difficult, because it messes up the shapes made by indentation, and horizontal scrolling slows down typing because you're always adjusting that darned scroll bar.

- *Quick recognition.* Formatting should produce code whose gross structure is apparent at a glance. Important features like flow of control and the presence of blocks should be obvious within a fraction of a second of seeing the code.

- *Careful reading.* Formatting should produce code that reads well in detail. You should be able to accurately read selectors. You should be able to understand the flow of control in detail.

These constraints are often in conflict. A good formatting style finds the right balance between them. I'm not saying that what follows is the be all and end all of formatting, but it is simple and consistent. If you disagree (and I'm sure some of you will), try to write up your own formatting style as patterns. Figure out what constraints you are resolving and how you are resolving them.

These patterns, and a whole lot more, also live on the Portland Pattern Repository, a Web server operated by Cunningham and Cunningham. Check them out by pointing your Web client at "http://c2.com/".

Type Suggesting Parameter Name

What should you call a method parameter?

There are two important pieces of information associated with every variable—what messages it receives (its type) and what role it plays in the computation. Understanding the type and role of variables is important for understanding a piece of code.

Keywords should communicate their associated parameter's role. Since the keywords and parameters are together at the head of every method, the reader can easily understand a parameter's role without any effect on the name.

Smalltalk doesn't have a strong notion of types. A set of messages sent to an object appears nowhere in the language or programming environment. Because of this lack, there is no direct way to communicate types.

Classes sometimes play the role of types. You would expect a **Number** to be able to respond to messages like +, -, *, and /; or a **Collection** to do: and includes:. Therefore,

Name parameters according to their most general expected class, preceded by "a" or "an." If there is more than one parameter with the same expected class, precede the class with a descriptive word.

An **Array** that requires **Integer** keys names the parameters to at:put: as

at: anInteger put: anObject

A **Dictionary**, where the key can be any object, names the parameters

at: keyObject put: valueObject

After you have named the parameters, you are ready to write the method. You may have to declare **Role Suggesting** Temporary Variables. You may need to format an **Indented** Control Flow. You may have to use a **Guard Clause** to protect the execution of the body of the method.

INDENTED CONTROL FLOW

You are writing a method following Type Suggesting Parameter Name.

How do you indent messages?

The conflicting needs of formatting to produce both few lines and short lines is thrown in high relief with this pattern. The only saving grace is that **Composed Method** creates methods with little enough functionality that you never need to deal with hundreds or thousands of words in a method.

One extreme would be to place all the keywords and arguments on the same line, no matter how long the method. This minimizes the length of the method, but makes it difficult to read.

If there are multiple keywords to a message, the fact that they all appear is important to communicate quickly to a scanning reader. By placing each keyword/argument pair on its own line, you can make it easy for the reader to recognize the presence of complex messages.

Arguments do not need to be aligned, unlike keywords, because readers seldom scan all the arguments. Arguments are only interesting in the context of their keyword. (This would be a good place for a diagram with an arrow going down the keywords in order to read **at:put:**, and another scanning left to right as the reader understands the message and its arguments.)

Therefore, put zero or one argument message on the same lines as the receiver.

```
foo isNil
2 + 3
a < b ifTrue: [...]
```

Put the keyword/argument pairs of messages with two or more keywords each on its own line, indented one tab.

```
a < b
   ifTrue: [...]
   ifFalse: [...]
array
   at: 5
   put: #abc
```

Rectangular Block formats blocks. Guard Clause prevents indenting from marching across the page.

RECTANGULAR BLOCK

How should you format blocks?

Smalltalk distinguishes between code that is executed immediately upon the activation of a method and code whose execution is deferred. To read code accurately, you must be able to quickly distinguish which code in a method falls into which category.

Code should occupy as few lines as possible, consistent with readability. Short methods are easier to assimilate quickly and they fit more easily into a browser. On the other hand, making it easy for the eye to pick out blocks is a reasonable use of extra lines.

One more resource we can bring to bear on this problem is the tendency of the eye to distinguish and interpolate vertical and horizontal lines. The square brackets used to signify blocks lead the eye to create the illusion of a whole rectangle even though one isn't there. Therefore,

Make blocks rectangular. Use the square brackets as the upper left and bottom right corners of the rectangle. If the statement in the block is simple, the block can fit on one line:

```
ifTrue: [self recomputeAngle]
```

If the statement is compound, bring the block onto its own line and indent:

```
ifTrue:
    [self clearCaches.
    self recomputeAngle]
```

Guard Clause

How should you format code that shouldn't execute if a condition holds?

In the bad old days of FORTRAN programming, when it was possible to have multiple entries and exits to a single routine, tracing the flow of control was a nightmare. Which statements in a routine got executed when was impossible to determine statically. This led to the commandment, "Every routine shall have one entry and one exit."

Smalltalk labors under few of the same constraints of long ago FORTRAN, but the prohibition against multiple exits persists. When routines are only a few lines long, understanding flow of control within a routine is simple. It is the flow between routines that becomes the legitimate focus of attention.

Multiple returns can simplify the formatting of code, particularly conditionals. What's more, the multiple return version of a method is often a more direct expression of the programmer's intent. Therefore:

Format conditionals that prevent the execution of the rest of a method with a return.

Let's say you have a method that connects a communication device only if the device isn't already connected. The single exit version of the method might be

```
connect
    self isConnected
        ifFalse: [self connectConnection]
```

You can read this as, "If I am not already connected, connect my connection." The guard clause version of the same method is:

```
connect
    self isConnected ifTrue: [^self].
    self connectConnection
```

You can read this as "Don't do anything if I am connected. Connect my connection." The guard clause is more a statement of fact, or an invariant, than a path of control to be followed.

You may need to return a **Nil Return Value** to signal an unusual condition.

SIMPLE ENUMERATION PARAMETER

What should you call the parameter to an enumeration block?

It is tempting to try to pack as much meaning as possible into every name. Certainly, classes, instance variables, and messages deserve careful attention. Each of these elements can communicate volumes about your intent as you program.

Some variables just don't deserve such attention. Variables that are always used the same way, where their meaning can be easily understood from context, call for consistency over creativity. The effort to carefully name such variables is wasted, because no nonobvious information is communicated to the program. They may even be counterproductive, if the reader tries to impute meaning to the variable that isn't there.

Call the parameter "each". If you have nested enumeration blocks, append a descriptive word to all parameter names.

For example, the meaning of "each" in

```
self children do: [:each | self processChild: each]
```

is clear. If the block is more complicated, each may not be descriptive enough. In that case, you should invoke **Composed method** to turn the block into a single message. The **Type Suggesting Parameter** in the new method will clarify the meaning of the object.

The typical example of nested blocks is iterating over the two dimensions of a bitmap:

```
1 to: self width do:
    [:eachX |
    1 to: self height do:
        [:eachY | ...]]
```

Nested blocks that iterate over unlike collections should probably be factored with Composed Method.

You may need Composed Method to simplify the enumeration block.

INTERESTING RETURN VALUE

When should you explicitly return a value at the end of a method?

All messages sends return a value. If a method does not explicitly return a value, the receiver of the message is returned by default. This causes some confusion for new programmers, who may be used to Pascal's distinction between procedures and functions, or C's lack of a definition of the return value of a procedure with no explicit return. To compensate, some programmers always explicitly return a value from every method.

The distinction between methods which do their work by side effect and those that are valuable for the result they return is important. An unfamiliar reader wanting to quickly understand the expected use of a method should be able to glance at the last line and instantly understand whether a useful object is generated or not. Therefore:

Return a value only when you intend for the sender to use the value.

For example, consider the implementation of topComponent. Visual components form a tree, with a ScheduledWindow at the root. Any component in the tree can fetch the root by sending itself the message topComponent. VisualPart implements this message by asking the container for its topComponent:

```
VisualPart>>topComponent
    ^container topComponent
```

ScheduledWindow implements the base case of the recursion by returning it-self. The simplest implementation would be to have a method with no state-ments. It would return the receiver. However, using Interesting Return Value, because the result is intended to be used by the sender, it explicitly returns self.

```
ScheduledWindow>>topComponent
    ^self
```

SUPER + 1

Smalltalk Report, MAY, 1995

You may have noticed me putting more and more personal comments at the beginning of columns. I think this resulted from getting more and more comfortable with my role as a columnist (even as I was losing interest—I didn't say I was straightforward).

I beat on the "inheritance, feh" horse a bit more in this column, but as before, I try to explain what to do about it, rather than just bash.

The other thing I noticed while rereading this column is the extra pattern thrown in at the end. I didn't do it to pad. I did it because I was honestly embarrassed to have missed it at the client and I didn't want other people to make the same mistake. This violates the "what one thing do you want to say" rule, but it doesn't bother me here. I'm very clear that there are two things to talk about, from the title on down. The power of any rule is when you understand it well enough to break it.

ONCE AGAIN, no garbage collectors. I've been busy paying the bills, so I haven't had a change to look in detail at the garbage collectors in the various Smalltalks. I'll get to it, but those college educations have to come first.

Smalltalk Solutions was a blast! Four hundred people packed into the hotel, giving the whole get-together quite a buzz. Of course, that could be because of the hordes of European and Asian tourists. I don't think I got onto an elevator and heard less than three languages the whole four days. Mark this one on your calendar for next year.

I had a great time talking on Wednesday of the conference. My performance-tuning talk was full, with lots of great give-and-take about performance issues. I gave a talk about patterns in the afternoon, and somehow we crammed even more people in. One thing I was uniformly surprised by during my talks was how open everyone was. It's hard to stand up in a room of 250 people and say, "I screwed up thus-and-so; how can I avoid it in the future?" The other thing I appreciated was how much dialog resulted. It wasn't me bringing down the stone tablets, it was more experienced and less experienced people sharing problems and solutions.

The best part of the whole thing was that when I got tired of talking and crowds, I went up to my hotel room and really cranked on code. It's been awhile since I've single-mindedly worked on something just for me. Now I remember why I love programming.

Well, the really best best thing about it was the cheesecake across the street. I must have consumed 10 Kcals having great talks with new friends and old.

And now, some content.

SUPER

A couple of years ago, I published a column about how to use "super" in Smalltalk. It turns out there are only a few legitimate uses, and several common mistakes. I've always liked that column, but I always thought it a shame that I wrote it before I was any good at writing patterns. I'm here to change all that. Because my pattern skills have improved, and because the readership of the *Smalltalk Report* has increased so dramatically in the last two years, I'll take another whack at talking about super, this time in terms of patterns. At the end, I'll throw in one more pattern that came up and smacked me in the face recently.

Before I jump in, let me first say that I think inheritance is vastly overrated. It is the least useful feature of the big three (encapsulation, polymorphism, and inheritance). If I had to do without one, inheritance is the one I'd drop.

However, inheritance is there, and when it is working well it is a joy to use. It results in code that is so highly compressed it is almost like reading poetry. I introduce these three methods and, voilà, I have an object that responds to 30 messages in a new and interesting way. This is the strength and weakness of inheritance. If you don't speak the language of the superclass, there is no way you will understand the subclass.

Three simple rules will keep you out of most of the trouble inheritance can cause:

1. **Keep it in the family.** This is Rick DeNatale's Law of Inheritance. If you are going to subclass, make sure that either the superclass is rock stable or the providers of the superclass are committed to bringing you forward as changes occur. It works best if you own both classes.

2. **Follow the rules.** Factored Superclass tells you to make superclasses only when forced to do so by duplicated concrete implementation, not merely speculation about the nature of the universe. The "super" patterns that follow help reduce coupling. Composed Method, when used in the superclass, ensures that subclasses needn't duplicate code.

3. **Never refactor a hierarchy twice in a row.** Early in my career I wasted more time twisting inheritance hierarchies this way and that, trying to share one or two more lines of code. If you do refactor an inheritance hierarchy, live with it for a while the new way. Be prepared to dump the refactoring if it doesn't go well.

Pattern: Super

How can you invoke superclass behavior?

An object executes in a rich context of state and behavior, created by composing together the contexts of its class and all its class's superclasses. Most of the time, code in the class can be written as if the entire universe of methods it has available is flat. That is, take the union of all the methods up the superclass chain and that's what you have to work with.

Working this way has many advantages. It minimizes any given method's reliance on inheritance structure. If a method invokes another method on self, as long as that method is implemented somewhere in the chain the invoking method is happy. This gives you great freedom to refactor code without having to make massive changes to methods that assume the location of some method.

There are important exceptions to this model. In particular, inheritance makes it possible to override a method in a superclass. What if the subclass method wants some aspect of the superclass method? Good style boils down to one rule: say things once and only once. If the subclass method were to contain a copy of the code from the superclass method, the result would no longer be easy to maintain. We would have to remember to update both or (potentially) many copies at once. How can we resolve the tension between the need to override, the need to retain the illusion of a flat space of methods, and the need to factor code completely?

Invoke code in a superclass explicitly by sending a message to "super" instead of "self." The method corresponding to the message will be found in the superclass of the class implementing the sending method.

Always check code using "super" carefully. Change "super" to "self" if doing so does not change how the code executes. One of the most annoying bugs I've ever tried to track down involved a use of super that didn't do anything at the time I wrote it and that invoked a different selector than the one for the currently executing method. I later overrode that method in the subclass and spent half a day trying to figure out why it wasn't being invoked. My brain had overlooked the fact that the receiver was "super" instead of "self," and I proceeded on that assumption for several frustrating hours.

Extending super adds behavior to the superclass. Modifying super changes the superclass's behavior.

Pattern: Extending Super

You need to extend superclass behavior.
How do you add to a superclass' implementation of a method?

Any use of super reduces the flexibility of the resulting code. You now have a method that assumes not just that there is an implementation of a particular method somewhere, but that the implementation has to exist somewhere in the superclass chain above the class that contains the method. This assumption is seldom a big problem, but you should be aware of the trade-off you are making.

If you are avoiding duplication of code by using super, the trade-off is quite reasonable. For instance, if a superclass has a method that initializes some instance variables, and your class wants to initialize the variables it has introduced, super is the right solution. Rather than have code like

Class: Super
Superclass: Object

```
Variables: a
Super class>>new
   ^self basicNew initialize
Super>>initialize
   a := self defaultA
Class: Sub
Superclass: Super
Variables: b
Sub class>>new
   ^self basicNew
      initialize;
      initializeB
Sub>>initializeB
   b := self defaultB
```

where the subclass has to invoke both initializations explicitly, using super you can implement

```
Sub>>initialize
   super initialize.
   b := self defaultB
```

and not have Sub override "new" at all. The result is a more direct expression of the intent of the code—make sure Supers are initialized when they are created, and extend the meaning of initialization in Sub.

*When you want to extend the meaning of a superclass method, override the method and invoke "**super**" as either the first or last statement of the method.*

☙ ❧

Pattern: Modifying Super

You need to modify a superclass's behavior.
How do you change the part of the behavior of a superclass's method without modifying it?

This problem introduces a tighter coupling between subclass and superclass than "Extending Super." Not only are we assuming that a superclass implements the method we are modifying, we are assuming that the superclass is doing something we need to change.

Often, situations like this can best be addressed by refactoring methods with Composed Method so you can use pure overriding. For example, the following initialization code could be modified by using super.

```
Class: IntegerAdder
Superclass: Object
Variables: sum, count
IntegerAdder>>initialize
    sum := 0.
    count := 0
Class: FloatAdder
Superclass: IntegerAdder
Variables:
FloatAdder>>initialize
    super initialize.
    sum := 0.0
```

A better solution is to recognize that IntegerAdder>>initialize is actually doing four things: representing and assigning the default values for each of two variables. Refactoring with Composed Method yields

```
IntegerAdder>>initialize
    sum := self defaultSum.
    count := self defaultCount
IntegerAdder>>defaultSum
    ^0
IntegerAdder>>defaultCount
    ^0
FloatAdder>>defaultSum
    ^0.0
```

However, sometimes you have to work with superclasses that are not completely factored. You are faced with the choice of either copying code or using super and accepting the costs of tighter subclass/superclass coupling.

Most of the time the additional coupling will not prove to be a problem. Communicate your desired changes with the owner of the superclass. In the meantime,

> When you want to modify the meaning of a superclass method, override the method and invoke "super" as either the first or last statement of the method.

COMMENTS

Here is where an interesting point about patterns comes in. Notice that these two patterns only tell you to invoke "super" with the same selector as the currently executing method. The original article discussed a couple of cases where it was marginally useful to invoke super with something other than the currently executing message selector. In trying to translate them to patterns, I wasn't convinced that they were actually good style, and they were terribly rare. Rather than write poor patterns that wouldn't be used often, I chose to leave them out (go browse all users of super in any stock image if you want to find how super is misused).

PLUS ONE

Here is a pattern morsel I'll throw in, mostly because I was so embarrassed recently when I missed it, and it took my clients to point out how much easier life would be once I reintroduced it.

Let me set the stage. I am writing a framework for this client that invokes one of many subclasses that they are writing. The protocol has been pretty unstable for a while, with names changing and parameter lists changing as we matured the framework. This resulted in the need for more communication than is productive, and slowed their development.

Now me, I'm willing to go through lots of pain to get to the right solution. If I have to go change 25 selectors because I found a better word for something, I'll do it. My assumption is always that the improved communication and resulting reduction in lifecycle cost is always worth the effort. In this case, my "self sacrifice" got the best of me. If I'd used "Parameters Object" about two months ago, the whole project would have sped up by about a week. Sigh…If only my computer would quit reminding me how little I really know.

Pattern: Parameters Object

How can you best write methods with many parameters?

Reducing the coupling between objects is good. Eliminating direct references from one object to another lets you use the two objects more independently. You can replace most direct references by passing extra parameters.

Going too far down this road leads you to code that doesn't communicate well. There are times when the communication between two objects is so pervasive, such an important part of your conception of the program as a whole, that you can't imagine not having a reference one to another. A Rectangle needs its Points. Further, even where you might be able to replace a direct reference with a parameter, passing extra parameters leads to difficult formatting and naming decisions and obscures the intent of the methods behind the host of keywords required.

If you have decided that you don't want a direct reference, but you still need several parameters, what do you do? The problem becomes worse if there are many implementations of the selector. During development, as you discover the need for more or fewer parameters in certain cases, you have to go around adding and deleting keywords from selectors in many classes.

In a collaborative environment, this redesign is unlikely to ever take place. One strategy is to pass every possible parameter everywhere on the off chance that it might be useful some day. This results in many messages being more complex than they need to be, obscuring the true intent of the code for later refinement or communication to others. The other strategy is to use global variables to short-circuit disciplined communication, thereby reducing the possibility that the code will ever be valuable on its own.

We need a way to decouple instability in the parameter list from instability in the protocol. As protocols change, they should change because of changes in intent. As the list of parameters change, the protocols shouldn't change just to accomodate the need of some particular implementation for extra information.

If you have three or more parameters that are passed three or more levels, or that are passed to five or more implementations of the same selector, create an object with one variable per parameter. Create an instance of the object in the highest-level sender and pass it around.

You may be able to use Composed Method to move computations into the "Parameters Object." Do so without regard to whether it "makes sense." If you send two or more messages to the "Parameters Object" in a single method and then compute with the results, move the computation.

For example, suppose we didn't have Rectangles. Everywhere we compute with Rectangles we have to pass four parameters:

...boundsTop: topInteger left: leftInteger bottom: bottomInteger right: rightInteger...
 ...area := bottom - top * (right - left)...
Introducing <u>Rectangle</u> as a Parameters Object, we now have:
...bounds: aRectangle
 ...area := aRectangle bottom - aRectangle top * (aRectangle right - aRectangle left)...

Far better to move the computation close to the data:

Rectangle>>area
 ^bottom - top * (right - left)
...bounds: aRectangle...
 ...area := aRectangle area

The resulting code is much more flexible, because we can change the implementation of area computation to suit the needs of the client without having to touch the client's code.

Another common implication of this pattern is that the method may be relying on sending messages directly to the parameters before you introduce the "Parameters Object." Use "Simple Delegation" in the "Parameters Object" to hide its existence from the method.

Between these two techniques, you will often find that the "Parameters Object" takes on an important role in the whole computation. These are the kinds of objects that thoughtful analysis will never reveal. As valuable as they are, you will only find them if you listen to what your program tells you.

CONCLUSION

That's it for now. Maybe I'll get to those garbage collectors next time. As always, please get in touch if you have comments, stories, complaints, rants, raves, or even just a good joke.

36

CLEAN CODE:
PIPE DREAM OR STATE OF MIND?

Smalltalk Report, JUNE, 1995

As with the previous column, this column has a strong confessional flavor. I like using my mistakes for columns, because I'm sure there is something to learn there.

The meat of the column is good stuff—refactoring and adding stuff becomes easy. I can't imagine how many times and ways I have said this in the last ten years. This is one of my better attempts, because it doesn't just say it, it shows it. (See "Make it Run, Make it Right" for another example.)

When I started writing this, I felt like I was getting preachy. Maybe that's what's so good about demonstrating from my mistakes—I can't be preaching if I'm explaining how I screwed up.

The personal material up front shows that I was aware that my attention was wandering. I'm glad I kept it together enough to say something important here.

IS IT MY IMAGINATION, or are these columns getting harder to write? I think I know exactly what I want to say, but I've started writing three different times without getting anywhere. Maybe this third time will work.

Simply put, here's what I want to say—the best programming style for Smalltalk is to have lots of little methods, and lots of little objects.

That's a pretty broad statement, broad enough that it can't possibly be true in all cases. What are the tradeoffs, the issues that affect programming style?

Why do I care? Why not just let a thousand different styles blossom? Here's what I've done over and over. I'll be asked by a client to help them figure out what's going wrong with a piece of code. The first thing I'll do is reformat the code in question so I can follow the flow of control. Then

I'll start breaking big methods into smaller pieces, asking the client to name the new methods I create.

At some point in this process the problem becomes obvious. The proposed name doesn't match what the method is doing. A computation that should happen once is happening twice. A computation that should be happening on only one side of a conditional happens on both.

I never get over feeling that a problem like this, where the solution is merely to clean up, didn't need to happen in the first place. It's not like what I do is profound—I don't have to go away and think hard. I mechanically apply a few simple patterns. The answer appears. I'm not there to give deep advice. I just provide permission.

Here are the important patterns for this kind of debugging:

- *Composed Method.* Give each method one simple job. Keep all the operations in the method at the same level of abstraction. This naturally results in many methods, most of them a few lines long.

- *Explaining Temporary Variable.* Communicate the sense of a complex expression by pulling a subexpression out and assigning its value to a variable named for the meaning of the subexpression.

- *Indented Control Flow.* For messages with two or more parameters, put each keyword and its argument on its own line, indented one tab. This makes multikeyword messages easy to spot and to read.

- *Rectangular Block.* Start blocks with two or more lines on a fresh line, indented one tab. This makes the shape of the control structures easy to scan.

Why don't these clients keep their code clean themselves? Why do I have to step in for them to do what is obviously (to me) the right thing to do?

Here are some reasons I've heard:

- *"I don't have time."* Folks will spend half a day working on a bug, trying various fixes without success. Often, 15 minutes of cleanup makes the problem obvious and improves the code for the future at the same time. Even if you don't find the bug right away, you'll be in a much better position to fix it when you do find it if the code is clean.

- *"I don't know how."* It might take a while to get accustomed to the patterns above, but a few hours' investment will pay off for years. If you don't agree with the details of the patterns, if you indent code differently, that's fine, but do it someway. Life is too short to continually make detailed coding decisions.

- *"It's not important."* The cost of a piece of code over its many-year life is dominated by how well it communicates to others. If it is easy to understand, it will cost your company less while bringing the same benefits.

- *"It's the wrong thing to do!"* Some people claim that many small methods and many small objects are harder to understand than fewer bigger objects and methods. Software engineering is all about mapping intention to implementation, moving from what to how. Every method name, every class name is an opportunity for you to communicate what is happening. Every method body and the code in every class is the means by which you specify how it is to happen. Big methods and big objects mean you are focused on how, not what.

I finally realize why this has been so hard for me to write. I'm frustrated. I keep explaining the principles of quality code over and over, and I keep getting the same arguments. I'm sure this reflects more on me than on anyone else, but I'm still frustrated.

TRUE CONFESSIONS

Confession being good for the soul, and all moralizing aside, do I really always keep my own code squeaky clean? I like to think so, and for the most part it's true, but every so often reality comes up and smacks me in the face (thanks, Reality, I needed that). Here's a nasty incident from my recent past that illustrates the value of clean code and how I sometimes resist it.

ORIGINAL CODE

I've been working on a new-from-scratch version of HotDraw, the graphic editor framework I wrote with Ward Cunningham at Tektronix lo these long and many. Anyway, here is the code that gets invoked when the mouse button goes down and the editor is in selection mode.

```
SelectionTool>> button1down: aPoint
    self originalPoint: aPoint.
    self previousPoint: aPoint.
    self figure: (self drawingPane figureAt: aPoint).
    self figure isNil
        ifTrue: [self drawMarquee]
        ifFalse:
            [(self selectedfigures includes: self figure)
                ifTrue: [^self].
            self resetSelections.
            self selectFigure]
```

There are two cases—if the mouse is over a Figure when the button goes down, the Figure should be selected. Otherwise, this should start group selection. This method is only eight lines long, it reads okay, so what's the problem? Well, it certainly violates the rule that a method should do one job. I wasn't satisfied, but it worked okay so I left it alone.

Here's the code for when the mouse moves while the button is down:

```
SelectionTool>> button1Move: aPoint
    [ delta ]
    self previousPoint: aPoint.
    self figure isNil
        ifTrue: [self moveMarquee]
        ifFalse:
            [delta := aPoint - self previousPoint.
            self selectedFigures do: [:each |
                each moveBy: delta]]
```

If we are selecting a group, track the mouse. If we are moving a Figure (or actually all the selected Figures), move them. Now I begin to get glimmerings of what is wrong. The conditional code "self figure isNil…" is repeated. Let's look at the "button up" code.

```
SelectionTool>>button1Up: aPoint
    self figure notNil ifTrue: [^self].
    self drawMarquee.
    self selectAll: self selectedFigures
```

Here the same conditional appears, but in a different guise. I worked with this code for about a month never realizing how hard it was to manipulate until I added Handles. Handles are like Figures because they live in the Drawing, but they are like Tools because they interpret input. When the selected Figure is a Handle, the Tool doesn't do anything itself, it just passes the input along to the Handle.

I started to extend the code above to implement the case where the mouse is over a Handle. It wasn't going well so I finally took a step back and asked myself "why?"

One simple change I could make is adding an "isSelectingGroup" method:

```
SelectionTool>>isSelectingGroup
    ^self figure isNil
```

I could replace the tests in the three input methods above so they read better. Then I could add a "shouldDelegateInput" method so I could tell if the Tool should delegate input:

```
SelectionTool>>shouldDelegateInput
    ^self figure acceptsInput
```

However, this doesn't solve the deeper problem, which is the repeated conditional code. All good programming style codes down to this: say everything once and only once. Having the same conditional code in three methods violates this rule.

STATE OBJECT

State Object is the pattern for eliminating repeated conditional code and adding flexibility at the cost of additional objects and messages. Here's how I did it. First I created SingleSelectionState and GroupSelectionState:

> Class: SingleSelectionState
> superclass: Object
> instance variables: figure previousPoint
>
> Class: GroupSelectionState
> superclass: Object
> instance variables: originalPoint previousPoint

Then I gave them each their portion of each of the three input methods. The instance variables figure and previousPoint moved from the Tool to the Single-SelectionState. The variables originalPoint and previousPoint moved from the Tool to the GroupSelectionState. The messages Tool>>selectFigure and Tool>>drawMarquee have to take an additional parameter because the Tool no longer stores these variables directly.

The way I added these methods was to mechanically copy each of the SelectionTool input methods to each state, delete the parts that didn't apply to that state, and then change messages to "self" into messages to "aTool" where necessary:

> SingleSelectionState>>button1Down: aPoint for: aTool
>   self previousPoint: aPoint.
>   (aTool selectedfigures includes: self figure)
>   ifTrue: [self].
>   aTool resetSelections.
>   aTool selectFigure: self figure
>
> GroupSelectionState>>button1Down: aPoint for: aTool
>   self originalPoint: aPoint.
>   self previousPoint: aPoint.
>   aTool drawMarquee: self marqueeRectangle

```
SingleSelectionState>>button1Move: aPoint for: aTool
    | delta |
    delta := aPoint - self previousPoint.
    self previousPoint: aPoint.
    aTool selectedFigures do: [:each | each moveBy: delta]]

GroupSelectionState>>button1Move: aPoint for: aTool
    aTool drawMarquee: self marqueeRectangle.
    self previousPoint: aPoint.
    aTool drawMarquee: self marqueeRectangle

SingleSelectionState>>button1Up: aPoint for: aTool
    "Do nothing"

GroupSelectionState>>button1Up: aPoint for: aTool
    aTool drawMarquee: self marqueeRectangle.
    aTool selectFiguresIntersecting: self marqueeRectangle
```

INVOKING THE STATE

Now I had to set up the right state in the first place:

```
SelectionTool>>setSelectionState: aPoint
    | figure |
    figure := self drawingPane figureAt: aPoint.
    self state: (figure isNil
        ifTrue: [GroupSelectionState new]
        ifFalse: [SingleSelectionState figure: figure])

SelectionTool>>button1Down: aPoint
    self setSelectionState: aPoint.
    self state
        button1Down: aPoint
        for: self
```

The other two SelectionTool input methods delegate to the current state:

```
SelectionTool>>button1Move: aPoint
  self state
    button1Move: aPoint
    for: self

SelectionTool>>button1Up: aPoint
  self state
    button1Up: aPoint
    for: self.
  self clearState
```

HANDLES

Now adding support for Handles is easy. First I add a new state that delegates to its Figure:

```
DelegationSelectionState
superclass: Object
instance variables: figure previousPoint
```

I make sure I create one of these states when the mouse goes down over a Handle:

```
SelectionTool>>setSelectionState: aPoint
  SelectionTool>>setSelectionState: aPoint
  | figure |
  figure := self drawingPane figureAt: aPoint.
  self state: (figure isNil
    ifTrue: [GroupSelectionState new]
    ifFalse: [figure acceptsInput
        ifTrue: [DelegationSelectionState figure: figure]
        ifFalse: [SingleSelectionState figure: figure]])
```

The input methods in the DelegationSelectionState delegate to the Figure:

```
DelegationSelectionState>>
  button1Down: aPoint for: aTool
```

```
        self previousPoint: aPoint.
        self figure
            button1Down: aPoint
            for: aTool

DelegationSelectionState>>
    button1Move: aPoint for: aTool
        self figure
            button1MoveBy: self previousPoint - aPoint
            for: aTool.
        self previousPoint: aPoint

DelegationSelectionState>>button1Up: aPoint for: aTool
        self figure
            button1Up: aPoint
            for: aTool
```

CONCLUSION

What can I conclude from all this?

1. **Simple code is its own reward.** When you're stuck, try cleaning up first. Chances are you'll get out of your jam more quickly, and your code will be a better place to live later.

2. **Use simple rules.** Cleaning up code is simple. Don't try to change the behavior while you are cleaning up. If you spot a mistake, wait until a reasonable stopping spot before filing it.

3. **These new robes are a bit breezy.** Don't worry if everything isn't clean all the time. It isn't for me, nor do I think it should be. Progress implies chaos, at least for a while. Make sure you clean up afterwards, though.

37

A MODEST META PROPOSAL

Smalltalk Report, JULY–AUGUST, 1995

This one seems like a real stretch now. Half the column is taken up describing a client and giving advice to other consultants. That's not what a Smalltalk Idioms column should be about, and it doesn't really fit. Not that the advice is bad; it just doesn't go with the rest of anything else I was saying.

The technical part still seems right on. I recently used MetaObject to extend tools for use with Gemstone, and it worked like a charm.

The other thing going on here was my shock at seeing myself quoted at length in an earlier Smalltalk Report. When I spoke at the first Smalltalk Solutions, I got pretty outrageous—taking digs at my friends and potshots at big companies. All this was dutifully reported, and it looked pretty stupid in print. I was both disappointed at myself for having said it, and disappointed that it was made so public. Well, so much more public.

The lesson for me out of all this is that if people are going to take what I say seriously, I'd better damn well take what I say seriously, too. That's tough to do without taking myself seriously, which would be fatal. Having four kids is a great antidote to ever feeling like you have everything under control, though, so I'm not too terribly worried.

I JUST GOT AN ISSUE of *Smalltalk Report* that had someone's written summary of one of the talks I gave at Smalltalk Solutions. I sound like a wild-eyed, fire-breathing, spiky-haired maniac! It is so strange to see how others see me, especially in public. I'll admit to being in rare form in New York, a little over the top on the outrageous meter, but really…

The other shock this month was news of the ParcPlace/Digitalk merger. I see the press release. I check the date. Nope, not April 1. Hmmm… Is this some kind of elaborate joke (badly timed and in extremely bad taste)?

Now that I'm over the shock, I can see positives and negatives in the deal. It makes sense for Digitalk because (as Robert Yerex from ObjectShare pointed out) they got a much better valuation than they would have on the open market. It makes sense for ParcPlace because their worst nightmare was Digitalk's technology married to somebody with cash and marketing clout.

The outlook for customers isn't so one-sided. If all goes well, the current products will get their holes filled. VisualWorks will get native widgets and better performance. V will get a better garbage collector and fuller application model. Digitalk's culture of getting stuff out the door married with ParcPlace's culture of striving for elegance could be a potent brew. On the other hand, if sales aren't going well there will be a lot of pressure to drop one or the other image before PPD can architect an orderly transition.

All this spells opportunity for the other vendors to invoke that good old FUD factor and pick up some quick market share. They'd better, because if they don't and PPD starts hitting on all cylinders—look out!

CLIENT: OOCL

I've gotten several questions about what it's like to be a consultant. By the time this is published, everyone on the planet who knows how to write Smalltalk may already be a consultant, but just in case, I thought I'd provide a short sketch of one of my clients and what I do for them.

Orient Overseas Container Ltd. (OOCL hereafter) is a $1.5 billion (US) global container shipping company headquartered in Hong Kong. Their business is delivering those standard-sized containers you see pulled by trucks on the highway from point A to point B, where A and B could be anywhere in the world. They own or lease hundreds of thousands of containers and chassis. They operate 30-some container ships. They run terminals, depots, and transshipment yards all over the world. They interact with hundreds of thousands of customers, all of whom rely on OOCL to get shipments delivered on time. They handle more than one million shipments per year.

While these aren't numbers to impress Federal Express (with a peak of three million shipments per *day*), they are pretty respectable, especially when you factor in the tremendous amount of capital involved in the form of containers, ships, and yards. Container shipping is heavily regulated worldwide, so small reductions in cost or improvements in productivity make a huge difference on the bottom line.

OOCL's current IS operation is centralized in Hong Kong, built around a large IBM mainframe. To gain flexibility, reduce cost, and better address local requirements (imagine having to satisfy a hundred different customs bureaucracies with one system), they decided to move to a more distributed, client/server system. They chose Smalltalk (VisualWorks) for the front-end implementation language.

The project, IRIS-2, is medium-scale by IS standards. They plan to have around 40 developers when things are in full swing. They located in Silicon Valley to be closer to Smalltalk talent.

I've been involved with IRIS-2 since it began its life in these United States. I've had a number of jobs as the project has matured:

- At first we were all just trying to figure out the architecture, so I was a design consultant. We slung CRC cards, acted the part of objects, and learned about each others' specialities.

- As the design became clearer, David Ornstein and I wrote an architectural prototype of a critical part of the design so we could be sure we weren't just making beautiful diagrams.

- I helped design and deliver the "Smalltalk Boot Camp," a three-day simulation of the entire software lifecycle, intended to bring teams closer together and promote good programming practices.

- OOCL has generously sponsored my pattern writing, using the Smalltalk Best Practice Patterns I have been working on as part of their developer guidelines.

- I have been visiting about twice a month all along to review code, suggest improvements, and tune performance.

I have learned a number of interesting lessons for myself and for projects like this, which are becoming the norm in the Smalltalk world. On my part, I have learned

- *A stand-up lecture is useless for teaching.* I have given a series of lectures about patterns that seemed to have no impact. To address this, we held a "Pattern Bowl," where teams were challenged to find patterns or the absence of patterns in existing code. I think everyone learned more in those two hours than in tens of hours of lecture before.

- *Be outrageous.* What we are doing is difficult. It is risky (does anyone know the source of the factoid that 50% of all software projects never deliver?) There is a lot at stake. Plodding along in a humdrum way doesn't cut it. If I want to have impact I have to go for risk and flash, not "just the facts." The Pattern Bowl is a good example. We had prizes, applause, an obnoxious timekeeper (me), tension, competition, and the all-important fuzzy animal to go into the keeping of the winning team. Hokey? Yes, but it works.

- *Don't be too hard on yourself.* A consultant can only do so much. In the end, the success of the project isn't my responsibility. I'm responsible for doing the best I can, and suggesting other things that I can see need doing. When a deliverable slips, it doesn't help to get caught up in the emotion. It's hard to care but not too much, but that's what it takes to be effective.

This project has shown me that Smalltalk has some serious holes. I have been swimming in Smalltalk for so long that I no longer see the water. Newcomers to Smalltalk find it anywhere from irritating to impossible. For the market to grow, the vendors absolutely have to address the issues raised by new Smalltalkers.

For projects, I learned

- *Baby steps.* Do one small thing, then one slightly larger thing, and on and on. The temptation to jump in with both feet is overwhelming. The argument always goes, "I have committed to this date. I can't do it with baby steps. I have to ramp up more quickly." The result is always disaster. Always. OOCL has done a good job of trying to stick to baby steps and of getting back to baby steps when they have gotten too big too fast.

- *Program in pairs.* The most productive form of programming I know (functionality/person/hour) is to have two people working with one keyboard, mouse, and monitor. Our educational system trains us not to do this, and some upper managers have a hard time with it ("Why did we buy all those workstations and cubicles if we don't use half of them?"), but it makes a bigger change in productivity than any other single change.

- *Follow standards.* There are two parts to this. First, you have to have standards. In writing patterns, I'm deeply embroiled in exactly what the standards should be, but honestly, it is far better to have adherence to good standards than deviation from perfect standards. Second, you have to follow them. OOCL has recently put in place a schedule of peer review that makes sure everyone's code is seen by a critical audience at least every couple of months. This ensures that everyone has a motivation to understand and follow the standards, if only to avoid being ripped in public.

There's a lot more, both to the project and what I've learned, but it will have to await another column. I'm running out of space and I still haven't gotten to my technical topic…

A MODEST META PROPOSAL

"Meta programming? Isn't that what PhD's do to get thesis? What does that have to do with getting my next deliverable out?" Even if you don't know it, you're probably already doing some meta programming. Meta programming is writing programs that manipulate not your objects, the way usual programs do, but the *representation* of your objects. For example, the fact that each object has a hidden "class" instance variable, and you can fetch any object's class and ask it interesting questions, is meta programming. IsKindOf:, respondsTo:, instVarAt:—these are all messages about how the receiver is represented.

Smalltalk makes meta programming easy. Too easy, in fact. When you meta program, you are no longer really programming in Smalltalk, you are inventing a new programming language that is an extension of Smalltalk. Used indiscriminately by application developers, meta programming is a disaster. Just as not everyone can write reusable software, not everyone can write new programming languages. When everyone is writing in their own Smalltalk increment, and all the increments are different, disaster lurks. You can no longer read a line of code and guess what it does correctly. Risk soars and so does the cost of maintenance.

On the other hand, the meta programming facilities of Smalltalk can come in extremely handy. They can even save a project. If having some new kind of control structure vastly simplifies your program, chances are you can implement it in Smalltalk and take advantage of it.

How then to provide the needed facilities without exposing them unnecessarily? The problem as I see it is that they are all implemented up there in Object. It's just too easy to stumble across isKindOf:, use it to solve a short-term problem, and never discover the powerful polymorphism lurking just around the corner. I propose to put up a wall between application programmers and meta programming by introducing a new class, MetaObject, upon which all the current meta protocol in Object (and some in Behavior as well) will be heaped.

This is not an original idea. I got the idea in 1987 from Patti Maes' OOPSLA paper. I don't remember the exact title any more, but it introduced the idea of meta objects. I've had the idea floating around in my head since then, but I didn't do anything about it until I was bored on a flight recently. Pulling out my trusty ThinkPad, I whipped together an implementation. I liked the result enough to publish it here.

MetaObject is an Adaptor on any object. An Adaptor changes the protocol that an object accepts by interposing an object with the changed protocol.

```
Class: MetaObject
   superclass: Object
   instance variables: object
```

You create a MetaObject by giving it the object to adapt:

```
MetaObject class>>on: anObject
   ^self new setObject: anObject
MetaObject>>setObject: anObject
   object := anObject
```

There is a Facade in Object, Object>>meta, for creating a MetaObject. Clients will use this interface.

```
Object>>meta
    ^MetaObject on: self
```

The infamous isKindOf: becomes "inheritsFrom:" in MetaObject:

```
MetaObject>>inheritsFrom: aClass
    ^self objectClass includesBehavior: aClass
```
ObjectClass replaces Object>>class:

```
MetaObject>>objectClass
    ^self object class
```

I don't have space here to show all the implementations of the **MetaObject** protocol. Table 37-1 shows the old and new meta protocol. In some cases, I'm

Table 37-1 Old and new meta protocol.

Object meta message	MetaObject message	Explanation
class	objectClass	Return the class the receiver instantiates.
changeClassToThatOf: aClass (VisualWorks)	objectClass: aClass	Change the receiver's class.
class allInstVarNames	keys	Return the named instance variables (MetaObject lets you treat an object like a Dictionary).
class allInstVarNames size	size	Return the number of named instance variables.
instVarAt: aNumber	at: aString	Return the value of an instance variable.
instVarAt: aNumber put: anObject	at: aString put: anObject	Change the value of an instance variable.
allOwnersWeakly: aBoolean (VisualWorks)	owners	Return a Collection of all objects refering to the receiver.
become: anObject	switchWith: anObject	Swap two objects identities.
isKindOf: aClass	inheritsFrom: aClass	Return whether the receiver inherits from aClass.
isMemberOf: aClass	instantiates: aClass	Return whether the receiver is an instance of aClass.

not thrilled with the new names. I'll happily entertain suggestions for better selectors.

This is certainly not an exhaustive list. It's just what I came up with in a couple of hours. It should be possible to move more meta programming protocol in MetaObject.

Given this amount of protocol, I was able to quickly produce an Inspector that used a MetaObject to display and modify instance variables.

MetaObject provides the following advantages:

- *It discourages casual use of meta programming protocol.* If you see "meta" in application code, you'll know to perk your ears up and make sure it really belongs.

- *It collects scattered protocol.* Some meta programming protocol is implemented in Object, some in Behavior, some in Class. MetaObject brings it all together in one place.

- *It is flexible.* If a particular class needs a different kind of MetaObject for some reason, it can override "meta." You might do this, for example, to give a uniform programming environment on Smalltalk and C++ objects.

- *It simplifies* Object. Let's face it. Object is too darned big. VisualWorks 2 (the Envy version, anyway) defines 166 methods on Object. Visual Smalltalk Enterprise 3.0 defines 348. IBM Smalltalk gets by with 101. MetaObject is a step in the right direction.

MetaObject has the following disadvantages:

- *One more class.* Don't we have enough classes in the base system already? We will have to teach people to use it and convert old code.

- *One more object.* Now, when you want to have access to meta protocol you have to create a whole new instance of MetaObject.

How about it? Next time you need meta programming, implement a little MetaObject first and see how it feels. Let me know if you like it.

38

USES OF VARIABLES: TEMPS

Smalltalk Report, SEPTEMBER, 1995

This is clearly recycled material from the patterns book. Not much more to say here.

THE TOPIC OF THIS and the next column is how to use instance and temporary variables. I came upon the information (some of it is patterns, some isn't yet) in the course of writing my forthcoming book of Smalltalk coding patterns. I looked at temporary variables first, and found patterns for four ways temps are used:

1. Reuse the value of a side-effecting expression (like ^SStream>>next^T).

2. Cache the value of an expensive expression.

3. Explain the meaning of a complex expression.

4. Collect the results of several expressions.

Success in hand, I went to look for a similar set of canonical uses of instance variables. No dice. I came up with a taxonomy of the uses of instance variables, but no patterns. Many of the uses are bound up in other patterns (like the instance variable that holds the current State object). Others are too vague to make good patterns. I'll present what I have so far, because I have found it useful even in its unpolished state.

Ward Cunningham and I had a good long talk about this. We decided that the reason I was having so much trouble was scope. In the first book I am looking for coding patterns, the tactics of successful Smalltalk. Choosing to use a temporary variable is a tactical decision. It affects nothing but the single method in which the variable is used. Choosing to use an instance variable is not a tactical decision (except in a few cases like caching). Instance variables are tied up with the bigger issues of making models in Smalltalk. I already had lots of patterns upstream and downstream of the temporary variable patterns, so they fit right in. The modeling patterns are not nearly so well developed (that's why I'm leaving them out of the first book).

PPDUC

Before I talk about variables, I'd like to give you an update from PPDUC.

I gave a half-day pattern tutorial the first day. Around 150 folks attended. I knew I wanted to cover a lot of ground quickly, so I tried something new for me: I programmed live while talking about coding patterns.

Let me recommend this as a technique to all you trainers out there. The great thing about programming and teaching at the same time is there is so much shared context. You create a class, then ask, "How are we going to represent instance creation?" Everybody is thinking about what they'd do, so when you introduce the pattern (Complete Creation Method), they can see exactly how it relates to their experience. The terrible thing about programming and teaching simultaneously is that you are trying to keep two stories going in your head at once—the development story and the teaching story. I found myself typing a few characters, talking for 15 seconds, typing a few more characters, talking some more. Really quite distracting.

I had been hacking like crazy trying to get a new release of Profile/V ready for the show (I didn't quite make it), so I was running on little sleep. The morning I left for the conference my wife reminded me "don't say anything you don't want to see printed in The Smalltalk Report." I'm afraid I blew that in the first couple of minutes. Oh well...

On a related note, a very angry developer came up to me at one of the breaks. A colleague of his had read some of my comments from Smalltalk Solutions in the *Smalltalk Report,* and understood them to mean that you don't have to design Smalltalk programs. The VAD blamed me for the resulting mess, which was now his problem since he had inherited the code.

I won't even argue about whose responsibility the ugly code is. If even one person misunderstood, however, the comment deserves a little explanation.

You have to design Smalltalk programs much *more* than programs in other languages, not less. You expect Smalltalk programs to *do* much more. However, you can't do all that design at the beginning of the project when you're ignorant. You have to get smart before you design. Effective design happens in *episodes* (Ward's word) throughout the life of a project. Just because you don't kill a whole bunch of trees in the first six months doesn't mean you aren't designing.

Back to the conference, many of the presentations were deadly dull. Next year I expect much better. I see lots of amazing things out there, so I know there's enough material. Two stand-outs were Ward's talk about how to decide to harvest frameworks from code and Roby's 1200cc presentation of "Smalltalk: The Web Server." Coming soon to a network protocol stack near you!

The booths were certainly lively. Everybody had lots of traffic. The attendees seem to be serious about looking for ways to protect and capitalize on their Smalltalk investment. That's good news to us third-party folks.

TEMPORARY VARIABLES

Smalltalk provides temporary variables to hold objects for the duration of a method. When I learned Smalltalk, I had to learn how to use them by reading examples in the image. Trial, error, and reading left me with a handful of ways to use temps, but the information was all subconscious. When I was looking for patterns of use, I went through every method in the image that uses temps:

```
| methods |
methods := OrderedCollection new.
Object allSubclassesDo:
[:eachClass |
   eachClass selectors do:
      [:eachSelector || node |
      node := eachClass decompile: eachSelector.
      node block body temporaries notEmpty ifTrue: [methods add:
eachClass printString , ' ' , eachSelector]]].
MethodListBrowser
   openListBrowserOn: methods
   label: 'Methods with temps'
```

I cycled through all the methods trying to classify each temporary variable. When I got to a variable I couldn't classify, I added a new category. Here are the results, written as patterns:

Pattern: Reusing Temporary Variable

How do you repeatedly use the same evaluation of an expression whose value changes?

Repeating an expression is often the simplest way to write a method. Reading a method without temporary variables is easier than reading one that has them. Occupying your mind remembering the assumed value of a variable provides a distraction from the work of comprehending the rest of the method.

Some expressions return new values for each evaluation because of side-effects. If you are relying on the same value, you cannot simply execute the expression again and get the right results. For example:

```
parseLine: aStream
    aStream nextWord = ^'one' ifTrue: [^self parseOne: aStream].
    aStream nextWord = ^'two' ifTrue: [^self parseTwo: aStream].
    ...
```

is not likely to be what you meant. Instead, you want to grab the first word in the line once, then use that word in subsequent tests:

```
parseLine: aStream
    | keyword |
    keyword := aStream nextWord.
    keyword = ^'one' ifTrue: [^self parseOne: aStream].
    keyword = ^'two' ifTrue: [^self parseTwo: aStream].
    ...
```

Other expressions, like "Time millisecondClockValue", change value because of resources external to Smalltalk rather than side-effects. They, too, must be stored in a Reusing Temporary Variable.

Store the value of the expression in a temporary variable. Use the variable instead of the expression in the remainder of the method.

Pattern: Explaining Temporary Variable

How do you clearly communicate the intent of complex expressions?

Introducing the complexity of a temporary variable may be worth the cost if there are complex expressions in a method. Readers must carefully study an expression with 5 or 10 messages embedded in it to understand its meaning. You can use a temporary variable to communicate the intent of part of the expression.

For example, you might need to compute the size of a widget by combining several factors:

```
extent
    ^self textWidth + self leftBorder + self rightBorder + self margin
@ (self textHeight + self topBorder + self bottomBorder + self
margin)
Compare that to:
extent
    | x y |
    x := self textWidth + self leftBorder + self rightBorder + self
margin.
    y := self textHeight + self topBorder + self bottomBorder + self
margin.
    ^x @ y
```

You can read the second version in three separate chunks, without having to understand the whole expression at once.

Store the value of a part of a complex expression in a temporary variable. Use the variable in place of the sub-expression. Give it a name that reflects the meaning of the expression.

Explaining Temporary Variables are often a prelude to Composed Method. The example above looks even better as

```
extent
    ^self width @ self height
```

Pattern: Caching Temporary Variable

How do you improve the performance of a method that repeatedly calculates the same value for an expression?

Often, redundant calculation makes for the most readable code. For example, if you haven't had any other excuse to introduce a temporary variable, you shouldn't use one just because you are redundantly executing an expression. For example, self bounds in the following code always returns the same Rectangle, but it reads best if it is executed repeatedly:

```
smallerChildren
    ^self children select: [:each | self bounds contains: each bounds]
```

If you measure that the repeated execution of bounds is slowing the whole computation down, and if this method is the only one for whom it is a bottleneck, the simplest solution is to compute it once and store the value in a temporary variable:

```
smallerChildren
    | bounds |
    bounds := self bounds.
    ^self children select: [:each | bounds contains: each
bounds]
```

The result is longer, more complex (because of the temp you have to keep track of), and more prone to breaking (what happens if the receiver's bounds change during the method?). However, if you need the code to go faster, the costs are likely to be a good investment.

Execute the expression once. Put its value in a temporary variable. Use the variable instead of the expression.

Pattern: Collecting Variable

How do you collect results across several expressions?

The enumeration protocol does a good job of relieving you of the burden of writing most looping code. You just write collect or select or whatever and the details are taken care of for you.

This is all well and good as long as you are working with a single collection at a time (which is 95% of all uses). When you need to coordinate several collections, or even collect results from several objects, you need to do a bit more of the coding yourself.

As with the other temporary variable patterns, if you can get away without them, you should. However, the only alternative in this case is to write a whole slew of enumeration methods, and keep extending them for every new application. Using a temp isn't so bad compared to that.

For example, say you need to return the concatenation of two collections, but the elements should be perfectly shuffled—an element from the first, an element from the second, an element from the first, and so on. Here's how you do it using a temporary variable:

```
couples
   | result |
   result := OrderedCollection new.
   self girls
      with: self boys
      do:
         [:eachGirl :eachBoy |
         result add: eachGirl.
         result add: eachBoy].
   ^result
```

Use a temporary variable to collect results. Initialize it, add to it, and return it as the value of the method.

CONCLUSION

In the next column I'll talk about the 11 ways I've found so far for instance variables to be used. See you next month!

39

VARIABLES OF THE WORLD

Smalltalk Report, NOVEMBER–DECEMBER, 1995

This column takes a little bit bigger chance. I never worked out the instance variable taxonomy to the degree I did with temps, but I went ahead and published what I had anyway (as a column, it's not in the book), because I thought it was interesting and potentially useful. Looking at it now, I can't see how terribly useful it is. Sigh. Anyway, I was about to quit as columnist, and this and the previous column were just about rock bottom.

IN THE LAST ISSUE, I presented the four ways temporary variables are commonly used. This time, I'll talk about how instance variables are used. The results for instance variables are nowhere near as tidy as those for temps. I'll speculate as to why after I've presented the information.

SOAPBOX

But first, I'd like to whine and complain a little. Here's the essence of my beef—it's getting harder, not easier, to write Smalltalk applications. This is not what I expected. Smalltalk had already raised the level of programming so much from what I was used to that I figured the trend would continue. Today's clichés would become tomorrow's abstractions and the day after that we would forget we ever had to program that stuff. Onward and upward.

Instead, I see my clients programming the same stuff time after time. Here are some examples:

- *Unit values.* If I want an object representing five days, I shouldn't have to create "January 5, 1900" or fall back on plain old "5." Five days ought to be five days. Decent unit values would catch lots of nasty semantic errors and eliminate code that is currently scattered through lots of domain models.

- *Time and date intervals.* "Every Thursday this month," "1 AM every night," "every month this year." Each of these expressions, used in almost all calculations, should be represented by an object.

- *Multi-currency calculations.* There is no reason Smalltalk applications should have to flinch at dealing with multiple currencies. Application developers should use a **Money** object to represent monetary values. Once the application knows it is dealing with money, supporting multiple currencies is a snap.

- *Drawing editors.* Interfaces where the connections between things are as important as the things themselves aren't effectively represented as lists, text, tables, or notebooks. A good framework for direct manipulation interfaces would go a long way toward distinguishing Smalltalk applications.

- *Active objects.* Time marches on, but not if you look at most of the Smalltalk library. I can't count how many times I've written an object that keeps hold of a **Process** and answers messages like "start" and "stop.". Doing a completely preemptive thread safe library is a lot of work. That's overkill for most applications. A little help writing and debugging active objects would go a long way.

One interesting question is why such obvious objects aren't part of the shared language of Smalltalkers. The boring answer is that buyers don't have these objects on their check lists, so the vendors don't produce them.

The more interesting answer is that the Smalltalk culture has shifted from producers of abstractions to consumers of abstractions. We have in our hands the best tool I've ever seen for creating reusable stuff, but we're all so busy writing apps that as a community we don't step back and make things that everyone can use.

Of course there is an economic rejoinder to this—it isn't possible to make money making reusable software. So what! Good abstractions are the product of experience and inspiration, not economics.

We need to change our culture. Application developers need to demand higher and higher levels of abstraction from their vendors. Framework developers need to create and publish abstractions, even if they don't make any money at first. Vendors need to aggressively search for, incorporate, and educate about the best new abstractions. In short, we have to start acting like a community, putting aside some short-term gain for the greater good.

I'm putting my time where my mouth is by putting my unit testing framework in the public domain. I'm also preparing my multi-currency framework for public consumption (it'll be a few months, but I'll get there).

INSTANCE VARIABLES

The temporary variables boiled down to a simple set of patterns. You can use a temp to

- Cache a value for performance.
- Hold a value of a side-effecting expression.
- Explain a complex expression.
- Collect results from a complex enumeration.

I discovered these uses by looking at every method in the system that uses temporary variables and classifying them. Pretty soon the first three classifications became clear. After a while I had to add a fourth.

When I tried to do the same thing for instance variables all I got was a muddle. I came up with nine uses. Where temps were clear, however, these nine uses are not. You can classify one variable as two or three at once. I also invented three (mostly orthogonal) styles of usage of instance variables.

Ward Cunningham and I tried to figure out why instance variables are so much harder to pin down than temps. I wasn't satisfied with our answer, but here it is: Temporary variables are tactical. They are created to resolve a set of constraints that only exist within the scope of a single method. Instance variables are often created to solve much bigger problems, problems that may span many objects.

In the process of writing a handbook for software engineering, we've been much more successful at canonizing coding practice than design or analysis practice. The decision to create an instance variable goes back to design or even analysis. It shouldn't be surprising that the result isn't crystal clear.

STYLES

Having successfully lowered your expectations, here are the three styles I've found so far:

1. Private

2. Public

3. Acquaintance

Private. These are instance variables that are a simple part of an object. They are used almost exclusively by the object itself within its own methods. A good example is the Visual Smalltalk version of OrderedCollection. It has variables startPosition, stopPosition, and contents. No object outside of the OrderedCollection has any need for the values of these variables.

Public. These are instance variables that are more complex parts of an object. They are often made available to the outside world for further processing. Frequently, they hold objects that are complex in their own right. However, if the referring object didn't exist, the object referred to by the variable wouldn't need to exist. Panes in Visual Smalltalk have an instance variable "pen" which holds a Pen. If you want to draw on a Pane, you need its pen. You can often improve your design by shifting responsibility into an object and making some of its public instance variables private.

Acquaintance. These are variables that are there for convenience, but don't imply the sort of ownership of a private or public instance variable. Stream's instance variable "collection" is an acquaintance. If you have an Array you need to stream over, you could send it along with every message to the Stream (nextPut:on:, nextFrom:). The protocol would be much uglier and there would be a greater chance of errors if you used different collections at different times. Thus, **Streams** get acquainted with one and only one collection.

USES

Here are the nine uses I've found so far:

1. Parent
2. Child
3. Name
4. Properties
5. Map
6. Current state/strategy
7. Pluggable selector/block
8. Cache
9. Flag

Parent. Sometimes an owned object needs to acquaint itself with its owner. The owner provides context for calculations. VisualWorks' VisualPart has an instance variable "container" that points to the containing **VisualComponent**. You can improve your designs by passing more context into the owned object and eliminating parent variables. This allows one object to be "owned" by several others.

Child. In tree structures, interior nodes need a variable to hold a collection of children. VisualWorks' **CompositePart** has a variable "components" that contains an **OrderedCollection** of **VisualComponents**.

Name. If everyone who refers to an object must use the same key to identify it, the object needs a variable (probably public) to hold the key. You wouldn't want two clients to access the same **Account** with different numbers.

Sometimes you can improve a design by replacing name variables with a Map (see below) in the owning object.

Properties. Every instance of a class has the same variables. What happens when every instance needs different variables? Visual Smalltalk Panes, for example, have a host of optional values that can be (but don't need to be) set. Such an object needs a variable to hold a Dictionary mapping names to values. Unlike a Map (see below), a Property Dictionary's values are heterogeneous. You can often improve a design by figuring out what the invariant state is, or finding distinct clusters of properties that can form their own objects (the pattern Whole Value addresses this issue).

Map. Objects hold all the state associated with them. That is, if the system has a number connected with a particular object, that object generally has an instance variable to hold the number. However, when an object is added to the system and it needs to associate new information with an existing object, adding a variable to the existing object would clutter it up. For example, Visual Smalltalk's ObjectFiler and VisualWorks' BOSS associate file offsets with objects. It wouldn't make sense to add a "fileOffset" instance variable to Object. Instead, each ObjectFiler keeps an IdentityDictionary mapping objects to file offsets. Unlike Properties, Maps have homogenous values. Sometimes you can improve designs by moving state out of an object and into a Map, or vice versa.

Current state/strategy. When you use the State Object or Strategy Object pattern, you need a place to put the current state or strategy. VisualWorks' UIBuilder has an instance variable "policy" that holds an object that will create user interface widgets.

Flag. When you have simple variable behavior where an object can be in one of two states, the object needs a variable to hold a Boolean to signify the state. VisualWorks' ParagraphEditor has a flag called "textHasChanged." It is true if the text has been edited. If you have lots of flags, or if a flag shows up in lots of methods, you can improve your designs by introducing a State Object or Strategy (see above).

Pluggable selector/block. Every instance of a class has the same behavior but different state. Sometimes you need a little variable in behavior, but not enough to warrant creating a whole new class. Objects with slightly variable behavior need an instance variable to hold either a Symbol to be performed or a Block to be evaluated. Visual Smalltalk's ListPane has an optional printSelector that is performed on the objects in the list to get the strings to display.

Cache. Sometimes an object returns the same answer over and over in response to a message. If computing the answer is expensive, you can improve the performance of the system by adding an instance variable to the object to hold the value of the expression. You will have to make sure the value is recomputed if the value of the expression ever changes, and you should only add a cache if a performance profile of the object running under realistic conditions shows that the expression is expensive. The variable "name" in Visual Smalltalk's Behavior (VisualWorks' ClassDescription) is an example. The message "name" could be implemented as

```
Behavior>>name
    ^Smalltalk keyAtValue: self
```

But because it happens so often, the value of the expression is cached in an instance variable.

CONCLUSION

That's it so far. Looking back at the list, it's obvious that there's still a lot of ground to cover. For example, sometimes variables have their values set when the instance is created and never change. If you've got a favorite trick with instance variables that isn't covered above, drop me a line.

40

PATTERNS 101

Object Magazine, JANUARY, 1996

I wrote this paper in one sitting in my favorite coffee shop in Boulder Creek, perched out over the creek sipping a mocha (several mochas, in fact). I was trying to come up with a catchy intro. When the time machine idea came to me, the rest of the article wrote itself.

I don't know whether it will reproduce in the book, but in the magazine, the words "Star Trek" in the fourth paragraph were done in the Star Trek font. I was impressed that someone had the time and ingenuity to put in that little touch.

The other lesson in this is that the coffee shop in question closed soon after. The building owner wanted to jack the rent way up once the shop was successful, and the shopkeeper closed down rather than pay. The shop had become a gathering place for the community. Our little town still hasn't recovered.

What I take from this is that even though as a businessman I have to pay attention to the bottom line, every decision I make also affects real people's lives. Once you're committed, not following through may have a huge cost for other people.

I WAS EXCITED WHEN Marie invited me to contribute a gentle introduction to patterns for this issue. Something as down-to-earth practical as patterns deserves the *Object Magazine* audience of folks trying to get the job done with objects.

I'll introduce patterns by running you quickly through a typical pattern-directed design session and then going through the same thing in slow motion to see how patterns contribute to design. Then I'll talk about what patterns are available today and where patterns are likely to go tomorrow.

Take 1

Let's take a trip five years into the future.

<<*High-tech, Star Trek-style sound effect*>>

We're in a windowless, gray-walled conference room. Nine ergonomic-looking chairs crowd around a table with a scarred oak laminate top. One chair, minus a wheel, leans drunkenly in a corner. What? Hasn't office architecture made any progress? Sigh… Anyway, that's not what we're here to see.

Technical-looking folks occupy six of the chairs. Business experts (you can tell 'cause of the ties) sit together in two others. The manager sits at the end of the table. There seems to be a technical discussion going on, perhaps some kind of design brainstorm. Let's listen in…

"You need to handle calculations in multiple currencies."

"What's the *User's Object*?"

"Call it a Money."

"To make it a *Whole Value* it will need both an amount and a currency."

"Currency is another *User's Object.*"

Nods around the table.

"What happens when you add two Moneys with different Currencies? We don't want to be doing currency conversions all over the domain model."

"We can create an *Imposter* for a Money, call it a MoneySum, that just holds the Moneys to be added."

"What happens when we need to display a MoneySum? There are lots of different exchange rates."

"We need a *Conversion Object.* Call it a CurrencyExchange. You pass it a Money or MoneySum and the Currency you want for the result and you get back a Money in that currency."

"That should handle it."

Take 2

Five years and how many galaxies? What language are they speaking? Why are those phrases in italics?

Those phrases are the names of patterns. Each pattern is a recurring decision, a thing that experienced developers do over and over. By giving them names and careful definitions, all the developers (and sometimes the business experts and managers) can share an understanding of precisely what a technical conversation like the above means.

Together, a set of patterns records a particular style of working with objects (although you can use patterns to describe any process with recurring decisions, not just software development). What do I mean by recurring decision? Let's look at the patterns used by our developers of the future.

"What is the User's Object?"
"Call it a Money."

Pattern: User's Object

Question: Where do you find your first objects?

Constraints: On the one hand, developers need to focus on the technical needs of the system. If the system doesn't work as a piece of software, the clients won't be happy. On the other hand, even the best engineered software in the world is a failure if it doesn't do what the clients want. Developers need to be encouraged to take the clients perspective as early as possible.

Solution: Start with objects the client recognizes. Trust the rest of the development process to refine them into a system that works well.

Let's look at User's Object as a pattern. Is it a recurring decision? Sure. Thousands of developers around the world make a decision exactly (or at least very much) like this every day. They may not do it for the same reasons. They may not even have thought of reasons; it just works well for them.

The pattern doesn't say exactly what to do, but it gives you a concrete approach to the decision. The pattern also gives you a way to check for its presence (ask the clients if they recognize the object). This is one of the most interesting things about patterns to me, that they both describe a thing and tell when and why to create it.

Back to the discussion:

"To make it a Whole Value it will need both an amount and a currency."

Pattern: Whole Value

Question: How do you put state together in an object?

Constraints: Every new object you create costs, both in execution space and conceptually, to teach it to developers and keep it running. You might want to make a few, large objects with lots of state to reduce this factor. On the other hand, the more smaller objects you create, the greater the chance you will be able to replace them with other objects and move them to new contexts. Well-written small objects are understandable in chunks, lowering the cost of maintenance.

Answer: Put state together in an object that only makes sense together.

"Currency is another User's Object."
Nods around the table.
"What happens when you add two Moneys with different Currencies? We don't want to be doing currency conversions all over the domain model."
"We can create an Imposter for a Money, call it a MoneySum, that just holds the Moneys to be added."

Pattern: Imposter

Question: How do you extend a system while changing it as little as possible?

Constraints: If you are going to modify a system cost-effectively, you have to do it without touching existing code. Otherwise, the probability that you have broken working code soars. The runtime binding of messages to methods provides you with the mechanism to "change without modifying." Having two implementations of the same message makes a system harder to understand, but good programming environment support and careful use of other factoring patterns like Whole Value mitigate the cost.

Answer: Introduce a new object into the system with the same protocol as an existing object but a different implementation.

"What happens when we need to display a MoneySum? There are lots of different exchange rates."

"We need a Conversion Object. Call it a CurrencyExchange. You pass it a Money or MoneySum and the Currency you want for the result and you get back a Money in that currency."

Pattern: Conversion Object

Question: How do you represent complex or variable object-to-object conversions?

Constraints: The simplest way to represent conversion is by sending a message to an object to convert itself. If you have an object representing some number of pounds, it makes sense to send it "asKilograms." When conversion isn't fixed the way pounds-to-kilograms or ASCII-to-EBCDIC are, you need more flexibility. Representing every variation as a method would result in a protocol explosion, one that would continue far into development. Even though you'd like to limit the number of classes in the system, in this case it prevents a worse problem. Therefore

Answer: Create a new class, instances of which take one object and convert it into another.

"That should handle it."

PATTERNS

You've seen four patterns:

- User's Object
- Whole Value
- Imposter
- Conversion Object

Each is solving a small part of the design problem. Together, they create (the beginnings of) a solution. What's going on here?

WHAT ARE PATTERNS?

Patterns are things. They are things that occur over and over in software. You've probably seen hundreds or thousands of User's Objects, hundreds of Whole Values, many Imposters, and maybe a handful of Conversion Objects. In going from system to system, you see the same configurations of objects used again and again, even to address vastly different problem domains. The same engineering that worked for container shipping works for pension administration.

Patterns are decisions. Any one engineer uses a handful of tricks that have worked well in the past. Amazingly, 90% of everybody's tricks overlap. I told my dad, a Silicon Valley engineer for 30 years, about patterns and he said, "Oh, I know all about that. But I'd never tell anyone my patterns. Those are my secret." His patterns were about stuffing a multi-tasking operating system into 4K of ROM, but he'd thought about it enough that there was little risk in writing "his" OS for a new chip.

Patterns are advice. If you were lucky, when you came out of school a grizzled, crusty, veteran engineer sat you down and said, "Forget all that school crap. Here's how we make software" and proceeded to show you the ins and outs of writing software that works. Patterns record the kind of advice new engineers need.

Patterns are a vocabulary. As you saw in the opening of this article, the names of patterns become part of the spoken vocabulary of a group that shares those patterns. You might not understand "a Composite is an Imposter for its elements" at first, but when you do, you understand a lot, and very precisely.

Patterns are a form of essay. Each pattern has to answer these questions:

- *Context.* What has to be true for this pattern to be valid? One simple way to communicate this is to talk about what other patterns ordinarily precede this one.

- *Problem.* What problem is addressed by this pattern? When you understand a pattern's problem, you will know when to apply it. The problem becomes your mental folder tab that helps you flip to the right pattern. You may even have several patterns that address the same problem.

- *Constraints.* What affects the solution to the problem? Every decision has technical and human constraints—space vs time, risk vs productivity, short term vs long term. Understanding a pattern's perspective on the constraints will give you confidence in its solution.

- *Solution.* What do you do to solve the problem? Patterns give you a concrete and unambiguous cookbook to help you solve the problem: Create a class, instances of which take one object and convert it to another.

The patterns in the section "Take 2" are really just thumbnail sketches of patterns. See the final section for pointers to more complete patterns.

WHAT AREN'T PATTERNS?

Patterns are not a style guide. Like patterns, style guides tell you what to do. Because they are focused on what and not why, style guides soon run out of gas. They are fine for describing how to format code and name variables, but writing a style guide for the content of requirements analysis or detailed design is futile.

Patterns aren't abstract principles. A deep understanding of the principles of software engineering is critical to advancing the state of the art. Unfortunately, a shallow understanding of the principles of software engineering is dangerous. If we held the Olympics of Software Engineering, "Abuse of Principles" would be a marquee event. You need to know how to do something before you can learn how to do it just right. Patterns are the things you need to know how to do.

Patterns aren't methodologies. A methodology tells you what kind of decisions to make and how to notate the decisions you've made, but it doesn't tell you what the decisions themselves will be. Patterns are the decisions. A pattern states, "You will encounter a situation where there are lots of ways of converting from one object to another, and when you do, create an object to do the conversion for you." That's a decision. Patterns and methodologies complement one another:

- The diagrams found in many methodologies can be a powerful way to present a pattern.

- When you use a pattern, methodologies provide good notations for recording the results of the pattern.

OKAY, YOU'RE CONVINCED; NOW WHAT?

I wish I could say, "All the patterns you'll ever need are in *The Big Book of Software Patterns* available now from SIGS Books." I can't. The effort to take software engineering, something we've done by the seat of our pants for a mere 50 years, and codify it has only just begun. The effort involves hundreds of people around the world, but there are imposing barriers of language and experience to overcome before we'll have anything like a single handbook.

That's the bad news. The good news is you can begin seeing some of the benefits of patterns now. I recommend that you begin by setting up a study group to read and discuss a pattern a week from *Design Patterns* (see below for details). Find each pattern in your software. Find places where it should exist but doesn't. Use the pattern in your development. Talk amongst yourselves.

Here's how you can learn more about patterns:

- *Design Patterns: Elements of Reusable Object-Oriented Software,* by Erich Gamma, Richard Helm, Ralph Johnson, and John Vlissides, Addison-Wesley, 1995, ISBN 0-201-63361-2. This is the book that sparked the current surge of interest in patterns.

- *Pattern Languages of Programs.* The annual conference for pattern writers and enthusiasts, to be held September 4–6, 1996 in Allerton Park, Illinois. Browse http://www.cpl.uiuc.edu/~plop/. See the sidebar by Dana Anthony for a report on the 1995 conference.

- *Patterns mailing list.* Send mail to patterns-discussion-request@cs.uiuc.edu with the body subscribe.

- *Patterns home page.* Browse http://st-www.cs.uiuc.edu/users/patterns/patterns.html for a potpourri of information about patterns.

- *SIGS columnists.* I write a column that often contains patterns in the *Smalltalk Report.* Jim Coplien writes about patterns in his column in the *C++ Report.* Ralph E. Johnson covers patterns in *JOOP.*

41

FAREWELL AND A WOOD PILE

Smalltalk Report, JANUARY, 1996

This *was my last column, and the one I'm proudest of. I have a habit of trying to take lessons from the world around me. If I see a tree leaning against another tree I say, "What is that like? Well, if one person leans on another too long, they both end up falling down." I always kept these little stories to myself, though.*

For my last column, I decided to break out. By now I was fully confident in my ability to describe a technical situation. I'd never tried to describe something from the real world in a publication before. This was my first attempt.

Looking at it now, it looks clumsy, but I still really like the underlying story. I've probably told the parable of the woodpile twenty times in the year since I wrote it.

In a way, this column represents the shift that I had been undergoing all along. I got completely away from technical stuff and completely into people stuff, and I did it in people-y, proto-literate way.

IT'S THE OBJECTS, STUPID

Sometimes it takes me a while to see the obvious. Sometimes even longer than that. Three or four times in the last month I've been confronted by problems I had a hard time solving. In each case, the answer became clear when I asked myself the simple question, "How can I make an object to solve this problem for me?" You think I'd have figured it out by now: got a problem? make an object for it.

Here's an example: I had to write an editor for a tree structure. There were several ways of viewing and editing the tree. On the left was a hierarchical list. On the top right was a text editor on the currently selected node of the

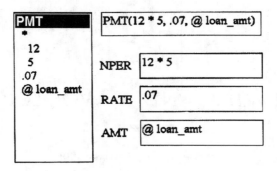

Figure 41-1

tree. On the bottom right was a list of text editors on the subnodes of the currently selected node (see Figure 41- 1).

Figure 41-2 shows the domain objects that live behind this view. How is the editor going to work? Let's say I have an editor on the value 5 (Figure 41-3). How are we going to write the code to parse and install a new function? The first part is simple enough:

```
FunctionEditor>>parse: aString
  | new |
  new := FunctionParse parse: aString.
```

But now we're stuck. If we just say

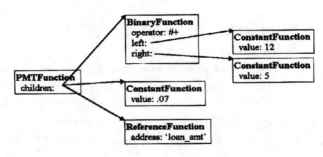

Figure 41-2

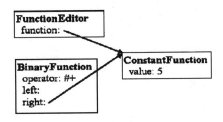

Figure 41-3

```
function := new
```

then the "right" instance variable of the BinaryFunction (which the editor knows nothing about) won't be updated.

"Make an object for it," that's the ticket. The object is an EditingWrapper. When you go to edit a function, you first wrap every node in the function tree, as shown in Figure 41-4.

Now the editor looks like Figure 41-5. And we can write the parsing method like this:

```
FunctionEditor>>parse: aString
    | new |
    new := FunctionParse parse: aString.
    function function: new
```

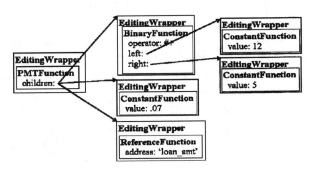

Figure 41-4

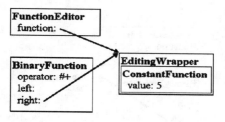

Figure 41-5

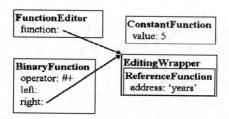

Figure 41-6

If we parsed the string "@years", the resulting picture would look like Figure 41-6. When the BinaryFunction unwraps its children, the right function will be in place.

As I said, several times in the last month I've faced baffling problems that became easy when I asked myself the question, "How could I make an object to solve this problem for me?" Sometimes it was a method that just didn't want to be simplified, so I created an object just for that method. Sometimes it was a question of adding features to an object for a particular purpose without cluttering the object (as in the editing example). I recommend that the next time you run into a problem that just doesn't seem like it has a simple solution, try making an object for it. It won't always work, but when it does it's sweet.

THE PARABLE OF THE WOOD PILE

The following is really about software. Really.

I live in the redwood forest. Fall in the forest has its own set of smells, distinct and different from the smells of every other season. Crushed dry ferns have a sharp, dusty smell. Rotting bay nuts are like psychedelic bay leaves. When we get our wood delivered, the smells of freshly split oak and madrone add to the mix.

My house is down by the creek, maybe 25 feet below the level of the driveway. There is a sheer cliff off to one side and stone steps directly in front of the house. When we get our customary two cords of wood delivered (for you city folk, that's a pretty damn big pile of wood, takes most of a two-ton truck to carry it), the easiest way to get it down near the house is to throw it over the cliff, one stick at a time, then go down later and stack it.

Wood chucking time has become something of a ritual for me. The smells of the fall forest, the filtered fall light through the surrounding redwoods, the ache of my generally desk-bound body, the knowledge that I'm keeping my family warm for the rest of the winter, all combine for a satisfying couple of days.

My driveway is long and narrow, so when the truck delivers the wood it makes a long pile, maybe 25 feet long and eight or nine feet wide. The end of the pile is right at the top of the cliff, so the first hour or so is easy—turn, pick up a stick, turn, throw. Once I get settled into a rhythm, I probably throw a stick every five seconds.

This year we had a dinner party to attend, and I didn't want to have to walk over pile of firewood all dressed up, so I wanted to at least get a path cleared quickly. Once I got the sticks close to the top of the cliff thrown, I noticed that my progress slowed down. Instead of "turn, grab, turn, throw" I was doing "walk, grab, walk, throw," where I was having to walk a few steps to get to the front of the pile. It may not seem like much, but it slowed down my throwing rate by half. The more progress I made, the further I had to walk, the slower I went, the further my goal of walking to the car without scuffing my shiny shoes receded.

I'm an engineer at heart, and repetitive manual labor leaves me plenty of time to think, so I wasn't about to let this state of affairs continue without at least trying to bring my productivity back up. I discovered I could throw light sticks down with one hand. On every trip to the front of the wood pile I began picking up two sticks, a heavy one in my left hand and a light one in my right. I'd throw the light one one-handed first, then heave the heavy one with both. This let me amortize my walking over two sticks. The pace picked up.

Pretty soon, though, I noticed I was still going slow. The front of the pile kept receding as I worked, so my time spent walking kept increasing. What I really needed was a way to get back to working like I had worked at first, just turning and throwing with no walking at all.

You've probably guessed the solution. I went to the pile and tossed sticks the 10 or 15 feet to the top of the cliff. I tossed 30–40 sticks, walked over, threw them down the hill, then walked back. This way my walking was amortized over so many sticks it didn't even count. I had to handle each stick twice, so my productivity was half of what it was at the beginning, but I could sustain the pace through the rest of the pile. No matter how far back the front of the pile got, it was always easy to quickly toss a little stack to the top of the cliff.

My wife and I made it to our party—shoes, suit, and dress unscathed.

When an experienced team starts a project in Smalltalk, the first few months go smoothly. The first cut at the domain model slides right in and away you go. Pretty soon, though, the team starts to bog down. Decisions they made without complete information begin to take their toll. The easy progress of the early days is soon but a fond memory. New functionality, rather than sliding in, has to be shoved in with a pile driver. Quality and predictability go out the window, because the team doesn't know if the next feature will fit with what's there, in which case all will be well, or it won't fit, in which case who knows how long it will take to shoehorn it in.

I have seen two unproductive reactions to this situation and one reasonable one. The first are the teams that keep walking back and forth to the wood pile, no matter how far it recedes. I call this "Smalltalk is more rope." These teams ignore the increasing risk and decreasing productivity, but Smalltalk is forgiving enough that they can keep their application sort of running while they add new features. Throw in enough *nil* checks and *isKindOf*'s and you can make almost anything work. The result is disaster deferred. Eventually the team is asked to do something that just can't be shoved into the system.

The shell-shocked veterans of "more rope" failures often turn the other way. Ignoring the sticks right there in front of them, they try to toss the whole pile close before they start throwing down the hill. They insist on creating the frameworks first. The application is divided into strict layers, and developers are only allowed to work on their own layer. The layers don't precisely fit because they are developed in isolation, but developers have no choice but to carry on as best they can. The result is again disaster deferred. The system gets big, because layers provide services no one needs and because there is no view of the whole system that would allow large-scale simplifications.

The sustainable solution is to find a balance between moving the pile and tossing the logs. Toss some, move some, toss some, move some, starting with tossing. (Jeff McKenna had a great article about this years ago, and Ward Cunningham has a pattern language called Checks about the same idea: http://c2.com/ppr). Take advantage of the quick wins to give you concrete information from which to generalize. Make it run, make it right, make it run, make it right.

FAREWELL

This is my last column, at least this go around, for the *Smalltalk Report*. It's been quite a ride, programming in Smalltalk and trying to write about it. When I started, when the *Smalltalk Report* started, we were the wild-eyed purveyors of what many people saw as a crazy language. Since then, Smalltalk has become the language of choice for many kinds of applications. Recently the Smalltalk market has been thrown into turmoil by the merger of ParcPlace and Digitalk and their subsequent disappointing financial performance.

From that standpoint, it seems like a strange time to quit. I'd like to go out on a high note, with noble Smalltalk standing proudly head and shoulders above the crowd. However, when I saw that I wasn't putting the thought or care into these columns that they, that you, deserve, I knew the time had come.

I'll still be involved in the Smalltalk world, in fact, more than ever. You won't get rid of me that easily! I'll be unveiling a one-day Smalltalk patterns course at Smalltalk Solutions in March. I'm working on a book, *The Smalltalk Best Practice Patterns: Volume 1, Coding,* due out in the first quarter next year. I'm scrambling to keep up with my products. I'm working on some fascinating contract programs. To top it off, consulting has picked up since OOPSLA. The only way you'll be rid of me is if I drop dead of exhaustion.

THANKS

I'd like to thank all the people who helped me during the last few years. In particular,

- Rick Friedman, for giving Smalltalkers a forum for our voices when we were far out in the wilderness.

- John Pugh and Paul White, for all their work making the *Smalltalk Report* work well.

- Elizabeth Upp and the production team at SIGS, for dealing with late submissions, raw ASCII, and requests for odd graphics.

- Liz St. Pierre, for hassling me in the gentlest possible way consistent with results.

- Ward Cunningham, for help refining many of my best column ideas.

- You, the *Smalltalk Report* readers, for support, encouragement, email, and ideas. Without you I could have written all the columns I liked, but no one would have read them.

So long. I hope I see you Smalltalkin' down the road.

AFTERWORD

————

WHILE A PROGRAM EXPRESSES intent, it is the computer, the hardware, that brings that intent to life. In order to have full control over your program's expression you must control the computer that runs it. Therefore, write your program for a computer with a plug. Should you be dissatisfied with the behavior of the computer, unplug it.

I'm working from memory here. This idea, the idea that you could unplug a computer, is an idea that has run in and out of our culture for about as long as there have been computers. I've expressed the idea as a pattern: a problem and its solution. I'm thinking about this pattern because it reminds me of programming with Kent.

I haven't got the words to this pattern quite right. It gives the impression that I fear computers run amuck. Does anybody remember that old film, *The Forbin Project,* where the U.S. defense computer gets to talking to the Soviet defense computer and they get the idea that they can run the world better than us? Well, that's not the problem. I first wrote the "don't program a computer you can't unplug" pattern because Kent and I needed a pattern at a large scale. We were looking for big advice for a new kind of developer. We imagined ordinary people taking their computing needs into their own hands. These people would use powerful languages to express themselves. But they would also need clear advice about using them. The "unplug" pattern says, *Before you start writing a program, get a computer that you can control for your own purposes.* It says, *don't settle for a computer in a glass room. Don't borrow time. Get your own computer. Make it yours.*

There is a lot of history to this pattern. Kent and I shared a vision of computing. We worked in a lab that used the sandbox approach to research. You know, give all the researchers the kind of computer that will be the norm in a decade and see what happens. We had dual-processor workstations with huge screens and graphics accelerators on every desk. And what happened?

Not too much. For some reason most people thought they needed permission to write programs. Not us. We made those machines our own.

We wrote programs together for a year and a half. We'd make up a problem over coffee on Monday, have a prototype struggling by Tuesday, and be dragging people into the office to see results by Friday. Yes, it was like that, except when it wasn't. Sometimes we'd get stuck. By Tuesday we would be over our heads and out of ideas. We had a program going nowhere. So we pulled the plug.

Kent and I could walk away from an undone program. We could because we were writing those programs for ourselves. We had no further use for them when they stopped giving back. Put another way, we expected the mere act of authoring to reward us, as it often did Then we found patterns. We both had Christopher Alexander on our bookshelves. We had noticed that our flip attitude about development was working, producing programs that were used, even reused. Alexander got us thinking that we could can what we were doing and share it too.

I remember Alexander's emphasis on piecemeal growth. It was fundamental to all of his work, and to ours as well. Alexander's vision went beyond our vision, though, in one important way. He recognized the incredible range of forces that bear on one's work. He knew that to make a house one must also know how to make a city, and a brick. Then he showed us how to link that know-how together, top to bottom. Awesome.

So that is how I came to be talking about computer plugs. We learned from Alexander that our advice had to be concrete. Who ever learned anything from advice like, "Make your program friendly"? We had recently had better luck with more concrete advice like, *Have one pop-up menu, containing verbs, for each pane. . . .*

The "unplug" pattern wasn't about plugs at all. It was about ownership and control. It said, "Take control of the environment in which you write programs." The point of plugs was just the test, something concrete that would lead you in the right direction without overly constraining what you do.

It's a good pattern, but not complete. The pattern really only works when surrounded with other patterns that actually give you the ownership and control you'll need. Kent and I fell into that. We didn't make it for ourselves. But we recognized we had it, and used it.

The pattern is anything but obsolete today. You're probably thinking that 99.9 percent of all software written is written on computers that unplug. But can you unplug them? I was thinking about workstations when I first articulated the pattern a decade ago. We thought they would be the locus of power. But it's turned out servers hold the power now. Can you unplug yours? Can you even get it on the phone?

I maintain an Internet presence that I set up with the help of a particularly enlightened provider. I have a server on my premises with a plug that I own. Although the bandwidth of my connection is modest, it is continuous. I've found the character of the whole configuration to be categorically better than simpler arrangements. On my machine I run programs that are unwelcome elsewhere: programs that open their own connections, or just run without stopping. I don't have to ask permission.

We are just consumers to the huge corporations of the computer and telecommunications industry. They want to sell to us alright, but they won't sell us everything we need; that is, they won't make us powerful . . . unless we insist. Pay attention to the pattern. If we computer users are to have and hold the kind of ownership Kent and I have known, we are going to have to watch those plugs.

—*Ward Cunningham*

INDEX